IN THE SHADO
LONE T1 __

THE FORGING OF THE 10TH GLOUCESTERS AND THE ORDEAL OF THE FIRST DIVISION AT THE BATTLE OF LOOS - 1915

Nick Christian

NICK CHRISTIAN

Copyright © Nick Christian 2012

ISBN 978-0-9528378-1-7

First published 1996 by Nick Christian
This revised edition 2012.

Printed by Orphans Press Ltd.
Arrow Close, Leominster Enterpise Park, Leominster, Herefordshire HR6 0LD

Contents

Your King and Country
NEED YOU.

A CALL TO ARMS.

TERMS OF SERVICE.

General Service for a period of three years or until the War is concluded. Age of Enlistment, between 19 and 30.

Full information can be obtained from Police Station, Cinderford, or

H. B. WOODMAN,

Woodlands, Cinderford,

Recruiting Officer for Cinderford and District.

118

Foreword

Foreword by the late Donald 'Lofty' Large, veteran of the 1st Gloucesters, prisoner of war in Korea and member of 22 SAS Regiment.

The Gloucestershire Regiment has more battle honours than any other infantry regiment in the British Army, and it would be easy to assume this record was attained by always having good, well-trained Regular troops. There is no doubt that in many battles victory favoured the Gloucesters because they were trained and experienced, but this was certainly not the case for most of the Gloucestershire battalions who fought in the 1914 - 18 War, and in any case, there has never been a war like it.

The 10th Gloucesters were a volunteer battalion of ordinary men from all walks of life, clerks, forestry workers, miners, farm workers, gardeners and shop assistants. It is one thing to volunteer in a popular rush to the flag, but something entirely different to be wet, cold, tired out of your mind and often absolutely terrified, and then climb from the comparative safety of a trench to rush towards what looks like certain death. To pit your flesh, bone and luck against a raging storm of lethal metal, flying rocks and earth whilst all around your comrades are being shredded. All this because someone blows a whistle and you won't let your unit down and most of all you won't let yourself down.

To put it into perspective, compare the sheer guts of almost any troops who fought on the Western Front between 1914 and 1918, either side of the line, with the spineless cowards of recent times who bomb and shell civilian populations, women and children, because they haven't got the guts to close their enemy and "do what a soldier is for."

In many respects the situation of the British Army has changed little in the eighty years since the Great War. Generals are now more accountable than were some of the idiots of long ago, but somehow, in my experience, we almost always were outnumbered by any opposition encountered. Our weapons and equipment often lag behind the times, and these deficiencies have to be made up by the same spirit displayed by the men of the 10th Gloucesters. But, it is doubtful that any troops from this country have ever before or since, been so badly let down by their Generals, training, weapons and equipment, as the men who fought in the Great War, "The Ultimate Hell" for the infantry.

This book helps the reader to people the names recorded in every city, town, village and hamlet in the British Isles, on memorials to those whose world ended in that "Ultimate Hell."

Hereford 1995

Sergeant 12532 Reginald James Betteridge, 10th Service Battalion, The Gloucestershire Regiment. Killed at the Battle of Loos - 25th September 1915, aged 25 years. Reg has no known grave and is honoured on the Dud Corner Memorial at Loos, Northern France.

Introduction

Reginald James Betteridge died on September 25th 1915. No one recalls the circumstances of his death, for he and those around him simply vanished amidst the smoke and carnage of battle, victims of machine guns, poison gas and exploding shells. His body was never recovered, at least not in an identifiable state. He may, however, have provided some of the thousands of unidentifiable human remains that were eventually collected and now lie beneath gravestones inscribed:

"Known Unto God"

Reg was my grandmother's elder brother. She mourned him deeply. I still recall the sadness in her eyes and the quaver in her kind old voice as she told me how Reg had joined the army many years before and was killed in a foreign land.

Within weeks of the outbreak of war in August 1914, Reg and 100,000 others eagerly flocked to the recruiting centres in response to Lord Kitchener's pointing gloved hand. Reg travelled from his home in the Forest of Dean to Gloucester where he took the King's shilling and found himself drafted into the 10th (Service) Battalion, The Gloucestershire Regiment.

A brief, hectic year of training followed before the battalion was ordered to France where it became part of the renowned but battle weary 1st Division of the Regular Army. Within a matter of weeks the 10th Gloucesters, together with the 8th (Service) Battalion, The Royal Berkshire Regiment, proudly led the Division's 1st Brigade 'over the top' at the Battle of Loos in September 1915, on a sector of the front known to the troops as 'Lone Tree'.

Lone Tree was in fact a wild cherry thrusting up from No Man's Land in stark isolation just in front of the enemy wire entanglements. The tree was destined to pass into legend and became a symbol of the tragic human suffering that exploded and raged around its gaunt and tortured frame on the opening day of the battle.

Not only was this dreadful battlefield hosed with deadly streams of machine gun fire and swept with bursting shrapnel and high explosive shells, but was also smothered with lung scorching chlorine gas. British Generals bore the responsibility for the release of this new and crude, unpredictable weapon, which, through bad planning and ill luck, inadvertently gassed hundreds of their own troops waiting to deliver the assault from the narrow, crowded trenches.

As one of the first New Army battalions to go into action on the Western Front, the novice soldiers of the 10th Gloucesters were tremendously eager to prove their mettle to the supporting Regular and Territorial battalions of their division. Indeed, their irresistible charge across the shambles of No Man's Land into the unknown, helped forge a path for the many hundreds of Britain's New Army battalions that were to follow in the terrible years ahead, ultimately buying victory with their flesh and blood. The 10th paid dearly and tragically for their bravery, for their dead and wounded fell in swathes across No Man's Land and in the captured German positions.

Sadly, the ordeal of such men is not unique, for many thousands like them perished or were maimed at Loos, and before those grotesquely bloody years of 1914 - 1918 were finally exhausted, millions more were destined to fall as casualties in the most pitiful and cruellest of circumstances. Yet, from what I have been able to discover, the ordeal suffered by the men of the 10th Gloucesters reveals a quite amazing human tale. The steady stoicism, unbelievable courage and sublime comradeship displayed by these men in the face of unimaginable savagery and carnage, epitomises the sheer bravery of all those that were forced to endure the utter horror of the Great War.

DEAN FOREST MERCURY
FRIDAY, OCTOBER 29, 1915.

SERGT. R. J. BETTERIDGE, CINDERFORD.

Official news came to hand on Wednesday of the death of a very popular and highly esteemed Forester, in the person of Sergt. Reginald James Betteridge, only son of Mrs. F. J. Baldwin of Steam Mills. He was attached to the 10th Battalion, Gloucestershire Regt. and he took part in the well-known advance on September 25th, in which he unfortunately, lost his life. With the official announcement received on Wednesday was a slip expressing the regret of the King and Queen. The news of the gallant sergeant's death was heard with great grief by his relatives and with feelings of no little sorrow also by all who had had the pleasure of his acquaintance. His was a character which many young men might well emulate – a thoroughly good fellow respected by those who were associated with him in his occupation, in life, popular with those with whom he played in the manly sports of football and cricket, and liked by everyone. In his youth he began his working life as a clerk in the Bilson office of the Lydney and Crump Meadow Collieries Ltd., at the time of his enlistment he was confidential clerk to Mr. M. Maclean, chairman of the Cannop Coal Company, Ltd. He was a total abstainer and a member of the "King of the Forest" Lodge of the Independent Order of Good Templars. He enlisted in the early weeks of the war, and his promotion was rapid, quickly attaining to the rank of Lance Corporal, and eventually being appointed Sergeant. Had he lived till next Tuesday he would have reached his 26th birthday. A brave young fellow, he nobly faced the path of duty and sacrificed a promising career in his country's behalf. The deepest sympathy will be extended to the relatives in their sorrow.

Preface to This Edition

In The Shadow Of Lone Tree was first printed and published privately in 1996. I was not able to interest an established publisher and so took a gamble on publishing it myself, having dismissed unhelpful comments describing my effort as "vanity publishing." The First Edition consisted of 500 copies that sold out within a year. The book's publication and resulting publicity encouraged a number of people to contact me with a wealth of interesting information about their forefathers who had fought at Loos. This, together with my continued fascination with every fact I can absorb about Loos and the Great War in general, has prompted me to take the plunge once again and to republish this considerably updated edition.

The book's First Edition owes its existence to a bundle of yellowing papers thrust into my hands in 1993 by my late father, John Christian. That evening I settled down to investigate this unexpected present and became electrified at what I read, for here was something quite astonishing.

The papers harked back to 1970 and proved to be the haunting testimonies of a number of former soldiers who as young men had been fortunate to survive the extreme violence of the Great War. Here was the fruit of my father's determined effort to piece together the circumstances surrounding the death of his uncle at the Battle of Loos. These now elderly gentlemen had responded to my father's appeal in the local papers for former comrades of the 10th Gloucesters to contact him. Without my father's efforts all those years ago and also the willingness of those brave veterans to recount such a harrowing chapter in their lives, *In The Shadow Of Lone Tree* would not have been written.

I had at that time no ambition to write a book, but merely harboured a vague idea to further this research and to produce a document for family posterity. However, my investigations led me to the archives of the local newspapers and to my utter amazement I discovered an absolute treasure trove of information, including dozens and dozens of photographs showing the 10th Gloucesters training in Cheltenham. Before my eyes, unfolded the fascinating story of local men, and teenage boys, who volunteered in response to Kitchener's stern challenge to serve their country in time of great need and who were destined to endure their baptism of fire at Loos.

From the autumn of 1914, the newspapers published long lists naming those who had stepped forward to volunteer. Then in early 1915, dozens of photographs appeared showing these smiling, confident young men posing happily in brand new uniforms and brandishing rifles and swagger sticks. Accompanying these photographs were patriotic articles, interviews and letters, describing their training and experiences as proud soldiers of Kitchener's New Army. Included too, were stirring accounts of the carnival like atmosphere as the 'Fighting Tenth' finally left Cheltenham in the spring of 1915, prior to serving on the Western Front; then, a total void descended until the autumn of 1915, when once again the papers were awash with images of soldiers. But no smiling faces this time, only individual formal portraits of serious looking men in uniform, accompanied by grim obituaries and long, long dismal lists naming those killed, missing, gassed and wounded in the "Great Charge" at Loos. The earnest faces of the dead gazed back through time, challenging me to tell of their sacrifice.

At Loos, so many of those smiling, eager faces vanished from this world forever, their bodies sprawled across the ugly wastes of No Man's Land and in the battered enemy trenches, or hung like grisly scarecrows on the enemy's wire entanglements. Proud men, so recently living, breathing, laughing individuals, butchered and reduced to anonymous hunched bundles of blood soaked khaki lying in machine-gunned rows with packs and tunic pockets turned out, photographs of loved ones and their cherished letters fluttering amongst the discarded rifles and equipment littering the battlefield. Their poor, lifeless bodies awaiting a hasty burial on the battlefield in a convenient shell hole or an abandoned trench, whilst all around the relentless toil of warfare ground by, leaving in its cold, ruthless wake, this sad, pitiful flotsam of wasted humanity. The bodies of others who fell and lay for years within the deadly arcs of enemy machine gun fire, decomposed into mere skeletons, shrouded beneath gas helmets and clothed in tattered, weathered khaki uniforms and webbing; their rifles, bayonets and entrenching tools rusting at their sides.

Fresh troops moving up could only pause to gawp in fascinated horror at this hideous mess of mass slaughter freshly strewn all around. The grim harvest of enfilading machine guns, poison gas and shrapnel shells left absolutely no one in any doubt that this could become their own personal, pathetic fate.

During the course of researching *In The Shadow Of Lone Tree*, the individual faces of these men have become so familiar to me. They are now no longer forgotten soldiers pictured in old discoloured newspapers, or anonymous names engraved on numerous weather beaten memorials. Their lives ended tragically and violently so many years ago, but their spirits were powerful enough to reach out to me and I cannot help but sense their individual characters, their hopes, aspirations and fears.

In The Shadow Of Lone Tree is therefore my personal tribute to the officers and men of the 10th Gloucesters, also to my late father and to all the soldiers of today, including my own beloved son, who, despite so called enlightened times, are still called upon to brave the same ordeals on the field of battle.

Nick Christian 2011

The Honour For The 10th Gloucesters

Private W.J. Williams 13445 10th Battalion Gloucestershire Regiment, 3 Company, 12th Platoon, BEF, France, 3.10.15.

Just a few lines from the front, or what people call somewhere in France, we call it a place unknown. We have been out of the trenches about three days after being in them for eleven days, and very thankful I am to have a few days rest.

I daresay you have been reading in the papers of the success of the Allies. Well we were in a bayonet charge at Hulluch. We battered and bayoneted the Germans for about two hours without stop and took four lines of trenches but at tremendous cost. We took about 1,700 prisoners with the help of the Scottish. There is one honour to the 10th, we led the charge and had a very fine name. We were told by the General we had done what no other regiment had done for the last ten months and that was routed the Germans from their snug abode because they can dig trenches like moles and make them like a palace.

I have got a few souvenirs, and if I can live long enough to see the old homestead once again, I will let you have some.

It was on September the 25th we started the advance and we stuck to our posts and not a man lacked courage. The smoke was very thick like a fog. You could not see far especially with gas helmets on. But we kept rushing on and on all eager to get at the foe not thinking of our own lives. Many a time did I lift up a prayer and ask Him above to save me from those death hunters. No one can tell what the feeling is, only those who have been through it. Some of the German prisoners were very well fed and clothed while others looked very weak with hardly a thing to their backs but very stubborn fighters too.

We want more men and still more men out here to help, the more the merrier and the quicker the war will be over. Tell them to buck up, pull themselves together and come and help us out a bit.

In some parts cigs are very scarce while in other parts they are plentiful. But we are without at present so if you will be so kind to let Tommy Atkins have a few he will be very grateful.

Well there is nothing more I can say at present so I must close now. Hoping this will find you and family in the best of health as I am fairly well at present.

I beg to remember yours most sincerely,

William J. Williams.

P.S. I think you have my name on the school honours board as Corporal Williams, but I have been recommended for good conduct on the field so I will write and let you know how it turns out. Our Colonel has gone back to England with shattered nerves. Remember me to all.

Twenty two year old Bill Williams penned this letter to John Emery, his old headmaster at Double View School, Cinderford in Gloucestershire. Sadly, by the time it was published in the Dean Forest Mercury on October 22nd 1915, Bill was already dead and would never return to his family homestead.

Bill fell on October 13th and has no known grave. The 10th Gloucesters lost 62 officers and men killed on that day, in a final, futile attempt to capture the village of Hulluch on the last day of the Loos battle. He was a brave and resolute young man, just one of many.

CHAPTER I

The Forging of a Battalion

They sell the pasture now to buy the horse;
Following the mirror of all Christian Kings,
With winged heels, as English Mercuries,
For now sits expectation in the air;
And hides a sword from hilts unto the point

King Henry V. Act I, Scene II

In August 1914, as the German Armies swept through Belgium and into France, Britain was hopelessly unprepared to fight in a European war, even though such a conflict was regarded as unavoidable as Germany flaunted its powerful military might. The Kaiser took a personal interest in the moulding of his armed services and was instrumental in the adoption of the Maxim machine gun into the German Army. Popular opinion in Britain, however, confidently expected that the Regular British Army would, together with Britain's allies, defeat the Germans by Christmas 1914. Field Marshal Lord Kitchener, Britain's Secretary of State for War, had the foresight to anticipate a much more bitter and protracted struggle, suggesting that such a war could continue for up to three years and require an army of up to seventy divisions.

The British press vied to print ever more shocking accounts of German atrocities, chilling tales of rape, murder and barbarity, graphically described under bold headlines such as, **"The Hateful Hun and His Handiwork"** and **"The Trail of the Blonde Beast."** Headlines designed to insult the decency of every true Briton and instantly inflame the Nation's fighting spirit.

Included too, were the supposed eyewitness accounts of bloody battles in which the brainwashed German troops stormed heedlessly into the attack suffering thousands of casualties but brutally murdering those who had honourably surrendered to them. Even their dead, according to these startling revelations, would not receive a Christian burial, but were instead stripped and removed to Germany by their countrymen and unceremoniously and callously incinerated in huge furnaces.

The Kaiser was branded as a madman; his evil desire to spread the **"Cult of the Fatherland"** threatened civilized Europe. In the opinion of the Medical Press and Circular:

> His recent acts are of such a nature as to suggest that he has lost the higher
> mental control that constitutes sanity.

Early August 1914 saw the now famous **"Your Country Needs You"** posters appear and by mid September 500,000 men from every walk of life had enlisted to fight for Britain in what was hailed in the press as **"A Just and Holy War."** The recruiting posters were equally as effective in Gloucestershire; many hundreds flocked to County enlistment offices in a surge of unprecedented patriotism. There were also those who saw army life as an adventure, an escape from the terrible grind of hard labour at pitheads or the misery of unemployment and poverty. Others thoroughly abhorred War but saw it as their unavoidable duty to enlist.

Among Gloucestershire's recruits were strong young colliers and agricultural workers from the Forest of Dean; David Hail from Greenbottom, Jack Kear from Ruardean Hill, George Evans, Francis and William Hawkins, all from Cinderford. There were men representing a profusion of trades from Cheltenham; David Hawling, employed by the Cheltenham Original Brewery, George Lea, gardener to Reverend Canon Goodwyn, Whittington Rectory, St. Stephen's and Frederick Bridgeman, a Clerk at Messrs. Frederick Wright and Co. tobacconists.

The call to arms.

With them too were eager young men from Gloucester, Stroud, Tewkesbury and remote Cotswold villages; Thomas Phelps, Thomas Trussler, Thomas Hall and George Larner representing volunteers from these areas. Yet this huge response was not good enough for the county authorities and dignitaries and recruitment in Cheltenham was described as "**disappointing.**" During August and September 1914 the Cheltenham Echo carried many letters denouncing young men for shirking their duty. One, signed 'Old Soldier' was most outspoken.

> **The stout working classes are not so much to blame although they are quite backward in coming forward. It is the class of young man who has the good fortune to be beyond the necessities of work that constitutes the young 'nut' or 'knut' class who may be seen any day walking up and down the prom very neatly got up and very superior. Are these young men too nice to shoulder a rifle and take their place beside our glorious Tommies whose boots they are only fit to grease?**

The men of the Forest of Dean bore the brunt of some savage criticism. A particularly vitriolic outburst appeared in the August 28th edition of the Dean Forest Mercury, under the headline:

DO YOU UNDERSTAND?

> Worst of all, recruiting falls flat. The Cinderford district has yielded four! And yet the Forest of Dean teems with young single men of just the type their country needs. Just as in the past they have shirked their duty by neglecting the Territorial Force so now they are deaf to Lord Kitchener's appeal. A good way to realise their numbers will be to tour the football grounds of the Forest next month and see how the company is composed. A few will be playing, but the majority will be standing in the puddles looking at the matches which are apparently going to proceed with all the usual enthusiasm as if there was nothing at all the matter. The fact is that the men of the Forest of Dean DO NOT UNDERSTAND.

Private John 'Jack' Kear, a young collier from Ruardean in the Forest of Dean, Gloucestershire.

David Hawling.

George Lea.

Thomas Phelps lived in Tredworth, Gloucester.

Thomas Trussler. He came from Stroud.

Thomas Hall. Lived in Tewkesbury.

George Larner. His home was at Bourton-on-the-Water, Gloucestershire.

One wonders if the author of this unjustified rhetoric ever stepped forward to serve at the front. Or later, when the killing was done, recalled his harsh, contemptuous words when the Forest's communities gathered to mourn the hundreds who volunteered and never returned.

During September 1914, it was almost a daily occurrence for crowds to gather and cheer the volunteers through the streets of Cheltenham to The Midland Road rail station where they were to embark for Horfield Barracks in Bristol. The Cheltenham Echo commented that many of these fine young men were Cotswold lads; their faces sunburnt from long hours of recent harvest gathering.

On Tuesday September 1st, Major Shewell, Cheltenham's recruiting officer, addressed 86 volunteers:

Mayor Skillicorne addresses volunteers at Cheltenham. Major Shewell stands to the rear.

We are in a bit of a tight pinch and you men have come forward willing to do all you can to get us out. Remember each man to do his own and do his very best. You can't do any more and that is all the Country wants. I hope you have the best of luck and all come back well, but don't come back if you don't do your duty.

Cheltenham volunteers. September 1914.

Headed by the Boy Scout Bugle Band playing 'Tipperary', friends and relatives accompanied the men to the rail station where they sang, 'Should Auld Acquaintance Be Forgot'.

On Thursday September 10th, 120 volunteers were escorted by the Mayor, Alderman Skillicorne and the Boy's Brigade Bugle Band, along the Promenade through Clarence Street and back to the Promenade via the Colonnade. Scouts from Gloucester Road School sang 'Rule Britannia' and 'The Marseillaise'. Parcels of bread, cheese and cocoa, along with a tiny khaki-bound copy of the Gospel according to St. John, were presented to the men. At the Midland Road station they were cheered aboard the waiting train and saluted with bugles and the firing of fog signals. That day, a number of men destined for the 10th Gloucesters left Cheltenham. Among them were Ernest Betteridge, Frederick Bridgeman, Arthur and Frederick Chandler and Walter Daffurn.

The following Friday, 162 men departed from Cheltenham in the same manner. Accompanying them was a young man called William Jennings.

Private William Jennings – 10th Gloucesters:

One day I was delivering bread for Coole's Bakery in the Bath Road, Cheltenham, when an aristocratic lady stopped me and said, "Young man you really ought to be in France." That evening I was out with my friends, we had all drunk a fair bit of cider and decided to go to the recruiting centre near the Norwood Arms. I was told to report to Horfield Barracks in Bristol with a whole crowd of others and stayed there for three or four weeks before being assigned to the 10th Gloucestershire Regiment and sent to Salisbury Plain.

Although just seventeen years old, farm hand Ernest Chadband, who was employed by a Mr. Leadbeater at Nineveh Farm near the village of Mickleton in north Gloucestershire, was keen to volunteer. Ernest, who rose to the rank of Sergeant, recalled in 1972:

We knew we would eventually join up, but not until the recruiting meeting in King George's Hall in Mickleton. Sergeant Beckett who was Carrier and Barber in Chipping Campden, an old soldier, was Recruiting Sergeant and of course was present with his red, white and blue ribands round his cap. I am afraid he got called different names after we found out that we should have received what they called 'ration money' from the time we enlisted until we were called to Horfield Barracks in Bristol, which I think was about 10 days.

A postcard from 1914 designed to shame young men into volunteering.

In Gloucester too, enthusiastic crowds gathered to wave their men folk off. On September 1st, 350 men formed up in long lines at the Shire Hall. The Mayor, Councillor Bruton, spoke sincerely and far more kindly than had Major Shewell to the men in Cheltenham:

Men of Gloucester, I shall call you the fighting men of Gloucester. I shall never forget the sight I saw in this room on Friday night. It did my heart good. Not that I ever doubted that the men of Gloucester would respond to their Country's call, but the response was such as no one anticipated. You are leaving in a few minutes, and I am not going to make a speech. I simply want to say how proud we are of you men, that at a time when you were wanted you volunteered to go in defence of your country. Now boys go and do your duty, and God bless you.

William Jennings.

Ernest Chadband was a born survivor. He cheated almost certain death at Loos and emerged unscathed from the murderous fighting at High Wood in 1916. By 1917 he had been promoted to Sergeant and in 1918, through sheer determination, he escaped capture despite a serious wound to his arm.

At Newnham-on-Severn's small rail station, lean, muscular, work hardened Forest of Dean colliers waited patiently on the platform. Many had walked several miles to board the steam train that would transport them from hard toil in the pits to what many hoped would be a great adventure. Reg Betteridge, Jack Arkell, Tom Hart, Charlie Murrell and the Hawkins brothers, all took their place amongst the throngs of their fellow colliery workers. Their families, proud fathers, tearful mothers and wives and bewildered children, accompanied the volunteers. Eventually, the train puffed into the station and with much clanking and a great hiss of steam, slowed to halt adjacent to the now animated crowd.

George Evans knelt and kissed his three young daughters. His wife Esther clutched his hand and with tear streaked cheeks looked up at him and once again begged him not to go. Of course it was

George Evans with his wife Esther and their three young daughters.

in vain, George had already told her he would **"fight as a volunteer"** and not as a **"pressed man."** And so, in all parts of Gloucestershire, Forest, Vale and Cotswolds, emotional, heartfelt farewells were exchanged as the men boarded trains that would transport them to an exciting but uncertain future.

Smiling volunteers leave Cheltenham for Horfield Barracks, Bristol.

Once at Horfield Barracks, the volunteers were accommodated in tents and allocated to either the 8th, 9th or 10th (Service) Battalions of The Gloucestershire Regiment. At that time, Service Battalions were being formed at locations all over Britain and as their name suggested they were formed to serve for the duration of the war. These battalions have become better known as New Army, Kitchener Army or Pals Battalions and shared the traditions and spirit of the Regular and Territorial Force units already fighting overseas, and after which they were numbered in sequence. Each battalion initially had an established compliment of about 1,000 men and eventually over 500 Service battalions would be formed during the Great War, massively expanding the strength of the British Army and buying victory with their civilian blood.

Volunteers parade at Horfield Barracks, Bristol, 1914.

The recruiting posters called for volunteers between the ages of 19 and 30. However, this was an era with very different standards and attitudes to those we aspire to today and it was not unusual for children to have already left school by the time they were thirteen years old and were helping to support their families by earning a small wage. Consequently large numbers of underage teenage boys presented themselves as volunteers.

Volunteers destined to join the ranks of a Gloucestershire battalion as cooks, pose with the tools of their trade.

At the start of the 20th Century, the British Army was still close to its long history of recruiting boys into the ranks. This is also reflected in the militaristic attitudes ingrained into boys of that era who were encouraged to join the Boy's Brigade, the Officer's Training Corps at Universities and Public Schools and the Territorial Force. After all, Britain required dynamic young Britons to uphold

Private Frank Gapper, age 17 on enlistment.

Private Hubert Butler, age just 16 on enlistment.

Private Edward Denley, age 19 on enlistment. Edward was originally from Eckington near Worcester where his mother had run the Bell Inn. He was drafted into the 8th Devons and was wounded at Loos on September 25th. Edward was later killed with the 1st Devons on June 2nd, 1916.

Corporal William Denley was Edward's younger brother. He enlisted at Cheltenham on September 6th 1914, giving his age as 19, which was accepted by the recruiting officer, Major Shewell. In fact William was still only 16 years of age. William was promoted to Corporal on March 24th 1915. He was wounded in the arm at Loos whilst serving with the 10th Gloucesters.

and maintain order in the far-flung corners of its Empire. It seems that on this basis, and the fact that they were paid for signing up each recruit, many recruiting sergeants were perfectly willing to turn a blind eye to those they suspected of being under age, and also to those who were over age.

A good number of these determined under age soldiers found their way into the ranks of the 10th Gloucesters. Frank Gapper, an under gardener to Sir Ashton Lister of Dursley, was seventeen, as was Dennis Gabb from Cinderford. Joseph King, who worked on the bookstall at W.H. Smith's in Cheltenham, Hubert Butler, who worked for Messrs. Fielding and Platt in Gloucester and James Gapper from Cheltenham were each only sixteen years old.

William Leaman of Aston in Birmingham was just fifteen years old when he enlisted and was still only sixteen when he was killed at Loos. Herbert Humphries from Balsall Heath in Birmingham was killed in the Ypres Salient on November 16th 1917. His grave at Divisional Collecting Post Cemetery near Ypres, states that at eighteen years old he was already the holder of a Military Medal for gallantry. As an original member of the battalion that went to France in August 1915, this would have meant that he was still only fifteen or sixteen years old when he fought at Loos. However, census details reveal that he was seventeen on enlistment and was in fact twenty years old when he was killed.

The parents of these youngsters also seem to have been complicit in this deception. Most were undoubtedly proud that their boys were answering the call of patriotism, whilst others let their young sons volunteer because their elder brother or brothers were volunteering and had foolishly persuaded themselves that the boys would be able to look after each other. Such was the tragic allure of the Pal's Battalion system.

Felix Stockwell was fifteen years old when he enlisted with his brother Sidney who was twenty years old. Felix was still only seventeen when he was killed in March 1916. William Hart from Upton-on-Severn, Worcestershire, enlisted having just turned seventeen and was posted to the 10th Gloucesters to serve with his father Sidney aged thirty-nine.

However, following the truly bloody casualties suffered by the British Army in the first months of 1915, 'the penny dropped' and many parents made frantic efforts to retrieve their sons from the army, or at least get them transferred out of the infantry. Even so, by the time the 10th Gloucesters went into action at Loos, all the under age lads mentioned above, and numerous others, remained with the battalion.

At the other end of the spectrum were those who were not obliged to enlist because they were beyond the required age. Again, as long as they appeared to be physically fit, there was no reason for the recruiting officers to reject them.

Forty four year old Arthur Harrison, an assistant schoolmaster at Holy Trinity School, Tewkesbury, enlisted at Christmas 1914 having previously been a member of the Tewkesbury Volunteer Training Corps. At Cheltenham, Frank Artus aged 39 probably left the security of working as a train driver to join his younger brother Richard, who had enlisted having formerly served with the 1st Gloucesters in the Boer War.

10th Gloucesters at Codford. Note the differing types of dress.

All those mentioned, found themselves with the 10th Gloucesters, however others were allocated to different battalions and regiments. Forest of Dean men, Tom Hart from Ruspidge, John Webb

Soon the men were issued with uniforms of blue, nicknamed "Kitchener Blue."

Also pictured at Codford, some of these men have been issued with khaki uniforms and cap badges.

A group of the 10th at Codford. George Evans, formerly a collier from Cinderford in the Forest of Dean, is kneeling in the front row second from left. George Lea, on the right with a cigarette, was a gardener in Cheltenham.

Sergeant Ernest Artus, killed at Loos, September 25th 1915.

Sergeant Horace Garner, killed at Loos, September 25th 1915.

A group of 1st Gloucesters pictured at a fortified position during the Boer War. Ernest Artus is marked with a cross.

from Whitecroft and Tom Pritchard from Ellwood, along with Harry Mills from Moreton in Marsh in the Cotswolds, went to the Regular 1st Gloucesters to help replace their massive casualties. Pritchard, Webb and Hart were all rushed to France on February 18th 1915, within seven months of enlistment and were still only partly trained. Others, such as Edward Denley from Eckington near Worcester and Albert Yemm from Steam Mills in the Forest of Dean, were drafted into the 8th Devon and 8th Royal West Kent (Service) battalions respectively.

The 9th Gloucesters were first formed from Cheltenham and district recruits, however, there was a surplus of men and these were sent to join the Warwickshire Regiment. However, as more Gloucestershire recruits flooded in, it became clear that there were practically enough men for a further battalion and so the 10th Battalion was formed and brought up to strength with recruits from the Midlands. The 10th therefore included a host of men from the Birmingham district, as well as men from all parts of Gloucestershire, the Cotswolds and the Forest of Dean, as well as a sprinkling from South Wales, Worcestershire, Wiltshire, Oxfordshire and Somerset.

During October 1914, the men allocated to the 8th, 9th and 10th Gloucesters were sent for initial training to the village of Codford St. Mary near Warminster on the edge of Salisbury Plain.

The men were all billeted in long rows of draughty bell tents and it rained so much that the men called the camp **"Codford-on-Mud."**

Sergeant Ernest 'Chaddy' Chadband – 10th Gloucesters:

> **At the ripe old age of 17 I endured the worst night I had ever experienced in my life. With about 17 in a bell tent, I eventually found myself sleeping under the flap of the tent. Anyway I refrained from taking my clothes off,**

which was as well because being used as a doormat I decided to take my blanket and sleep under the trees in the camp. I think it rained day and night the whole time we were there.

The conditions were so primitive and unpleasant that the men refused to suffer it for long.

Sergeant Ernest Chadband:

> Codford was a terrible place to pitch a camp. Well, we all rioted and went on strike, as we could not sleep. Wet ran down the hill and through the tents so we protested to go to bed. The 8th, 9th and 10th Gloucesters guards turned pick handles but with no avail. We let the tents down on those who would not come out and in almost three days the 9th and 10th were billeted in Cheltenham and the 8th in Weston-Super-Mare.

Wisely, the regimental authorities took immediate steps to calm the situation and on Monday November 16th 1914, the 10th Gloucesters arrived on two trains at Cheltenham's Great Western rail station. A reporter from the Cheltenham Echo witnessed their arrival and contrasted the appearance of the battalion with that of the 9th Gloucesters who had preceded the 10th to Cheltenham:

> It was observed that the 10th had not the khaki great coat, but wore overcoats of miscellaneous cuts and patterns that had been served out to them pending the coming of the orthodox one, and their caps were not all of the same style. Here and there a case denoted a musical instrument in it.

Men of the 10th Gloucesters form up in Cheltenham prior to being marched to Lansdown Crescent.

Mayor Skillicorne accompanied by Lt. Col. Pritchard lead the 10th Gloucesters through the streets of Cheltenham. Lt. Ivan Richard Gibbs is the officer on the left of the column.

Nevertheless, the local population cheered the men of the 10th Gloucesters, as they marched through Cheltenham to Lansdown Crescent where they were to be billeted.

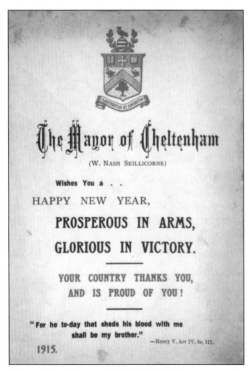

Happy New Year card for 1915. Each man serving with the 10th received one.

Sergeant Ernest Chadband:

How well I remember how we were welcomed and made at home. I picture the Rotunda with 'Soldiers Welcome' posted all around and these kind ladies certainly made us welcome with cups of tea, cocoa and all good things to eat, games, writing and everything one needed, with hymn singing on Sundays. I have made several visits to Christ Church where we used to parade on Sundays and where the cross from High Wood is placed. We sang 'Hark the Herald Angels Sing' at Christmas 1914 and nearly lifted the roof.

Following the weeks spent in tented misery at Codford St. Mary, the men found the spacious four storey buildings of the Crescent a complete revelation.

Christ Church, Cheltenham.

Sergeant Ernest Chadband:

> We spent six months in Cheltenham, which we enjoyed very much after a
> few weeks in the mud, to come into clean streets and billets, which were
> empty houses.

These buildings provided excellent billets and the large grassed area fronting the Crescent made a fine parade and training ground. Those who lived nearby were allowed the luxury of reporting for duty from home.

It seems that the Regency Crescent also suited the officers and one discovered a colony of Roman snails thriving amongst the ivy-covered walls in the Crescent gardens. Private Reginald Fennell was most amused to be sent out hunting for these French delicacies, which were afterwards served in the Officer's Mess.

Private Fennell was shortly to become a minor celebrity in his native Forest of Dean when he gave a most glowing account of his new life to a reporter from the Dean Forest Mercury.

WHAT A BLAKENEY SOLDIER THINKS OF ENLISTING

> Mr. Reginald Fennell, New Road, whose name appears in the 'Mercury'
> amongst others a few weeks since, having been granted four days leave, came
> home, and his many friends and acquaintances were very interested in all
> the things he had to say of his barrack life experiences and daily round.

In respect of food, Mr. Fennell is content that the provisions served are both plentiful and varied. Everything provided is absolutely clean and the cooking leaves nothing to be desired. Mr. Fennell, in fact, speaks in high praise as to the provision made for the sustenance and contentment of the recruit.

Discussing the question of clothing, especially at night, our informant says that from the point of view that a soldier ought to "endure hardness" the fact that he was provided with as many blankets as he wanted was sufficient for him. He acknowledged sleeping on the floor was not exactly how they arranged things at Honey Bee Cottage, New road, Blakeney, but then, to have it all too comfortable would not be soldiering.

He mentioned incidentally that just then the company to which he

Private Reginald Fennell.

belonged were accommodated in a large mansion in Cheltenham. All the vacant residences in the Garden Town had been secured by the military as

Servants of the officers mess. Reginald Fennell is in the back row second from the left.

domiciles for them. Mr. Fennell spoke in highly complementary terms of his Colonel, who, he said, was among other things a teetotaller. He took more than a military interest in his men.

There were hours every day when the men were free to follow their own bent, but the Colonel had been wonderfully successful in his appeal to the townspeople to do what in them lay in the provision of accommodation where they could meet and enjoy social recreation, amid a sound, healthy environment. The special activities of the Y.M.C.A., which was doing right good work amongst them, care being for their material advantage as well as spiritual good, was very highly spoken of.

Of the drilling and the marching and the routine of his daily life, Mr. Fennell says that, if it means "putting on flesh," as is the fact in his case, then his exercises are not overdone. To put the whole case shortly, and merely from the point of view of the experiences gained, and the advantages, which he hopes discipline will have on his future life.

Mr. Fennell strongly advises all eligible young men to join Kitchener's Army, this apart from the question of the grave national crisis and the duty which he enjoined on everyone to rise to the occasion, and to come forward and offer himself freely and readily to do his defence of King and Country.

Mr. Fennell, who is the younger son of the family, returned last weekend, leaving home in the best of spirits and of health. He never "felt so fit" he said.

Soon the men of the fledgling battalion were issued with complete uniforms, but had to be content with obsolete Lee Metford rifles, a type that had been replaced in 1902 by the Long Lee Enfield rifle, which in turn was replaced by the Short Magazine Lee Enfield rifle. Other equipment was very limited, but gradually as war production improved the men became fully kitted out, having the appearance at least of a disciplined and effective fighting force.

Some of the men billeted in Eckington House.

Cooks of the 10th. A motley crew.

Crowds gathered in Lansdown Crescent to watch the soldiers carrying out bayonet practice. The battalion's standard route march took them from Cheltenham to Tewkesbury, then on to Gloucester and back to Cheltenham. Here their Colonel would meet them on horseback at Arle Court and march them into Cheltenham. What a fine, heart swelling sight they must have presented, marching resolutely along the country roads, earning the admiration of all they passed.

Sergeant Ernest Chadband:

> It was great fun to us youngsters. We had a few boys from Birmingham transferred from Worcester who were good pals and we had lots of fun together, forgetting that we were training to fight a war.
>
> I always picture Sammy Moss and Jimmy Hill, two small boys, but oh so full of life! I remember going on a route march to Gloucester Cathedral, having our lunch in the square afterwards. We proceeded through the cathedral in single file and Jimmy was just in front of me. We came across some huge statue of some Lord. I burst out laughing when Jimmy said, "wake up mate, don't you know there's a war on." I can still see those two boys coming out of High Wood in 1916, a little older perhaps but still able to smile and joke and see the funny side, if there was one to be found!
>
> Afterwards, marching back to Cheltenham, we had a really grand time, free teas on Sunday after we had sung all the well-known hymns, (and lots we had made up.) Several Soldiers Clubs were opened for us, one in particular at the top of the Promenade and called the Rotunda, now Lloyds Bank.

The battalion's main training ground was on Cleeve Hill, just outside Cheltenham where the men could regularly be seen charging from the summit down towards Winchcombe, or storming make believe enemy positions.

Sergeant Ernest Chadband:

> At Gloucester road where 'B' Company went for company training, the
> fields we used are now no more, but Cleeve Hill and Leckhampton Hill are
> still there.

In Cheltenham the press had already incongruously dubbed the battalion "**The Fighting Tenth.**"
Their commanding officer was Lieutenant Colonel Henry Edward Pritchard, an experienced Indian
Army officer brought out of retirement. His second in command was a New Zealander, Major James
G. Kirkwood, a veteran of Brabant's Horse and Kitchener's Fighting Scouts of the Boer War.

Sergeant Ernest Chadband:

> The Colonel, who had just returned from commanding a unit in the Indian
> Army, must have thought he still had Indians to deal with as a favourite
> word of his always before he gave a word of command was, "10th
> Gloucesters, not a move" and he never gave way until everyone ever stopped
> blinking. He was very popular just at that time.

Officers of the 10th Gloucesters pictured in Cheltenham.
Back: 2nd Lt. F.A. Carnegy, 2nd Lt. G.W. Robinson, 2nd Lt. C.A. Symons, 2nd Lt. A.S. Whitworth, 2nd Lt. E.H.
Sale, Lt. W.R. Paterson, 2nd Lt. W.S. Gange.
Middle: 2nd Lt. S.G. Stephenson, Lt. (QM) J. Hewins, 2nd Lt. L.W. Hastie, 2nd Lt. H. Enriquez. Lt. I.R. Gibbs,
2nd Lt. G.G. Leary, Lt. A.A. Langley, 2nd Lt. J.W.C. Tongue.
Front: Capt. H. Anderson, Capt. W.P. Brough, Capt. R.L. Williams, Lt. Col. H.E. Pritchard, Capt. L.C. Lawrence,
Capt. J.G. Kirkwood, Lt. (Adj) K.A.R. Smith.

Back row: second from left David Hail. Middle row: from the left Herbert Page, John 'Jack' Kear, John 'Jack' Arkell, Frank Haile. Front row: second from left Thomas Wood, fifth from left Frank Artus, sixth from left Dennis Gabb.

A group of 10th Gloucesters from Painswick near Stroud, Gloucestershire, including Private Albert Higgins seated with the dog. Young men from Painswick were happy to be known as 'Bow-Wow Boys' following a feud with their counterparts in Stroud. The legend is that to seal a supposed truce the Painswick men baked the unwitting Stroud men a meat pie - with the meat from a puppy dog. Albert Higgins did not survive Loos, falling on September 25th.

Two platoons of the 10th Gloucesters pose at Lansdown Crescent. Many of these men were destined to become casualties at Loos. Seated together second from right, Sergeant Reginald Betteridge, third from right Sergeant Ernest Artus, fourth from right, Lieutenant Geffrey Leary. All three died at Loos.

The battalion consisted of five companies, including an HQ company. The four fighting companies each had an establishment of about 240 men. The senior NCOs were likely to be experienced former soldiers that had re-enlisted or were reservists called up quickly to replace casualties at the front and to staff the fledgling service battalions. On August 11th 1914, the re-enlistment of former senior NCOs up to the age of fifty was authorised. Further NCOs were sometimes picked from the volunteers on the dubious basis of who could shout the loudest. A service battalion of the Northamptonshire Regiment picked theirs on previous service as vague as having been a boy scout.

Subalterns were often newly gazetted Second Lieutenants who had been trained in the Officer's Training Corps at universities or junior cadet units at public and grammar schools. Junior commissions were also handed to under graduates, senior schoolboys and those who it was considered held responsible positions in civilian life. Of course demand for new officers outstripped the supply and so in early 1915 it was decided that volunteers recommended by their commanding officers would be given a short course of four weeks and then, if deemed suitable, commissioned.

Awkward and unsoldierly at first, these 'civilian soldiers' were marched and drilled until the relaxed nature of their former existence was driven from them. Many of the newly gazetted subalterns, some still in their teens, were as inexperienced as the men, but were guided by experienced sergeants such as veterans Horace Garner and Ernest Artus.

Sergeant Ernest Chadband:

> **Much of the training was routine, musketry, platoon and company drill,**
> **which most of us already knew through the Boy's Brigade. Here I was put**

into the tug of war team under a P.T. sergeant who soon found out how old I was, just 18 and far too young to hang on to oak trees for 20 minutes at a time so I soon got put back to company. We all got vaccinations and injections and eventually got transferred to khaki from 'Kitchener's Blue' and we were issued with rifles for training. Of course when we could present arms, general salute etc. we felt like business, but we had no ammunition, we were still firing blanks, which was perhaps just as well.

Courtesy Paul Hughes.

A group of the 10th pose with their Boer War vintage rifles. There was no ammuntion available and live firing didn't take place until a few weeks before the battalion finally crossed to France.

All the photographs taken of the men and officers at the time reveal them to be proud and cheerful in their comradeship, the very essence of Britain's strength and fortitude. Little did anyone guess that every ounce of these attributes would be needed in the coming months and years to carry them through the unimagined horrors that lay ahead.

Winter passed and Kitchener's gloomy vision of a long and terrible struggle had come to pass. There was to be no hoped for victory by Christmas 1914, indeed some desperate fighting had barely saved the French, British and Belgian armies from collapse. Advances and counter advances of the first months of the war had finally bogged down in the winter of 1914 and the Germans had consolidated the territory they had captured. On the Western Front they now faced the French, British and Belgians from the cover of deep, carefully prepared trench systems, protected by festoons of barbed wire, machine guns and meticulously registered artillery. This defensive line presented a single front from Nieuport on the Belgian coast, to Switzerland.

By May 1915, the 10th Gloucesters were ready for Divisional training on Salisbury Plain. On the Wednesday evening before their departure, the Sergeants and Warrant Officers held a farewell party at Cheltenham Town Hall. Two hundred and fifty relatives and friends attended. They danced to Hambling's Band and Mr. Marfell of the Cosy Corner restaurant provided the catering.

A well deserved rest on Cleeve Hill.

A group of men collecting rations. Private Hubert Butler is standing at the front second from left and Sergeant Ernest 'Dick' Betteridge is far right.

Soldiers of the 10th train on Cleeve Hill near Cheltenham.

In preparation for the laying of a water main, the new soldiers hone their trench digging skills in Sandford Road, Cheltenham.

Aged just 19 years, Private Charles Richard Newman died of pneumonia on February 18th 1915. Charles lies buried near his home at Minchinhampton, Gloucestershire.

At 10am on the morning of May 6th, the battalion marched from Lansdown Crescent to St. James' Square Station, headed by bugles and drums. Here, tearful relatives and the cheering population of Cheltenham, led by Mayor Skillicorne, bade them a heartfelt farewell.

The train took them to Wiltshire and they went into camp at Longbridge Deverill near Longleat, and later to Camp 6 at nearby Sutton Veney. Here the early summer was spent attached to the 26th Division, digging trenches in the hard, dry, chalky soil. The Germans had already demonstrated the super efficiency of the machine gun, and yet, because there were no tactics available to counter this menace, the men were still taught to advance in extended order with rifle and bayonet at high port. General Sir Douglas Haig, who was to command the offensive at Loos in which the 10th would be first committed, reputedly once stated, "**The machine gun is a much over rated weapon.**"

Whilst at Sutton Veney, the battalion was issued with modern Short Magazine Lee Enfield rifles. The 10th were now equipped for combat, however, unbelievably, their practice with the new weapons amounted to firing only half a dozen rounds or so on the ranges.

A great air of comradeship radiates from these men about to leave Cheltenham. Sergeant James Taylor from Cheltenham is standing left of centre with a cigarette.

Friends and relatives gather to see the new soldiers off.

In contrast to the broad grins of the men, the seriousness of their farewell can ben seen on the faces of these officers and their realtives.

"6" COMPANY
10TH GLOUCESTERS ON THE MARCH
ON SALISBURY PLAIN.
1915
J.G.K

'C' Company of the 10th Gloucesters with Lt. Sale and Major Kirkwood at their head.

Sergeant Ernest Chadband:

> We had bags of Company and Battery formation which made us fed up to the teeth until one dreadful day we were ordered to parade early in the morning through Warminster. We did not know why until too late. We and

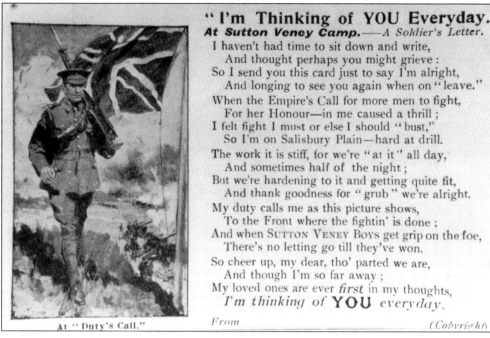

A patriotic postcard sent home by Evan Davies. On the reverse he wrote, "The water we drink has been poisoned by someone, it has made some of the lads bad."

A group of the 10th at Sutton Veney, Salisbury Plain. Private Evan Davies from Blakeney in the Forest of Dean is seated front centre.

the 8th Royal Berkshires were picked out by the Big Man himself to replace the Grenadiers and Coldstream Guards in the 1st Division in France. Some honour we thought at the time, but we were allowed only 48 hours to fire ball ammunition and 24 hours leave.

The frustrating months of route marches, night manoeuvres, bayonet practice and trench digging were almost done, when at the end of July 1915 Lieutenant Colonel Pritchard received orders to prepare his battalion for active service in France. The long awaited news electrified the men. Each, as a volunteer, yearned to get to the front and fight for Britain, but now that the order had finally arrived, few failed to grasp the possible tragic implications.

Officers and men alike, each found quiet moments to write home, all claiming to be happy and in good health, but also painfully reassuring their loved ones that if the unthinkable should happen they would be provided for.

Men of the 8th Royal Berkshire Regiment pose at Sutton Veney.

Many of those hailing from simple rural backgrounds or city slums had never learned to read and write. They often quietly approached a friend handier with a pen to scribble a few lines for them. Others, like George Evans, whose best skills lay with a pick and shovel deep in the dark depths of a Forest of Dean coal mine, wrestled with dimly remembered rules of grammar. His anxious wife received the following letter; its touching simplicity does not obscure his deep love and affection for Esther and his three tiny daughters:

> Sutton Veney nr Warminster Wilt. My Dear wife and children father and mother I now write these few lines to you hoping that they will find you in good health as it leaves me at present and my arm is much better now we

due for some long marching to do but I shall be home on Saturday they have stop on all pass this week and we are in the second army and I may be home any times. I do not now went I shall be home and we are under order to go away from here and I have made my will out for you to have all I got and we are have our new rifle sometimes this wekk and I got the money and fags alright this morning. Write back soon my Dear wife and I hope that nelle and lena and little annie is alright so good night and god bless you till see you again.

Courtesy Paul Hughes.

Private William Hedges pictured on his last leave home with his family at Campden in Gloucestershire. William was killed on September 25th 1915, alongside his cousin Private Thomas Smith. Neither has a known grave.

Courtesy Vic Morris.

Lance Corporal Edmund Lord was gassed at Loos and finally captured in 1918 whilst serving with the 8th Gloucesters. Here he is pictured on his last leave home in 1915 with his family at Erdington, Birmingham.

Men of the 10th Gloucesters leaving Cheltenham for Sutton Veney following their last leave before crossing to France.

Courtesy Paul Hughes.

Private Thomas Smith was the cousin of William Hedges. Tom fell at Loos on September 25th 1915 and has no known grave.

CHAPTER II

To War

**Now thrive the armourers and honours thought
Reigns solely in the breast of every man**

King Henry V. Act I, Scene II

Finally, after nearly a year of training, the eagerly awaited orders were issued. The 10th were to sail and take their place alongside the hard-pressed Regular and Territorial battalions of the British Expeditionary Force. Once in France, the 10th, together with the 8th Royal Berkshires, were to join the prestigious and already battle hardened 1st Brigade of the 1st Division. A battalion each of the Scots Guards and the Coldstream Guards were to be withdrawn from the Division and it was the unenviable task of the 10th Gloucesters and 8th Royal Berkshires to replace them.

In August 1915, Major General Arthur E. Holland commanded the 1st Division. It contained three infantry brigades each made up of the following battalions:

1st Brigade	2nd Brigade	3rd Brigade
10th Gloucester	2nd Royal Sussex	1st South Wales Borderers
1st Black Watch	1st Loyal North Lancashire	1st Gloucester
8th Royal Berkshire	1st Northampton	2nd Welsh
1st Cameron Highlanders	2nd King's Royal Rifle Corps	2nd Royal Munster Fusiliers
1/14th London Scottish	1/9th King's Liverpool	

On August 8th 1915, the 10th Gloucesters departed from Sutton Veney aboard three trains bound for the port of Southampton, and at 5pm they boarded a steamer bound for Le Havre. The crossing was to be conducted at night to avoid detection by German submarines. According to the battalion War Diary it was an uneventful crossing.

Lance Corporal Leonard Freeman – 10th Gloucesters:

> We did not start until well into the night, we had rather a good voyage across, although the sea was rather rough at times. We had our first glimpse of France when we arrived at Le Havre in the morning and disembarked and set our feet on French soil. However we hadn't much time to spare so it seemed as we hastily fell in and marched from the docks and through the town to a little place some way out. We camped there for a day or so and eventually moved off and arrived at the station where we boarded but not in railway carriages, but in cattle trucks.

The morning of August 9th dawned bright and clear, promising a continuation of the swelteringly hot weather. Finally at 7am that morning, the excited soldiers stepped expectantly onto French soil. The soldiers were halted on the quayside for an hour whilst the battalion disembarked and formed up for the march to No.5 Rest Camp at Le Havre.

Arriving at the camp, the men thankfully released the uncomfortable burden of their chafing equipment and kicked off fire hot boots, before collapsing in perspiring heaps. The march had been too much for some of the newly vaccinated men, who fell out on the way.

The battalion strength amounted to 30 officers and 985 other ranks, only 10 below established strength. The four fighting companies were commanded respectively by Captain Ivan R. Gibbs; Lieutenant Hay Enriquez; Lieutenant Edward Hanson Sale and Captain W.R. Paterson. The battalion possessed three Maxim machine guns commanded by Second Lieutenant J.A. Royds. Second Lieutenant George Walton Field was the Grenadier and bombing officer and Second Lieutenant Frederick Harry Turner was the Signalling Officer, whilst Second Lieutenant J. Hewins was Quartermaster and Lieutenant R. O'Dowd the Transport Officer. Second Lieutenant Stanley G. Stephenson acted as the Adjutant and faithfully recorded in the battalion's War Diary the events that came to pass.

The sea crossing to France and following march had been tedious, but the second leg of their journey was to be even more arduous. At 9am on the following morning, the 10th fell in once more with full kit and marched to the Gare des Merchandises. Here, they entrained into covered cattle trucks, forty men to each truck. It was past noon when the train ground ponderously out of the station and rattled its way northward along the coast through Etaples, Boulogne and Calais, then inland through the night to G.H.Q. at St. Omer on the Franco – Belgian border. It was 7.30am in the morning when they finally arrived. Here ended their journey on wheels. It had been stiflingly hot and water had been in short supply. Burdened by packs and equipment, rifles jarring and jagging every obstruction, all were glad to emerge into the fresh air and put into practice the traditional labour of the infantry - marching. A Staff Officer met them with orders and they marched two miles to Tatinghem where they were shown their billets. At Tatinghem clean water was difficult to obtain and sanitation was bad.

The 10th remained at Tatinghem until August 16th and whilst there received orders to join the 1st Division and replace the 1st Scots Guards in the line. On the 16th therefore, they marched to Aire and spent the night billeted in some old Napoleonic barracks.

Lance Corporal Leonard Freeman:

> **When we eventually arrived at our destination, which was a rather large town called Aire, our poor feet had suffered from the road. The French roads are much different to ours, the majority are cobbled with rough surfaces, not like our smooth tarred roads we have in England.**

The following day the battalion marched on through Molingham, Ham en Artois, Lillers, Chocques and finally to the town of Béthune in northern France, six and a half miles from a relatively quiet sector of the front. Béthune was described as a **"jolly town"** and very little damaged, unlike some of the war ravaged mining settlements extending eastward towards the sound of the guns.

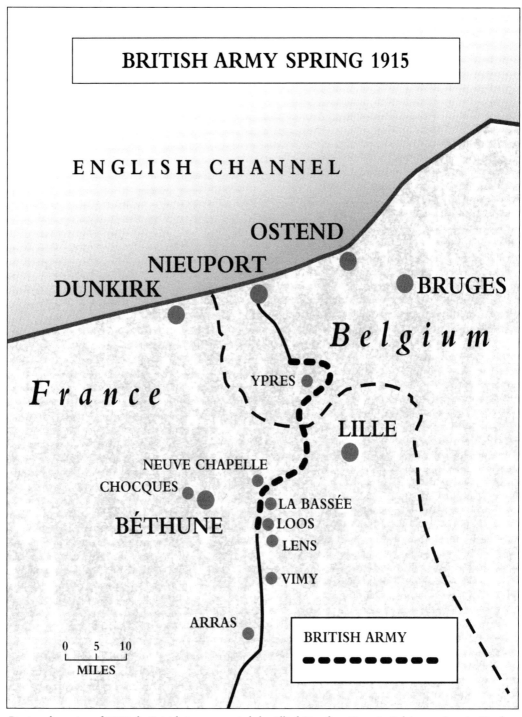

BRITISH ARMY SPRING 1915

ENGLISH CHANNEL

OSTEND

NIEUPORT

DUNKIRK

BRUGES

Belgium

France

YPRES

LILLE

NEUVE CHAPELLE

CHOCQUES

BÉTHUNE

LA BASSÉE

LOOS

LENS

VIMY

ARRAS

BRITISH ARMY

0 5 10
MILES

During the spring of 1915 the British Army occupied the Allied Line from Ypres in Belgium to Lens in Northern France.

The British held town of Vermelles lies in ruins. The flat, open nature of the Loos battlefield lies to the east.

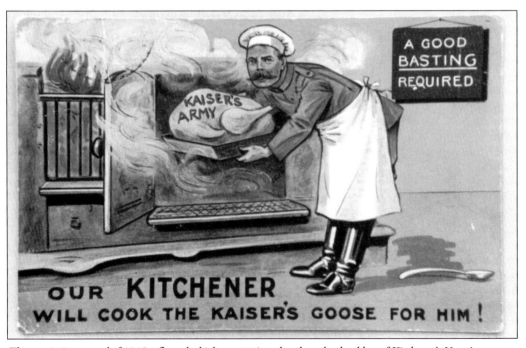

This patriotic postcard of 1915 reflects the high expectation placed on the shoulders of Kitchener's New Army.

At 6am on August 18th, the men experienced their first taste of the violence of war and suffered their first casualties inflicted by enemy action.

Corporal Albert Carter – 10th Gloucesters:

> Whilst we were billeted in Béthune, the battalion and men of other units were lying out in a field when a plane flew overhead. Everyone gazed up at it curiously. As it came over I saw the pilot lean over the side and let go of a bomb. It exploded amongst us killing an artilleryman and wounding some others, including two from the Gloucesters.

Private William Jennings:

> As the plane passed overhead, some French children nearby began pointing upwards and shouting excitedly, "Allemande, Allemande." Of course, we did not know what they meant and just sat there.

On August 19th, Battalion Headquarters was established at the small mining village of Sailly Labourse and that night the 10th formed up and were marched two and a half miles towards the flickering flashes of gunfire and the eerie arcs of rising Very lights that rose to fitfully illuminate the battlefront. On reaching the shell blasted ruins of Vermelles town, the battalion was met by a guide who led them into a maze of unfamiliar communication trenches that zigzagged a tortuous route to the front line.

In the pitch dark, burdened with rifles and haversacks, the bewildered soldiers stumbled their way over broken duckboards, slipped into slimy sump pits and snagged their rifles on sagging lengths of telephone cable. The Gloucesters would soon learn to negotiate such obstacles by quietly passing back down the line a warning of impending hazards.

Here, an officer of the Welsh Guards describes how his company were led into the trenches from Vermelles in October 1915:

> The Battalion was distributed about the ruins of Vermelles, which was continually shelled by the enemy. It was a bright moonlight night, with a faint distant haze – a ghostly kind of haze – and there was no movement to be seen, and no skyline – we seemed to be marching towards nothing; but outside the empty fields of our vision there was a noise, far away cannon, rumbles of French 75s and occasionally a whine overhead as a big shell passed on its journey.
>
> The flat chalky plain was covered with rank grass, and I can remember the muffled tramp on the hard ground, and the swish of the men's feet as they cut through the long grass.
>
> The moon deceived us with its brightness, revealing distances that were false, and the mist, an accomplice, enveloped us so softly that we did not know it was there: grey mounds and banks showed up ahead and on our flanks. With surprising suddenness we were made aware of human

presences. While skirting one of the mounds a glint of light would show through a crack in the earth – it was a dugout. Or, on approaching a bank it would open into a wriggling, shallow, tumbled trench, and a motionless shadow would move and speak! Everything was unexpected; we went into a slight dip where there was a hedge and what looked like a gateway leading into a narrow cutting. This was a communication trench.

Here we pause as the company formed into single file to begin, seemingly, an endless journey along the twisting trench, which was so deep I could not see over the top. Eventually we came to a cross trench, with troops and dugouts: they told us we were in the third line. And so to the second line, and finally to the firing line.

Here, we were met by some more guides who led each platoon to the post it had to relieve, and the relief was carried out without confusion, though with a certain amount of mental uncertainty.

At length, the disorientated men arrived in the front line trenches, which were designated Y1, Y2, Y3 and Z1. These trenches formed the British forward positions on a sector of front a mile east of Vermelles town. The area was also known to the troops as the 'Lone Tree' sector, because a single tree grew out in No Man's Land.

Lone Tree was in fact a large, wild cherry tree. Its sad, shell blasted frame stood starkly in front of the German wire entanglements, deep in No Man's Land. At Loos, the Lone Tree was to become a symbol of death and destruction, just as Lone Pine became infamous during the Gallipoli campaign in Turkey.

Legend had it that one night earlier in 1915, a young Lieutenant of the Seaforth Highlanders had crept out from the British trenches with the intention of securing a Union Jack in the upper branches of the tree. This he managed to achieve but was trapped in the light of a flare and the Germans riddled him with machine gun bullets. His body hung in the branches for several days in full view of the British trenches. Attempts to retrieve the body failed and so the artillery was ordered to destroy the tree. In this they failed, but left the tree blackened and splintered.

Each company of Gloucesters was seconded to an experienced battalion already in the line. No.1 Company went to the 1st Gloucesters; No.2 Company went to the 1st Cameron Highlanders; No.3 Company went to the 1/14th London (London Scottish) and No.4 Company went to the 1st Scots Guards. These tutor battalions had been engaged in vicious fighting since 1914 and were now old hands at the bloody task of surviving in the trenches. Lessons had been cruelly learned the hard way against a determined and organised enemy equipped with grenades and trench mortars of a type vastly superior to anything then possessed by the British. The eager, green soldiers of the 10th had a lot to learn and precious little time in which to learn it. Bitter experience would eventually teach them much.

During daylight hours their new world was confined to the narrow, chalky trench systems and the meagre shelters hollowed into the sides of the trenches. Dugouts were not usually placed in the front line as they were vulnerable to gas, which would sink down into them and officers felt that it would take too long to get troops out of them in an emergency. The dugouts were instead situated in the support trenches and were mainly reserved for the use of officers.

Due to the persistent attention of enemy snipers, it was folly to peer over the trench parapet into No Man's Land. Soon the men began to rely on their judgement of sound, but at first, much to the mirth of veterans, they would dive to the trench duckboards on hearing the clattering approach of a shell. After a while they learned to gauge just how closely it would fall and to take cover accordingly.

Courtesy The South Wales Borderers and Monmouthshire Regimental Museum, Brecon.

The 'Lone Tree' pictured soon after the capture of Lone Tree Ridge.

The Welsh Guards officer:

> **Shells and bullets made different noises according to the distance they had travelled, and you seldom heard the discharge of the rifle or gun that was fired at you. Bullets from a great distance whispered; nearer they swished; close they cracked like a whip. Small shells usually came with a swish and a crash – a whiz-bang: a kind of drawn out groaning sound, not long, and a thundering 'whump' - one of the biggest kind. Overhead you got anything from the soprano whine of small shells to the deep bass growl of a monster.**

The battalion officers soon learned that to stave off boredom it was necessary to keep the men occupied. As dawn approached the order was given to 'Stand to' when every man would occupy his allotted fire position until it was fully light and 'Stand down' was ordered. The idea behind this was to keep the men on the alert during what was believed to be the most vulnerable times of the day to a surprise enemy attack. Breakfast was then eaten, followed by rifle and equipment inspection. Men who were not posted for sentry duty were free to sleep until midday when lunch was eaten. Others were detailed to work within the trenches carrying out repairs and improvements. More improvement work followed until an evening meal was consumed at 6pm.

Sanitation was deemed essential and sandbags were hung in the trenches for the men to deposit refuse. The sanitary squad emptied these bags, and also collected the latrine buckets from slits in the trench sides. The contents were removed and buried in a selected place behind the line.

At night the rules would change. Under the cover of darkness it was possible to carry out many tasks that would be impossible and suicidal to attempt in daylight. Shadowy 'listening parties' would crawl stealthily out along saps, shallow, narrow trenches which ended in a crudely prepared forward listening post closer to the enemy and protected all round by a tangle of wire. Others would worm their way further out towards the enemy positions and take cover in a convenient shell hole. These parties usually consisted of two or three men and their function was to report back on any enemy activity that they could see or hear.

Sentries would be doubled and work parties sent out to repair the wire or to dig new saps out into No Man's Land. They were protected by groups of face blackened riflemen who kept a sharp eye out for enemy patrols and the sudden shower of sparks that heralded the firing of flares, the light from which would reveal the hive of activity in No Man's Land to the lurking snipers and machine gunners. With the approach of dawn, this secretive, nocturnal activity would recede back into the relative safety of the trenches. Tired, jittery sentries would tense and anxiously demand the password from the returning parties.

The 8th Royal Berkshires had already preceded the 10th Gloucesters to the front, arriving at the Lone Tree sector on August 17th. They too had been farmed out to the front line battalions and had completed their first stint in the trenches on the morning of August 19th. Their War Diary proudly comments that at 4.15am on the morning of the 19th, Major Brakspear shot a German sniper who lay camouflaged in No Man's Land.

This then, was the immediate and ugly face of modern warfare with which the 'Civilian Soldiers', for at heart they remained civilians, had to speedily adapt to and master.

The new soldiers received a mixed reception from the officers and men of the Regular battalions. Some weary veterans admired their keen spirit and fresh optimism, whilst others were openly contemptuous. Robert Graves, at that time serving as a young officer with the 2nd Welsh, claimed that many were of the opinion that, **"The New Army divisions can't be of much military use."** This cantankerous attitude, which was also initially directed at the battalions of the Territorial Force, would very soon prove to be unfounded; rather the outraged pride of hard-bitten veterans who had conveniently forgotten their own baptisms of fire. The outstanding bravery and sacrifice displayed by the men of the New Army, the Territorials, and later the conscripted men, would buy Britain victory with their blood.

When the 10th Gloucesters and 8th Royal Berkshires finally joined the 1st Division, Graves commented, **"We met the battalions of the New Army, and felt like scarecrows by comparison."**

Despite Graves' cockiness, the morale of the 1st Division by mid 1915 was certainly at a low ebb. Massive casualties suffered since the outbreak of war had seen to that. Graves said of the Division, **"Its spirit in the trenches was largely defensive, the policy was not to stir the Germans into more than their usual hostility."** There was even a rumour circulating suggesting that the Division's morale had failed completely. However, Graves did not agree, commenting, **"The Division will fight, but with little enthusiasm."**

According to Graves, in eight months of almost continual fighting, the 2nd Welsh had lost their fighting strength a staggering five times over. The casualties were first replaced with reservists and then, when there were no more to recall, with volunteers from 1914. Finally, by the summer of 1915, the battalion was receiving men recruited that spring. Many of these had completed only three weeks training and had never fired on a musketry range.

The terrain encompassing the 1st Division's immediate battle front was agricultural land, open and desolate, with small mining settlements, associated mine buildings and slag heaps dotted behind the opposing lines. In No Man's Land, a couple of small, scrubby, shell blasted patches of woodland provided the only relief on the chalky soil.

The German front line trenches lay on a low ridge about 700 yards distant from the British trenches and protecting the fortified village of Hulluch nestling in a shallow valley beyond. Long communication trenches connected the German's deep and well prepared front line to a second line skirting the western reaches of Hulluch, approximately 2,000 yards to the rear, beyond the crest of the ridge and out of sight to the British. The enemy held town of Loos-en-Gohelle also lay in the shallow valley ¾ of a mile to the southeast. The town's massive iron latticework, twin pit head winding towers, connected by two huge gantries and standing over a long slag tip, became the iconic symbol of the offensive that was to rage at Loos. Indeed, the British named it 'Tower Bridge' because of its close resemblance to the famous London landmark.

Up until the summer of 1915, this sector had been regarded as being relatively quiet, the main fighting having taken place in 1914 when the French Army had finally halted the German advance and forced them to dig defensive positions. The 'live and let live' policy of the 1st Division had resulted in very little shelling and consequently the British trenches were very well built and generally in a good state of repair.

To reduce the effects of grenade and shell blast, and enemy enfilade fire, British front line trenches were constructed in a crenulated pattern to a depth of six or seven feet with firing bays every few yards, topped to the front by a thick sandbagged parapet that was capable of stopping rifle and machine gun bullets. A 'firestep', which was a ledge on which sentries could stand to fire over the parapet or through sandbagged loopholes, was dug into the side of the trench. To the rear of the trench, the excavated earth was piled higher than the parapet to form a parado. This helped to stop

The infamous 'Tower Bridge' at Loos.

sentries becoming silhouetted and gave a modicum of cover to those occupying trenches to the rear by catching some of the bullets fired at the front line trench.

Rain and the effects of the weather would quickly cause a trench to collapse inwards and so the sides were normally revetted with wooden stakes, planks and wire netting, as well as being faced with sandbags. Trenches were not normally very wide, just wide enough for a stretcher to pass through. The flooring of these trenches normally consisted of wooden 'duck boarding', which allowed water that collected in the trenches to flow underneath into sump pits that could be pumped out if necessary.

The soil around Loos was of a chalky nature and drained fairly well, allowing the trenches and dugouts to be excavated to a fair depth, unlike the waterlogged breastworks that characterized the Ypres Salient and French Flanders, just a few miles to the north.

The enemy trenches were constructed in much the same fashion; however the Germans had carefully chosen the positions on which they were sited, often on high ground and enjoying superior arcs of fire and observation. From a tactical point of view they were much more effectively designed for defence and counter attack than those built by the British and French. Their front line trenches were wider and deeper than the British equivalent and on the Lone Tree sector consisted of two supporting parallel fire trenches connected every 50 yards or so with short communication trenches. Further long, snaking communication trenches connected these with the German second line skirting Hulluch.

In their front and support lines, the Germans had no qualms about constructing deep, sophisticated, shellproof dugouts as well as cleverly concealed machine gun posts roofed with sheets of steel and covered with earth and sandbags.

German barbed wire was liberally strung out in No Man's Land, just in front of the fire trench and indeed it was also strategically positioned behind their forward trenches to hinder an enemy breakthrough and to aid their own defence and counter attacks. The wire was usually erected in the form of belts approximately ten yards wide four feet high, and strung between wooden or metal stakes. Some of it was nailed to wooden frames known as 'knife rests'. These belts did not always present a direct barrier to an advancing enemy, but were arranged at oblique angles or with gaps to cleverly funnel enemy troops into a 'killing zone' where they would be trapped and at the mercy of machine gun and rifle fire.

To add a further dimension to their defences, the Germans dominated No Man's Land with extra machine guns cleverly positioned in saps, lengths of trench line extending out into No Man's Land from their fire trench and often ending in a 'hammer head' redoubt. These saps, which were protected with further belts of wire, allowed the Germans to fire obliquely down the length of No Man's Land and into the flanks of attacking infantry with devastating effect.

The 10th Gloucesters completed their first spell in the front line on the morning of August 22nd. Just before dawn they were relieved, filing back along the communication trenches and then marched to their billets in a former orphanage at Béthune. Here, amongst friendly, civilized cafés and cake shops, each man would have ample time to reflect on these bewilderingly new experiences.

On August 31st, the 1st Brigade left the delights of Béthune and marched westward for twelve miles to the small country village of Ferfay. Here the 10th Gloucesters and 1st Black Watch were allocated billets. The accommodation was reported as being poor and cramped and the Gloucester's No.1 Company had to continue a short distance to Bellery to find suitable billets. The water was not fit to be drunk without boiling and to the great annoyance of the battalion three horse drawn field kitchens broke down when their axles snapped due to the constant battering inflicted by the cobbled French roads.

Lieutenant General Haking, commanding the Guards Division, inspected the Brigade on September 1st. The Brigade as a whole was complemented on its turnout; however, Haking remarked that the clothing of the men of the 8th Royal Berkshires was dirty. The Berkshire's War Diary goes to some lengths to explain that the grubbiness was unavoidable due to grease from **"cooking pots and mess duties"** which, **"could not be brushed off."**

On September 2nd, in the fields and woods around Ferfay, the Brigade began field service training for attack and defence. The hard marching and bad sanitation had taken its toll, for by the following day 20 or 30 men from the 10th Gloucesters were reported sick with diarrhoea or sore feet.

The following officers were promoted on September 3rd. To Temporary Captain: Lt. Stephenson, Lt. O'Dowd, Lt. Sale and Lt. Tongue. To Temporary Lieutenant: 2Lt. Robinson, 2Lt. Carnegy, 2Lt. Leary, 2Lt. Gange, and 2Lt. Riddle.

Training continued until September 15th, during which time the men benefited from some brief but desperately needed rifle practice and bomb throwing instruction. The vicious close-quarters combat nature of trench warfare had proved the usefulness of the hand grenade to clear trenches, dugouts and machine gun posts. As usual the Germans were far in advance of the British and were quickly issued with a variety of different grenades. The British were at first reduced to making their own bombs out of empty jam tins and filled with gun cotton, scrap metal and bullets. A burning fuse ignited these makeshift bombs and there was always a good chance of a premature explosion, often resulting in the death of the bomber and the maiming of those nearby.

Eventually, by the summer of 1915, British troops were issued with the 'cricket ball bomb'. Officially designated as the No.15 Ball Grenade, it was a smooth, round grenade, about the size of a cricket ball but weighing a

No. 15 Ball Grenade, the infamous 'Cricket Ball Bomb'.

hefty 1½ lbs and fitted with a short fuse projecting from the top. The fuse was ignited by lighting it with a match struck on a brassard, a sheet of emery paper strapped to the bomber's wrist. In the coming battles these bombs were to prove tragically unreliable, the matches failing to light when the brassard became damp.

Private A.S. Dolden – 1/14th London (London Scottish):

> **These bombs had a detonator jutting out of the top covered with a piece of sticking plaster. On our wrist a band was worn, to which was attached the striking part of a box of matches. The procedure was as follows – to take the bomb from the pocket of the kilt apron, tear off the sticking plaster on the detonator, strike a match on the wristband and light the charge, hold**

> the bomb for three or four seconds, then throw as far as possible. I do not know what genius devised this bomb with its farcical method of ignition, but I am very doubtful if he spent a night in the pouring rain and tried to strike a match on his wristband, since even dampness put the striking band out of action. However, I have no doubt that he must have received some sort of reward for his services to the nation!

A defective fuse led to the death of Private Charles Goodhall of the 1st Gloucesters, whilst receiving bombing instruction at Béthune on 14th August. In the same incident, Second Lieutenant Philpott was dangerously wounded and another man lost an eye. It was noted with typical British understatement, **"Our bombs were most indifferent."**

By the summer of 1915, the window of opportunity to launch an offensive in favourable weather was beginning to close. Earlier, in the spring, Field Marshal Sir John French, commanding the BEF, had aggressively launched his Regular Army Divisions into offensives at Neuve Chapelle, Aubers Ridge and Festubert. These operations had fairly limited objectives aimed at gaining the strategic advantage of some high ground on the Aubers Ridge in French Flanders. Success would help to relieve his weary troops from living in foul, flooded trenches where the overlooking Germans held all the advantages. A small advance of the line was achieved at an enormous cost in casualties, but the ridge remained uncaptured. The bravery and determination of the infantry could not be faulted and the failure was largely put down to a serious shortage of artillery shells. At this stage in the war, Britain's capacity to manufacture the huge quantities of shells needed to repel enemy attacks and to support even the most modest of offensives was totally inadequate.

The BEF had now become seriously depleted in trained manpower, and following further heavy casualties in the Ypres Salient in May and June, desperately required several months respite to replenish, reorganise and dramatically increase its fighting strength. Unfortunately, General Joffre, commanding the French Army, had other ideas and was enthusiastically planning a new offensive. He wished to keep up maximum pressure on the enemy and the projected launch date for the new offensive was initially planned for July 1915. Joffre implacably insisted that the British must take part to increase the chances of success. The main thrust of the French assault was planned for the Champagne region of northern France near Rheims, north east of Paris. It was to be supplemented by a further powerful attack in the Artois region, where the French Army joined the British 1st Army, which was at that time commanded by General Sir Douglas Haig.

Naturally, Sir John French had very serious misgivings about British participation in this offensive. In his opinion the New Army divisions being hastily trained in Britain and which represented his main pool of fresh manpower, would not be adequately trained or supplied for a full-scale offensive until the spring of 1916.

To add to Sir John's deep concerns, Joffre was demanding that the British would direct their offensive efforts over terrain near Loos, immediately to the north of the French Artois thrust. The landscape around Loos consisted of relatively flat and featureless farmland; however, it was also sprinkled with mining villages and associated colliery buildings, bordered by large slag tips. The British referred to these villages by the French term of 'Corons' and the slag tips as 'Fosses' or 'Crassiers'. Ominously, the Germans had taken full advantage of these features, turning the villages and slag tips into formidable redoubts and placing their forward trenches on any available ridges or rising ground.

Left to right, Field Marshal Sir John French, General Joffre and General Sir Douglas Haig.

The tall winding towers of the colliery buildings provided their artillery observers with excellent views and to add depth to their defences a powerful second line had been constructed to the rear and placed largely beyond the reach of the British artillery. Clearly all the advantages lay with the Germans and the likelihood of success on this sector therefore seemed very doubtful. A perturbed Sir John consulted General Haig and quickly received this forthright assessment:

> **The enemy's defences are now so strong, that lacking sufficient ammunition**
> **to destroy them, they can only be taken by siege methods – by using bombs**
> **and by hand to hand fighting in the trenches – the ground above is so swept**

by gun and machine gun and rifle fire that an advance in the open except by night is impossible.

Plainly, the Germans had carefully transformed the entire area into a deadly killing ground. Joffre, however, was not to be swayed by such trifling arguments and brazenly approached Kitchener for support. Kitchener, who was well aware of the serious weaknesses of the British Army, nevertheless upheld Joffre's patriotic call to regain every inch of French soil, and in the interests of Anglo - French relations he ruled that the British Army would comply with Joffre's demands.

Extremely heavy casualties inflicted on the infantry in the spring of 1915 had convinced the British Generals that future offensives would have to be preceded by an extensive and thorough artillery bombardment. Sir John French and his Generals had now accepted that their artillery needed to 'conquer' the enemy's increasingly sophisticated defences and break the crust of enemy resistance before the infantry, and cavalry, could occupy, consolidate and then exploit the captured ground. However, since critical artillery and ammunition shortages hampered the British capacity to deliver such a barrage, clearly some kind of supplement was required.

In their spring offensive against the Ypres Salient, the Germans surprised the Allies by releasing toxic chlorine gas from metal cylinders placed in their forward trenches. Its use produced howls of outrage in the British press, which seized upon the incident as further proof of the **"Hun's ruthless savagery"** and exhorted Britons to rise and oppose this **"Hunnish devastation."** Long diatribes appeared in British journals exploring in depth the **"Soul of the modern Hun."** The soul of a nation that was driven to create monstrous Gothic cathedrals and to admire the **"Berserker Spirit"** above all regard for the **"Spirit of Fair Play."** Little was it realised that later in this lunatic second year of the war the Allied Commanders were prepared to adopt these very methods to break the deadlock in the trenches. Sir John French was ready to order the use of chlorine gas to make up for the limitations of his artillery.

The release of gas from trench-based cylinders had one great disadvantage and that was the total reliance on a strong enough breeze to carry it in the right direction and through the German lines. Furthermore, the attacking infantry required protection against their own gas. Being

The primitive gas/smoke helmet of the type issued to the 1st Division at Loos.

ahead at this stage in gas technology, the Germans were better equipped than the British and French. The Germans possessed masks of a fairly effective pattern, whilst the British at first employed crude devices amounting to pads of lint soaked in bicarbonate of soda or even urine tied over the nose and mouth. Later, the efficient sounding gas/smoke helmets were issued. These were detested by the troops and still relied on being soaked in a solution of glycerine, hyposulphite and bicarbonate of soda, issued to each man in a bottle. This solution was liable to leach into the eyes of the wearer causing severe irritation.

Corporal Albert Carter:

> **The gas helmets were just flannelette bags, which covered the head and tucked under the tunic collar. There was an oblong mica panel to see through but it soon got steamed up and the whole thing was very uncomfortable.**

There is no doubt that Sir John French feared that the recent huge casualties suffered by his Regular and Territorial battalions had seriously eroded their offensive spirit. This view seems to be corroborated by Graves' assertion that the 1st Division would fight, but with little enthusiasm. Clearly, if the artillery barrage and the surprise use of gas was to be effectively exploited in the manner planned, the utmost determination and commitment would be required from the leading assault troops. To this end, French and Haig judged that the New Army soldiers with their tremendous and as yet undimmed spirit would be most effective as shock troops spearheading the van of the attack.

On September 10th, the 10th Gloucesters were officially informed that they were to take part in a huge offensive. Six British Divisions were to storm the German trenches along a six-mile front and the 10th Gloucesters and 8th Royal Berkshires would spearhead the attack of their division's 1st Brigade. The renowned but battle weary Regular battalions of the 1st Cameron Highlanders and 1st Black Watch would provide support and exploit the rupture in the enemy defences. A year of hard training and endeavour was about to reach fruition.

The excited soldiers were told that the attack was vital to help divert German pressure from Russian troops sorely pressed and in retreat on the Eastern Front. It was also revealed that the Germans would be treated to a dose of their own medicine; poison gas was going to be used by the British for the first time.

Preparations now began in earnest and thousands of British soldiers, including working parties from the 10th Gloucesters, toiled night and day to complete the myriad tasks required to successfully launch the troops into battle.

An unfortunate accident occurred on September 14th. Second Lieutenant Eric Coe George, assisting with the digging of gun emplacements, was accidentally shot and mortally wounded in the stomach by a subaltern of the 117th Royal Field Artillery, whilst taking part in the popular pastime of hunting rats. He died the following day at No.1 Casualty Clearing Station, Chocques aged just 19.

Although the British trench systems facing the Germans were already extensive, the monumental task of bringing forward into battle positions 75,000 assault troops of six divisions required their massive extension. To make matters worse, any obvious increased activity near the front was likely to attract heavy artillery fire from the Germans. Consequently, the bringing forward of supplies, digging of new trenches and movements of men had to be conducted at night and with the utmost quiet and secrecy.

Thirteen hundred yards behind the British front line on the Lone Tree sector was a large farmhouse named Le Rutoire. The farm itself had been reduced to ruins during the heavy fighting of 1914, however, its extensive cellars remained intact and it was here that the 1st Gloucesters had established their battalion headquarters. It was described as an **"excellent place,"** but any movement around the farm buildings during daylight produced hostile shelling. During the coming battle, Le Rutoire Farm would also become the headquarters of the 1st Division's 2nd and 3rd Brigades.

The grave of Second Lieutenant Eric Coe George at Chocques near Béthune.

Here on the Lone Tree sector, No Man's Land varied in depth from between 650 and 800 yards. This was a huge obstacle for the assaulting troops to cross in the open, all the while at the mercy of machine gun, rifle and artillery fire. To reduce this distance orders were given for a continuous line of assault trenches to be dug some 200 to 300 yards out into No Man's Land. These new trenches were also required to serve a further purpose. Tests had shown that the toxic effects of the chlorine gas rapidly diminished after travelling 400 yards from the point of discharge, it was therefore

Courtesy Jean Fouquenelle.

Le Rutoire Farm lies in ruins.

imperative that the gas cylinders should be placed as near to the Germans as possible to obtain maximum effect.

All along the front, night after night, men on detail quietly emerged from the trenches like swarms of wary rabbits. With picks and shovels they would creep cautiously out into No Man's Land to find the long lengths of tape laid down by parties of Royal Engineers. Covered by armed parties of their comrades, they would gingerly begin digging along the tape, which marked the position of the required assault trenches. The pick men would begin first, wincing every time a stone was struck, whilst the shovel men lay prone with the shovel blade held in front of the head in case the Germans got wind of what was going on and let loose a hail of bullets. When the earth was loosened, the shovel men would quickly remove the soil to form the beginning of a crude trench with a raised parapet. As the trench was dug deeper, it gave the men a little more cover from hostile fire and somewhere to crouch and hide from the enemy flares.

The alert Germans were quick to realise what was going on as the freshly disturbed chalky soil of the Artois region showed up in brilliant white ribbons for miles. The extent of the digging left them in no doubt that a major attack was being prepared. The Germans quickly responded by digging extra saps out into No Man's Land from their forward trenches. In mid September, patrols from the 1st Gloucesters, then occupying the Lone Tree sector, reported that the two copses of La Haie and Bois Carré, situated in No Man's Land, had been strung with extra wire entanglements and turned into formidable redoubts by the enemy. Indeed, the Germans lost no time in erecting lots more wire, which, by the eve of the battle, protected their front in belts 4 feet high and up to 10 yards wide.

Of equal importance to the British were the assembly trenches needed to protect the battalions that would be waiting to move forward to support the initial waves of assault troops. In early September the 1st Gloucesters spent cold, clear nights digging these trenches between Le Rutoire

Farm and Vermelles. The task was made unpleasantly grim when they began to disinter the putrefying corpses of German soldiers killed and hastily buried during the fighting around the Farm in 1914. According to Albert Carter, the Regulars took gruesome delight in showing the curious down into a cellar beneath the farm where the mouldering bodies of German soldiers had been piled. Near Vermelles the equally unpleasant decomposing remains of fallen French soldiers were uncovered.

By September 18th, sixteen miles of extra trenches had been dug in preparation for the offensive. Sir John French was now ready to order the placing of the gas in the assault trenches. The gas was contained in cylinders and arrived by train concealed in wooden boxes. It was unloaded at the Gorre railhead near Béthune and then dispersed at night by horse drawn limbers to local dumps nearer the front. The 10th Gloucesters were ordered to provide a work party consisting of 6 officers, 20 NCOs and 284 men led by Captain John Tongue, to manhandle the gas at night from Vermelles to the front line trenches, a distance of well over a mile.

The traditional three-man party was used. Each cylinder, six feet long and weighing 125 to 160 pounds, was slung from a pole carried between the shoulders of two men. They rotated at the blowing of a whistle, one man resting at each leg.

Lance Corporal Leonard Freeman:

> We were loaded with a huge cylinder on a pole, two men to each. The weight was terrible, but anyway we managed alright for a time as we were on top of the ground. We arrived at Lone Farm, a solitary farm and buildings, but there was not much of it left. Passing into the farmyard we descended into a trench, this is where the real struggle began. The trenches were full of water and it had been raining all this time and we were getting fairly wet. Well, we ploughed through it as best we could, but it was very difficult because the trenches were dug in a zigzag. So you can see it was most awkward to get these huge cylinders around the corners.

On average each team took four hours to cover one and a half miles. Having reached the forward trenches, the cylinders were positioned in specially prepared emplacements located every 25 yards along the narrow assault/gas trench. The emplacements were dug into the side of the trench beneath the parapet and shored up with timber. Twelve cylinders nestled upright in each emplacement and were covered with sandbags to help protect them from shellfire and aerial observation. The cylinders were sunk down two feet below the floor of the trench, allowing easy access to the gas valve at the top of each one. It was necessary for troops occupying these trenches to have to climb out and lie over the parapet whilst the cylinders were being positioned. This effort, it is estimated, cost each division between four and ten men killed each day.

Lengths of iron piping and rubber tubing were then supplied to facilitate the release of the gas over the parapet and out into No Man's Land. The long lengths of piping also proved difficult to move along the awkward winding trenches and each section had to be carefully cleaned of the mud that inevitably became lodged inside.

L.G. Mitchell – Royal Engineers:

> At Vermelles we were given the pipes, of which every man had to carry six. I shall never forget that journey down the communication trench. In order to localise the effect of shell explosions, the communication trench zigzags from beginning to end. The result was that we had to carry the pipes right above our heads in order to get them along the trench, otherwise at every corner they would get stuck.

It was imperative to deny the enemy any inkling that gas was being deployed, and so the piping would not be placed over the parapet or connected to the cylinders until just before the gas was due for release. The pipes were therefore kept out of the way by being temporarily pegged along the trench walls.

The work of the fatigues parties was arduous and backbreaking and the men were often kept short of sleep. However, they were able to wash away the sweat and grime of their endeavours at the pithead showers in the local collieries, or even in local breweries. An anonymous account records:

> I remember after my first horrible spell up the line in the Loos affair, the battalion were marched to a disused brewery at the Le Brebis. The baths consisted of a row of about ten enormous barrels cut in half, which had about 12 soldiers per barrel – in front of this array there was a long line of small half barrels which held but one soldier per barrel. All barrels were heavily impregnated with Jeyes fluid, and the single barrels were almost solid with Jeyes, and I remember wondering why these particular men had arranged such favourable treatment, but to my surprise I saw they were all sitting in their tubs with their shirts on and not looking very comfortable. Then the truth dawned on me, these chaps were so infected with lice that their shirts had stuck to their scratched flesh and this was the only hygienic way to get them off.

Sergeant Ernest Chadband:

> I was taken ill there (Béthune) after going to the mining baths. I and one or two others indulged under the shower baths too long and didn't dry ourselves properly. The next day or so the battalion had to parade for General Rawlinson before the Battle of Loos and after standing at the 'present arms,' which seemed an eternity, I eventually collapsed and fell down just as he was riding past. This was a terrible let down for 'B' Company. I had never reported sick since joining up but the Sergeant reported me sick in billets and the M.O. had to come to me and said, "Evacuate at once" and ordered a tube full of castor oil for me. I was taken to Lillers to the casualty clearing station where they kept me for three or four days. I must have been very ill as I recollect getting out of bed and walking out of the marquee which was used as a hospital. The nurses sat

> up with me and fed me with a feeding cup and one put a bar of chocolate under my pillow when they carried me out on the stretcher.
>
> I landed at Versailles where I stayed for three weeks and learned that I had pleurisy and pneumonia. I think I was three weeks in hospital at Versailles, then travelled on barges down the River Seine to Rouen and then on hospital ship to Southampton.
>
> A poor shell shocked lad jumped overboard and the 2nd Officer of the ship jumped after him and a rope ladder was lowered to bring him up on deck, a very brave action I thought.

Finally on September 20th, the last of 5,243 cylinders was in position. The gas was now the responsibility of the Royal Engineers whose very recently formed Special Companies were tasked with releasing the gas just before the infantry went over the top. The men of these Special Companies were issued with armbands coloured red, green and white, which distinguished them from the assault troops. For obvious security reasons it was ordered that the gas should strictly be referred to as "**The Accessory**."

Now that trench digging and gas carrying was complete, the utterly exhausted soldiers of the 10th were pulled back from the front. As troops earmarked to make the assault, they needed to be rested. On September 21st they were marched to Ferfey near Béthune and bivouacked in the relative peace of Le Morquet Wood.

That day too, witnessed the opening of the British artillery bombardment in preparation for the assault. At 7am, 110 heavy guns and 841 field guns thundered out, shattering the tranquil peace of Le Morquet Wood. The guns would sustain a steady bombardment night and day, finally rising to a concentrated crescendo just prior to the infantry assault and then lengthening their aim to concentrate on secondary targets in support of the planned break through.

Captain Wyllie – Royal Scots Fusiliers, 9th Division:

> It was an extraordinary sight to see so many guns as far as one could see on each side, recoiling under the force of the charge as often as a shell could be rammed into the breech. The men were stripped to the waist and were streaming with perspiration, and no doubt very thirsty.

Tellingly, despite a great improvement in the manufacture and supply of shells, it was estimated that the quantity now available to the British artillery still fell well short of what was required to adequately destroy the enemy wire and trench systems on the whole six-mile Loos battle front. French and Haig were gambling heavily on the effectiveness of the gas to help make up for this serious deficiency. General Sir Hubert Gough, who commanded one of Sir John French's Army Corps during the battle, summed up the position:

> At this time, however, the prospects of the battle were materially altered by the possibility of our being able to use gas. The artillery and ammunition at our disposal were entirely inadequate to justify launching any infantry to

the attack at Loos, but the arrival of an ample supply of gas made it possible
not only for the attack to be made but for it to be successful.

Even so, this bombardment would be the heaviest that the British had yet delivered in the war. It
needed to be because gas would not destroy wire entanglements.

An officer of the 1st Gloucesters witnessed the awesome spectacle of a 15 inch howitzer
bombarding the town of Loos:

It was thrilling to watch its projectile weighing over 1,400 pounds sailing
up into the air from the muzzle of the terrifying weapon.

British Field Artillery in action.

The artillery had two tasks. The heavy guns, consisting of 6 inch, 9.2 inch, 8 inch, 12 inch and
15 inch howitzers, were required to disrupt supply routes, bombard portions of the distant enemy
second line and to smash the more immediate redoubts and trenches with high explosive shells. The
much lighter calibre field artillery of 4.5 inch howitzers, 13, 15 and 18pdr guns, were to concentrate
mainly on breaching the enemy wire, principally with shrapnel shells, a job that had to be completed
thoroughly or the assaulting infantry would be trapped in No Man's Land.

As the Germans held the advantage of better observation positions situated on Hill 70, Tower
Bridge and numerous slag tips, the heavy guns of the Royal Artillery were sited in camouflaged gun
pits at least 4,000 yards to the rear of the British front. The open nature of the Loos area forced the
gunners to place the lighter Field Artillery in positions up to 3,500 yards behind the forward
trenches. These distances seriously hampered the accuracy of the guns and also meant that the

German second line was mostly beyond their range. However, where possible, field guns were manhandled at night close to the British front line where they were camouflaged inside ruined houses or in gun pits amongst the trenches. These guns were to remain silent until the approach of zero hour when they would open up rapid fire into the enemy wire over open sights.

The Germans could now be in little doubt that an attack on the Loos sector was imminent. All the signs were present, the furious digging and now a terrific and lengthy bombardment. The British had sacrificed any advantage of surprise in the hope that the gas and artillery could indeed 'conquer'.

To aid the planned destruction of German troops, a ruse described as a "**small show**" was sprung at 8.55am on September 22nd. On the Lone Tree sector, the methodical bombardment was to intensify for ten minutes and then slacken away. At this moment the 1st South Wales Borderers and 2nd Welsh, occupying Y1 trenches in front of Le Rutoire Farm, were ordered to cheer loudly and raise their bayonets over the parapet. It was expected that the Germans would emerge from their dugouts and man their fire trenches where they would be slaughtered by an immediate resumption of the British bombardment. The tactic proved to be of doubtful value as the War Diary of the Welsh reported the loss of four men wounded in the inevitable enemy artillery retaliation. The South Wales Borderers War Diary merely states that the exercise was "**successful.**"

Though the intentions of the British were now obvious, the finer details of the attack needed to be concealed from the enemy, as is made clear by an order issued by the Adjutant of the 2nd King's Royal Rifle Corps entitled, "**Leakage Of Information.**" Troops were warned that spies both male and female were abroad and that they were not to speak of anything military in the presence of civilians. "**It is their duty to know nothing.**" Infringement of this order was punishable by court martial.

Bivouacked in Le Morquet wood, the soldiers of the 10th tried to relax. This relatively slack time after so much intense endeavour allowed them to ponder the coming events. The incessant thunder of gunfire from nearby batteries never spared their minds to wander too far from the test that each faced. Even their dreams were set to a symphony of shellfire. A thoughtful calmness descended on the men. Each realised that the battalion would inevitably suffer casualties. Their sobering experience at Béthune and the brief sojourn in the trenches, where unseen enemy machine guns regularly raked the sandbagged parapets or swept the rear areas, had seen to that.

Each man spent time isolated within his own thoughts and memories of family; dear mothers, fathers, brothers, sisters and children, living out their homely lives far away in bustling cities, busy Gloucestershire towns, sleepy Cotswold villages and oak bordered Forest hamlets. Brothers, fathers, sons and cousins would seek each other out and sit closely together in murmured conversation of home. Such was the nature of a Kitchener battalion.

All along the British front at Loos, the scenes were repeated. The New Army boys contemplating the terrible unknown, the Regulars, some veterans of Mons, Neuve Chapelle, Aubers Ridge and Festubert, resigned to facing the inevitable barbed wire and machine guns yet again. Would their luck finally run out? An officer of the 1st Gloucesters sensitively recorded:

> **The average man always felt a gentle melancholy at the approach of big battles, not because he feared their result as regards himself, but because he knew that in them he must lose many with whom he had served in great good fellowship.**

Brothers Harry, Frederick and Arthur Chandler from Alderton near Winchcombe, Gloucestershire, served as transport drivers with the 10th Gloucesters. They all survived the Great War.

On the other hand, Robert Graves, speaking about the old hands in the 2nd Welsh, was brutally cynical:

> **They look forward to a battle because that gives them more chance of a cushy one in the leg or arm than trench warfare.**

Divisional padres were issued with 'Burial Registration' books and special 'green envelopes' were distributed. In these envelopes the men were afforded the dignity of being able to send home private, uncensored letters, just before being committed to battle. The envelopes had printed on their flaps:

> **I certify on my honour that the contents of this envelope refer to nothing but private and family matters.**

Lieutenant Clement Symons, a young officer of the 10th Gloucesters and formerly an employee of Lloyds Bank in Lydney, Gloucestershire, wrote optimistically to a friend in Bath:

A very few lines before the fun starts. I have been up in the trenches since the 14th bringing up all sorts of things to the firing line. We were a fatigue party and have had about twelve hours sleep in the last three days. We moved back last night to join up with the rest of the battalion. We are now on the march for either death or victory. All are in good spirits.

We are taking things easy for an hour in a wood near the large town that we were in on leaving the trenches for the first time. We feel so happy, everything points to a great success. The Huns are being strafed terribly and will be for a day or two longer.

We went up to a certain fatigue work and reached the badly shelled village about 9.40pm and were working from then until 1pm the next day, without food and no rest. I now know that part of the trenches, which we are about to hold. We bivouacked four nights in some trenches, which have been dug by the French miners as the last line trenches, fine dugouts and good trenches. It was bitterly cold; I shall be able to tell you full details in a few days, I hope. Look out for good news in four or five days from now.

Lietenant Clement Aubrey Symonds. Killed in action September 25th 1915 aged 22 years. Before departing for France he wrote down these lines from an A.E. Houseman poem.

The Conflict

The queen of air and darkness
Begins to shrill and cry,
"O young man, O my Slayer,
"Tomorrow you shall die."

"O queen of air and darkness,
"I think 'tis the truth you say,
"And I shall die tomorrow,
"But you shall die today."

Lieutenant Symons, reflecting the feelings of all the men and officers, was obviously striving to face up to his own mortality, but tempering the sacrifice that he might have to make with his faith in the success of the offensive.

Despite his apprehension on the eve of battle, Corporal Arthur Harrison didn't forget the generosity of the boys of Holy Trinity School, Tewkesbury where he was an assistant schoolmaster, for he wrote to them to thank them for their kind parcel of food and woollens.

Whilst out of the line, battalion officers and NCOs were taken to view a scale model, prepared from aerial photographs, of the terrain they were to assault. It must be remembered that when in the trenches the troops had very little idea of where they actually were. Movement during daylight hours had to be conducted along the winding communication trenches, leaving all disorientated.

To glance over the trench parapet was likely to invite a bullet between the eyes. It was therefore a revelation to see from a bird's eye view, the detail of their own front line, the relatively small expanse of No Man's Land and the maze of German trenches bolstered here and there with strong points and redoubts.

The trenches were represented by sprinkled lines of chalk, woods by twigs, buildings by bricks and slag heaps by mounds of coal. Here in miniature was the battlefront allocated to the 1st Division revealing its particular features, Le Rutoire Farm, Daly's Keep, the Northern Sap, Sap 81, Lone Tree, the wooded areas of Bois Carré, La Haie, Bois Hugo and the village of Hulluch.

General Haig's Plan of Attack

General Haig's objectives for the coming battle were extraordinarily ambitious, allowing for a spectacular rupture of the enemy's front and an advance of up to 40 miles in support of an equally victorious French Army to the south. Clearly Haig was thinking in terms of sweeping aside a demoralised and increasingly desperate German Army in much the same way the Germans had advanced through Belgium and into France in 1914. The inevitability of his troops foundering against unsubdued lines of entrenchments, defended at every point with machine guns and artillery, was not yet a scenario that he seriously cared to consider.

The 1st Division was to attack the enemy sector north of Loos from the Northern Sap, northward to the Vermelles to Hulluch road. The Division's 2nd Brigade would form the right wing of the attack, from the Northern Sap to Lone Tree at Sap 81, a frontage of 600 yards.

The 1st Brigade, to which the 10th Gloucesters belonged, formed the left wing of the attack, which was to be made on a further 600 yard frontage from Lone Tree to the Vermelles to Hulluch road. This brigade's orders were to advance directly eastward and overrun the German firing line. The brigade would then continue the advance and cross the La Bassée to Lens road, penetrate the enemy second line and capture the primary objective, namely the southern portion of Hulluch village. The village was to be immediately placed into a state of defence. The brigade would also construct two strong points on the line of the La Bassée to Lens road, just west of Hulluch. Having captured Hulluch, the infantry were to signal their success to British planes overhead, by placing strips of 'shooting' arranged in a 'V' pointing towards the enemy. If they were driven out of Hulluch, the 'V' was to point back towards the British lines.

The 2nd Brigade's orders were to overrun the enemy firing line and advance south east to the La Bassée to Lens road, where they were to occupy Chalk Pit Wood and its associated Chalk Pit and also the nearby colliery buildings of Puits 14Bis. These positions were to be turned into strong points. Success was to be signalled with a 'T' pointing towards the enemy and with the 'T' reversed if they had been driven out.

It was realised that the bulging configuration of the 1st Division's newly dug assault trenches would quickly direct the two brigades against their objectives opening up two unprotected flanks. Between these flanks the Germans would be unopposed and capable of directing enfilade fire and counter attacks on both brigades. To counter this threat, two Territorial battalions, the 1/14th London (London Scottish) and the 1/9th King's (Liverpool), both under the command of Lieutenant Colonel Edgar Green and designated 'Green's Force', were detached from the 1st and 2nd Brigades respectively. Green's Force received orders to advance eastward across the captured

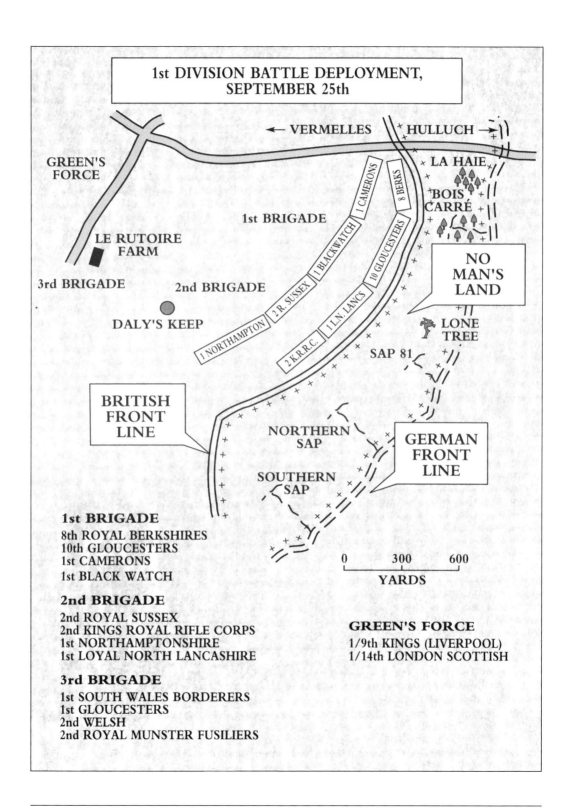

1st DIVISION BATTLE DEPLOYMENT, SEPTEMBER 25th

← VERMELLES

HULLUCH →

GREEN'S FORCE

LA HAIE

BOIS CARRÉ

1st BRIGADE

1 CAMERONS

8 BERKS

10 GLOUCESTERS

LE RUTOIRE FARM

NO MAN'S LAND

3rd BRIGADE

2nd BRIGADE

1 BLACKWATCH

2 R. SUSSEX

1 L.N. LANCS

LONE TREE

DALY'S KEEP

1 NORTHAMPTON

2 K.R.R.C.

SAP 81

BRITISH FRONT LINE

NORTHERN SAP

GERMAN FRONT LINE

SOUTHERN SAP

1st BRIGADE
8th ROYAL BERKSHIRES
10th GLOUCESTERS
1st CAMERONS
1st BLACK WATCH

0   300   600
YARDS

2nd BRIGADE
2nd ROYAL SUSSEX
2nd KINGS ROYAL RIFLE CORPS
1st NORTHAMPTONSHIRE
1st LOYAL NORTH LANCASHIRE

GREEN'S FORCE
1/9th KINGS (LIVERPOOL)
1/14th LONDON SCOTTISH

3rd BRIGADE
1st SOUTH WALES BORDERERS
1st GLOUCESTERS
2nd WELSH
2nd ROYAL MUNSTER FUSILIERS

THE LOOS BATTLEFIELD IN DETAIL

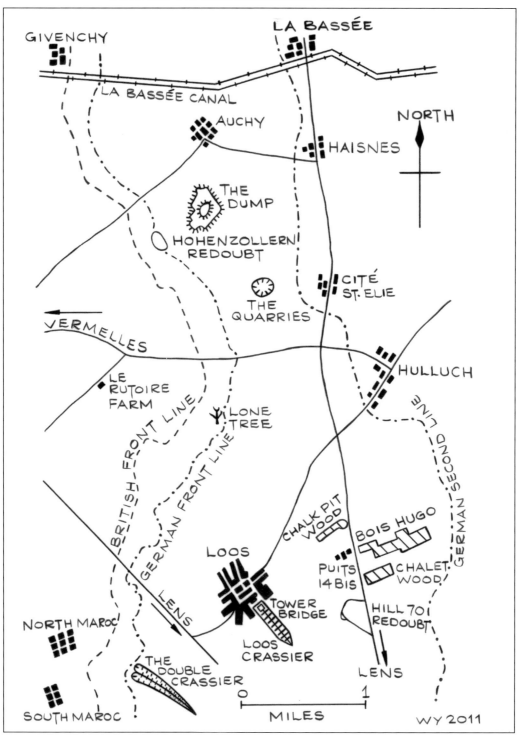

German firing line in the wake of the 1st and 2nd brigades and establish a strong point on the La Bassée to Lens road, midway between the strong points already constructed by these two brigades.

Once these objectives had been gained, the Division as a whole would advance eastward with the 1st Brigade capturing the colliery of Puits 13Bis and outflanking the remaining German second line to capture its strongpoint of Stutzpunkt III. Green's Force would advance against Stutzpunkt IV in the centre and the 2nd Brigade would pass through the wood known as Bois Hugo to break into the second line at Bois de Quatorze, Stutzpunkt V. In this they were to be supported by the 3rd Brigade.

To the north, the 7th, 9th and 2nd Divisions respectively, would advance likewise with the 2nd Division securing the left flank. To the south, the 15th Scottish Division would capture the town of Loos and Hill 70 then advance to threaten the city of Lens. The 47th London Division would secure and protect the right flank.

In theory the Germans would now be on the run. With their strong points and entrenchments left far behind, a state of 'open warfare' would prevail, allowing the British

Corporal Arthur Harrison. Killed in action September 25th 1915. He was an Assistant Schoolmaster at Holy Trinity School, Tewkesbury, Gloucestershire.

infantry reserves to advance another five miles to the village of Pont á Vendin. Here, they were to seize the crossing over the Haute Deule Canal allowing the cavalry to break out and ride an astonishing 35 miles into the hinterland to penetrate enemy occupied territory and seize river crossings between Condé and Tournai.

The tactic of reducing the width of No Man's Land by digging assault trenches closer to the Germans meant that the 1st Brigade would have to advance for about 400 yards before reaching the main enemy firing line. But first the Berkshires would have to neutralise enemy machine guns positioned in the sap which snaked out to the small scrubby copse of La Haie and the Gloucesters had the even more formidable task of storming the enormous 'hammerhead' sap situated near the slightly larger wooded area known as Bois Carré.

The 2nd Brigade only had the relatively minor obstacle of Sap 81 to overcome. However, No Man's Land was wider on their frontage, 450 to 500 yards and for the most part the enemy trenches and protective wire entanglements were obscured by a very slight swell in the ground.

Tests carried out on captured German personal anti gas equipment suggested that their effectiveness lasted for approximately 40 minutes. It was therefore imperative that the Germans should be forced to wear their masks for at least this period of time. As each cylinder contained only enough gas for two minutes discharge, smoke bombs and candles were to be ignited between gas discharges to produce the illusion of a continuous flow of gas. A final discharge of smoke would commence 2 minutes before the first troops went over the top. In theory this gave the gas previously released time to clear No Man's Land and reach the Germans, at the same time concealing the emergence of the troops from their assault trenches and allowing them to form up for the advance.

An aerial photograph of the British trench systems immediately to the east of Le Rutoire Farm. Taken on September 24th it shows Le Rutoire Farm in the top left corner with Daly's Keep just left of centre. No Man's Land is in the bottom right corner.

On September 20th, 1st Division H.Q. issued the following directive:

> The best wind for the gas is 4 – 5 miles per hour. Thus during the last 2 minutes of smoke discharge the last of the gas will have travelled 250 yards. There is therefore no fear of our own men running into the gas before reaching the German trenches. There is no danger in following up gas in the open, but no one should enter a German trench, dug out or cellar without having his smoke helmet properly fastened, as the gas sinks into these and remains there until dispersed with vermorel sprayers. No food or water found in German trenches should be used, as it will be poisoned by the gas.

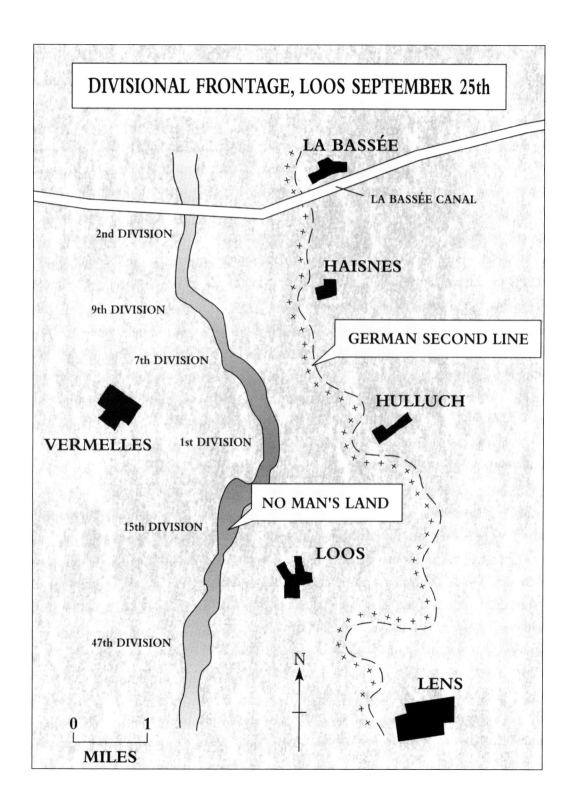

DIVISIONAL FRONTAGE, LOOS SEPTEMBER 25th

LA BASSÉE

LA BASSÉE CANAL

2nd DIVISION

HAISNES

9th DIVISION

GERMAN SECOND LINE

7th DIVISION

HULLUCH

VERMELLES

1st DIVISION

NO MAN'S LAND

15th DIVISION

LOOS

47th DIVISION

N

LENS

0   1

MILES

1399, Box 60, Courtesy Imperial War Museum.

Taken on September 12th, before the British artillery bombardment had begun, this photograph shows the 1st Division's battle front in its entirety. The British trenches on the left face into No Man's Land where the three enemy saps of La Haie (top), Bois Carré (centre) and Sap 81 (bottom) can clearly be seen snaking out into No Man's Land. The German trenches to the right show signs of being heavily fortified with numerous dug outs and strong points.

On September 18th, a German soldier deserted and came over to the British lines. Unusually talkative, he claimed to be serving with the 157th Regiment of the 117th Division. According to the prisoner, his company were poorly trained and were in his words, **"no great warriors."** They would be glad to escape, as he had done, from the hard work and too severe discipline. Paradoxically, he revealed that the German trenches were amply defended by well-concealed machine guns protected by overhead iron sheeting and covered with earth.

1465, Box 60, Courtesy Imperial War Museum.

Three days into the British artillery bombardment the effects of shrapnel shells fired mainly at the enemy wire entanglements, can clearly be seen scarring the ground either side of the German trench systems.

At Hinges, seven miles back from the front, General Haig sat back satisfied. The signs were extremely encouraging. The artillery was believed to be delivering death and destruction on an unprecedented scale, the quality of some of the opposing troops was suspect and the massive use of chlorine gas had the potential to asphyxiate thousands of Germans. Soon the eager infantry would storm through the enemy fortifications and the cavalry would gallop forward to fan out and ride down the retreating Germans. Such a stunning victory would push back the enemy for many, many miles.

On the morning of September 22nd, the 10th Gloucesters broke camp and marched to the village of Gosnay, south of Béthune, where, with the 8th Royal Berkshires they dumped their personal belongings and unnecessary equipment in a brewery. Along with his rifle, bayonet and entrenching tool, each man was to carry into battle a filled water bottle, two sandbags, two gas/smoke helmets, one waterproof sheet and 220 rounds of ammunition. The bombers carried 100 rounds less but were issued with five of the hated cricket ball bombs, which were carried in a special vest with pockets. The waterproof sheet was packed into a haversack along with a mess tin and iron rations of bully beef and biscuits. Steel helmets had not yet been issued to British troops so each man would go into battle wearing a rolled up gas/smoke helmet and with his field cap slung through his equipment.

At 11am the same day, the Gloucesters and Berkshires marched a short distance to Vaudricourt Wood where they bivouacked until the evening. It was raining heavily and the wood was seething with troops. Some of the bivouacs were trampled on in the darkness and the men became exceedingly wet. Later that evening, the men were marched to assembly trenches positioned near Vermelles. Here they remained for the night and for the best part of the following day until 7pm on September 23rd when the two battalions moved forward to relieve the 2nd Welsh in Y1 trenches. The surviving veterans of this Regular army unit knew full well what the two inexperienced New Army battalions were in for and gravely wished them the best of luck in the coming assault.

Remaining at Gosnay, under the command of Lieutenant Frederick Carnegy, were 95 men from the 10th Gloucester's No.1 Company suffering from mumps. These men were no doubt extremely frustrated to miss their battalion's opening battle, but for the time being their lives were safe.

A terrific thunderstorm broke that night, filling the trenches with mud and soaking the apprehensive troops crowded into the meagre shelter of the newly dug assembly trenches. Overhead, the British artillery was sending over huge numbers of shells that clattered and shrieked off into the darkness, drowning out the relatively gentle rumble of thunder.

The wet and tired men spent Friday September 24th checking and rechecking equipment, rifles, machine guns, ammunition, bombs, gas/smoke helmets, wire cutters, whilst the officers studied their maps and clarified their orders. Every officer, rifleman, bomber, bayonet man, machine gunner, signaller and stretcher-bearer was required to know his role.

Optimistic reports filtered to the men from the forward artillery observers who believed that the enemy wire and forward trench systems were being comprehensively destroyed, giving hope to the notion that the attacking infantry would have little trouble crossing No Man's Land. The War Diary of the 8th Royal Berkshires states that safety pins and elastic was distributed to help the men quickly secure the tails of their gas/smoke helmets around their throats.

Sergeant Ernest Linden 'Dick' Betteridge, killed on September 24th 1915 by a shell that landed on a dug out. His grave in Dud Corner Cemetery gives his date of death as 25th September. He was a plumber in civilian life and he also played as centre forward for Cheltenham Town.

The German artillery was largely quiet, however, Sergeant Ernest Betteridge became the 10th Gloucester's first battle fatality when a shell landed on the dugout in which he was sheltering.

The gut-wrenching hour of battle was fast approaching, whilst overhead the barrage howled and increased to mind numbing proportions. At 7.30pm British soldiers all along the battlefront filtered forwards and took up their places in the assault trenches to await dawn and the order to deliver the assault.

THINKING OF YOU

(A SOLDIER'S LOVE SONG.)

I am thinking of you as I sit here alone,
Dreaming of you when the daylight has flown;
Ever before me your dear face I see,
And I know, little girl, you are thinking of me.

THE GLOUCESTERSHIRE REGIMENT.

(28th Foot and 61st Foot.)

BATTLE HONOURS.

The Sphinx, superscribed "Egypt."

"Ramillies," "Peninsula,"
"Louisburg," "Waterloo,"
"Guadaloupe, 1759," "Chillianwallah,"
"Quebec, 1759," "Goojerat,"
"Martinique, 1762," "Punjaub,"
"Havannah," "Alma,"
"St. Lucia, 1778," "Inkerman,"
"Maida," "Sevastopol,"
"Corunna," "Delhi, 1857,"
"Talavera," "Defence of
"Busaco," Ladysmith,"
"Barrosa," "Relief of
"Albuhera," Kimberley,"
"Salamanca," "Paardeberg,"
"Vittoria," "Nivelle," "Nive," "South Africa,
"Pyrenees," "Orthes," "Toulouse," 1899 1902."

HISTORY AND TRADITIONS.

The Regiment was formed in 1694. Proceeding to Spain it took part in the battle of Almanza in 1707, where it suffered severely. It fought at Fontenoy, 1745, and took part in the capture of Louisburg, 1758, and Quebec, 1759. Its gallantry at Alexandria in 1801 won for it the unique distinction of wearing the badge at the back as well as the front of the cap. It fought with great gallantry at Maida, 1806. During the Peninsular War, 1809-14, it served with conspicuous bravery at Talavera, Salamanca, and Toulouse. It particularly distinguished itself at Quatre Bras and Waterloo. In the Punjaub campaign, 1848-9, it fought at Chillianwallah and Goojerat. During the Crimean War, it was engaged at Alma, Inkerman, and the siege of Sevastopol. In the Indian Mutiny it took part in the siege of Delhi. During the South African War, it shared in the defence of Ladysmith, the relief of Kimberley, and the battles leading up to the capture of Bloemfontein.

CHAPTER III

Zero will be 5.50a.m.

**Now set the teeth and stretch the nostril wide
Hold hard the breath and bend up every spirit
To his full height**

King Henry V. Act III, Scene I

The 1st Brigade – 10th Gloucester, 1st Black Watch, 8th Royal Berkshire,
1st Cameron Highlanders.

In the early morning of Saturday September 25th, rain again soaked the restless soldiers tightly crammed into the crude and muddy assault trenches that offered only a modicum of protection from shellfire and none from the natural elements. The crush was made even more uncomfortable by the nests of bulky gas cylinders attended by the men of the Special Companies charged with releasing the gas at the allotted hour.

General Haig had become concerned for at 3am the wind speed was only 1mph. He consulted Captain Gold, his meteorological officer, who was of the opinion that the wind speed should increase just after dawn at about 5.30am. However, at 5am the wind had dropped away to nothing more substantial than a slight movement of air detected in the smoke of cigarettes. Nevertheless, at 5.15am Haig took the weighty decision to order the Special Companies to release the gas at 5.50am.

Meanwhile, as the first bright streaks of dawn silhouetted the great gouts of earth and smoke erupting all over the German lines, the forward Field Artillery gunners cast aside the camouflage concealing their guns and added to the deafening cacophony in an effort to complete the destruction of the enemy wire.

Lance Corporal Leonard Freeman:

The morning arrived, a fearful, cold September morn with a little mist. A jar of rum was passed along, each fellow having a little of it.

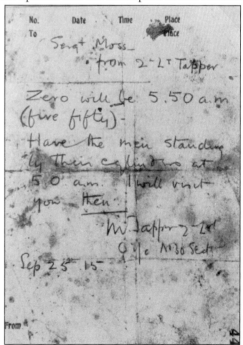

A memo detailing 5.50am as 'Zero' for the release of gas.

Captain Edward Hampton Moss, he blew the whistle that sent the first wave of Gloucesters 'over the top'. He died in the attack.

Private Bertram Taylor, aged 20 from Draycott near Chipping Campden, Gloucestershire. He was killed by machine gun fire as he left the British trenches.

Promptly at 5.50am, the Royal Engineers of the Special Companies turned on the gas cocks and 150 tons of chlorine gas began to hiss out into No Man's Land. Within minutes a dense, sinister, yellowish-green cloud, 30-40 feet high, had formed over the six mile battlefront. Each gas emplacement was manned by two men from the Special Companies, who, although wearing their smoke hoods, soon found themselves affected by the gas which leaked from the joints in the piping. Furthermore, when each cylinder was empty, the pipe had to be unscrewed and fitted to a fresh one. The gas remaining in the pipe seeped back into the trench. One of the Special Company Corporals commented:

> To attach a pipe to twelve cylinders in succession and turn the tap on and off in a period of 38 minutes does not sound difficult a task, for the gas took less than 2 minutes to flow out of each cylinder and we had two pipes. However, working as hard as we could, and without intermission while smoke was being sent over, we managed to empty only ten cylinders, which we later discovered was more than average. The difficulty was caused by the release of the pressure making the nuts so cold that they would not fit easily onto the new cylinder.

Disaster then followed, for in many places the fickle breeze never approached the anticipated 4 to 5 miles an hour and the gas merely hung malevolently in No Man's Land, or even worse, billowed back into the British lines. Here it immediately sank down into the muddy trenches causing alarm and dismay amongst the packed waiting assault troops. The Gloucesters and Berkshires were immediately ordered by their officers to roll down their gas/smoke helmets and to stand fast. However, the order did not come in time to prevent dozens of men collapsing in convulsive heaps, victims of their own gas.

The Germans, now fully alerted to an imminent attack by the now intensified British barrage and the clouds of gas and smoke issuing from the British lines, released coloured flares to call down a terrific artillery barrage. Their infantry donned their gas masks, which consisted of goggles and a special chemically soaked gauze pad taped over the nose and mouth.

Despite the massive four-day bombardment, most of the German troops had survived, sheltering in deep, well prepared dug outs created to withstand such an onslaught. Only the heaviest of British shells stood a chance of bursting deep enough and with sufficient violence to entomb them. Aiding the enemy's survival was the absolutely abysmal quality of the British shells. Inadequate fuses allowed the shrapnel shells to bore into the earth before exploding, rather than detonating amongst the wire. Others simply failed to explode and the attacking infantry found No Man's Land and the German positions littered with duds.

At 6.10am, the four platoons of the 10th Gloucester's No.2 Company, occupying the 300 yards of the battalion's battlefront, were given the order to fix bayonets. Each man swiftly drew his from the scabbard and fitted it to his rifle. For what seemed an eternity the hooded infantrymen stood shoulder to shoulder at their posts in the narrow, muddy trench; each man aware of the thumping of his heart and belaboured breathing amplified within the confines of his gas/smoke helmet, as he anxiously waited for the sound of the whistle which would be the signal to climb the ladders and go 'over the top'.

"**Two more minutes,**" came the word down the trench. Men instinctively tightened white knuckled grips around their rifles and offered up a quick prayer to God for their safety.

Finally at 6.30am, above the frenzied pounding of their hearts, the men heard Captain Moss blow his whistle. To the muffled encouragement of their platoon officers and NCOs and with a heady swirl of adrenalin, the men scaled the ladders positioned against the parapet. With boots slipping and sliding in the greasy earthworks and to the sound of their own bugles and the distant ranting pipes of the 15th Scottish Division to their right, No.2 Company took their dressing, loomed off into the forbidding smog and were gone, erased in a vast, hellish void.

German bullets were already tearing into the sandbagged parapets and singing off the wire as two more waves of Gloucesters climbed from the trench and moved forward to close with the enemy across the rank wastes of No Man's Land.

Events were sudden, immediate and terrible, like a kaleidoscope of violent images, woven into the distorting wreaths of gas and smoke, liable to change at every explosion of shell or stutter of machine gun fire. What happened at more than a few yards distance to left and right was out of each man's orbit.

Private William Jennings:

> **The gas caused a lot of trouble and men were lying in the trench bottom foaming at the mouth. On the whistle we climbed out of the trench up stepladders. Our own barbed wire was supposed to have been cut during the night by sappers, but the only gap I could see was on my right. Private**

> Bertram Taylor was next to me and as he tried to pass through the gap he was shot dead. I crouched to see how I could get through, but a bullet shattered my rifle and took away my left thumb and forefinger. Another bullet grazed my chin and tore a hole in my gas helmet. Someone crouching on my left was also hit and fell. I bent down to help him, but an NCO ordered me back into the trench. I tore off my gas helmet and splashed some water on my face from the trench bottom onto my bleeding chin, not realising I was breathing in gas lying in the trench. I crouched there, shocked and dazed until a soldier of the Black Watch came by and put a field dressing on my hand. He had moved off along the trench a little way when a shell exploded, knocking me down and killing the Scotsman.

The German infantrymen were now at their posts and opened fire, unleashing belt after belt of machine gun bullets into the eerie cloud. Opposing the 1st Brigade, the enemy in La Haie and Bois Carré redoubts, survived long enough to rake the ranks of advancing Berkshires and Gloucesters with machine gun fire before being overwhelmed and dispatched with the bayonet.

Emerging from the gaseous gloom, the hideously becowled infantrymen paused momentarily to adjust their dressing and direction of advance. Through steamed up eye panels the German line appeared little more than an indistinct tangle of wire backed by mounds of chalk, now some 200 yards to their front. To the rasping of their air starved lungs, masking the furious sound of rifle and machine gun fire, the men advanced to the command and direction of their surviving officers and NCOs. The German machine gunners and riflemen, presented with such an obvious target, hammered out a message of oblivion to the ragged lines of advancing Gloucestershire and Berkshire

British shells burst on the German positions at Loos.

British troops advance into gas and smoke at Loos.

boys. Whole lines crumpled to the ground as machine guns traversed left and right, here and there leaving a man to advance alone, surprised at his sudden seclusion.

Men pitched forward as if tripped by a hidden wire. Private Richard Hanks had only just cleared the British wire along with other members of his platoon when a huge explosion threw him to the ground along with men to left and right. Feeling a heavy blow to his leg he glanced down to see blood welling from a tremendous gash in his knee where a piece of shrapnel had caught him. Lying nearby were a number of dead men. One he recognised as Francis Hawkins, a young collier from the Forest of Dean. The shell blast had blown away his gas helmet and fatal shrapnel wounds bloodied his head and face. Discarding his rifle, webbing and pack, Hanks crawled back through the tangle of British wire toward the relative safety of the trenches. As he crawled, grimacing with pain, the following wave of Gloucesters swept out of the smoke and pounded off towards the German wire, hardly giving the fallen soldier a second glance.

Bullets were still whining overhead as he dragged himself over the parapet to slide into the muddy trench. Nearby was a huddle of pale faced, blood splattered men from the 10th. George Larner wounded in the foot and head; Ernest Wheeler, wounded in both legs and Thomas Wood, who, like Hanks, was wounded in the knee. Dazed and in considerable pain, each was suffering the mild effects of gas which still hung around in the trench bottom.

Strange voices and the clink of equipment heralded the approach of men filing along the trench. Around a traverse emerged kilted soldiers of the 1st Black Watch. These were men of the supporting battalion moving up in the wake of the initial assault. The hardy Scotsmen took up positions awaiting their order to advance. Cigarettes were lighted and thrust into the mouths of the Gloucestershire men, while expert hands applied field dressings to their wounds.

Perched high up on a crassier behind the British front, Philip Gibbs, correspondent for the Daily Telegraph, was able to observe the opening stages of the offensive:

Presently, when our artillery lifted, there were new clouds arising from the ground and spreading upwards in a great dense curtain of fleecy texture. They came from our smoke shells, which were to mark our infantry attack. Through them and beyond them rolled another wave of cloud, a thinner, whiter vapour, which clung to the ground, and then curled forward to the enemy's lines. "That's our gas," said a young voice on one of the slag heaps, amidst a little group of observers. Across a stretch of flat ground beyond some of the zigzag lines of trenches, little black things were scurrying forward. They were not bunched together in close groups, but scattered. Some of them seemed to hesitate, and then to fall, and lie where they fell, others hurrying on until they disappeared in the drifting clouds. It was all that one could see of our infantry attack, led by the bombers. The enemy were firing tempests of shells. Some of them were curiously coloured of a pinkish hue, or with orange-shaped puffs of vivid green. They were poison shells giving out noxious gases.

Advancing at the head of his platoon, Second Lieutenant William Tate had almost reached the German wire when he was struck down by flying earth and stones from a nearby shell burst. As he lay dazed and helpless with a fractured thigh, Private Frederick William Smith came to his aid. Kneeling over his officer, Private Smith was almost immediately struck by a bullet and fell dying onto the officer. Here they lay for the remainder of the day whilst the battle raged all around.

Second Lieutenant William Tate survived Loos and later joined the Tank Corps.

Private Frederick William Smith. Shot and killed whilst tending the wounds of 2nd Lt. Tate. Frederick was from Beckford near Tewkesbury, Gloucestershire.

Meanwhile, groups of the dwindling infantry stumbled over their fallen comrades to reach the edge of the German wire, but to their horror they discovered that much of it was virtually intact. The shrapnel shells had proved to be largely ineffective against the wire, which was of a thicker gauge than the British equivalent. Here and there the heavy shells had heaved up sections of the wire and with blind courage the surviving officers and NCOs rallied the few men that still remained and led them into these thickets of death, not pausing to consider what fate lay ahead.

Lieutenant Clement Symons arrived breathless at the enemy wire. Just a handful of his platoon remained; most of them lay sprawled in No Man's Land a few yards south of Bois Carré redoubt, victims of a machine gun. Into the vicious barbs Symons plunged at the head of his men. Bursting through the final strands he found himself on the enemy's parapet. Turning to urge his men forward in a bayonet charge, he fell, caught in a fusillade of bullets. Fearful at the emergence of these resolute, devilishly clad soldiers, a German machine gun crew had swiftly traversed their gun and scythed down Symons and his platoon at close range, where they slumped to hang in the wire's steely embrace.

On the extreme right flank of their attack, towards Lone Tree, the Gloucesters found the wire totally impenetrable and the enemy fully alert behind their machine guns.

Private William Collins – 10th Gloucesters:

> I was detailed to act as a bayonet man to the bombing section of No.4 Company because the sergeant said I was "strong in th' arm and thick in th' 'ead." I was to rush into the German trench after the bomber had thrown his bombs and mop up.
>
> We reached the German barbed wire in front of their parapet; it was still there, undamaged. We couldn't get through it so we lay down in front of the wire. A German machine gun was firing over our heads, they were so close we could hear them chattering away between bursts. It was lucky for us. Some of the battalion got through the wire further along and the Germans surrendered.

But on their left flank and also in the centre, the Gloucesters managed to thrust a way through the jagged maze, scrambling over the strewn bodies of their comrades to rush the last few yards and tumble headlong into the deep German positions. To their left, the Berkshires also lost many men in the wire, but were successful in getting into the enemy trenches.

Twenty seven year old Corporal William Ingles reached the enemy wire only to find much of it intact and the Germans exacting a heavy toll on the men trying to cut a path through. Using his bombs to good effect, he bought enough time for his comrades to get into the trench and put the enemy to flight. The citation for the award of his Distinguished Conduct Medal reads:

> For conspicuous bravery on 25th Sep 1915 in front of Hulluch. Whilst the battalion was assaulting the first line of German trenches, Pte Ingles took a position, by himself, immediately in front of the German parapet, and by skilful and continuous throwing of bombs, successfully prevented the enemy from bombing or firing upon the troops, whose advance was impeded by heavy uncut wire entanglements. His bravery and devotion to duty gave a fine example to all ranks.

Small groups of grimy, sweating, exhausted men, crouched in the German trench, with teeth gritted, rifles, bombs and bayonets at the ready, expecting at any moment to become embroiled in a frenzied, stabbing bayonet contest with hordes of ruthless Germans. When the fire breathing Germans did not materialise, bands of men, led by junior NCOs, as many of the officers and sergeants were dead or wounded, began to work their way cautiously into the enemy trench system, clearing each traverse as they went.

In the main they found that the Germans had evacuated their front line trench, taking their machine guns to their support line just 80 yards to the east. From these trenches they unleashed a renewed storm of gunfire forcing the severely depleted Gloucesters to renew their bayonet charge in which many more of them fell. The bombing officer, Second Lieutenant George W. Field, was killed along with many of his grenadiers when their bombs were found to be useless. The bayonet men had to try and carry out their bloody task without them. The 10th Gloucester's War Diary explains:

> Our bombers suffered severely, their bombs in the main refusing to explode, the Brock lighters having got wet with the rain, which fell in the early morning. Nevertheless the attack was pushed home with the utmost resolution over the 2nd line into the 3rd and up the flanking communication trenches to the east

The Germans were quickly forced to flee down their communication trenches into the sanctuary of their second line and the village of Hulluch, some 2,000 yards to the east. In their wake they left a number of dead and a few prisoners.

Sergeant Harry Thomas of Blakeney in the Forest of Dean was one of the first men to reach the enemy firing line, and at the head of his platoon he pursued the Germans into one of their communication trenches. One of Harry's wounded comrades later recalled:

> They were making their way up a German communication trench when an enemy officer suddenly sprang out upon them from a dug out, and coming up behind, shot Harry between the shoulders. They were only separated by a few yards, but the wound was such a severe one that his death was practically instantaneous.

Not only did the machine guns reap a harvest of death but the enemy artillery had carefully ranged on No Man's Land to sweep its flat expanse with high explosive and murderous shrapnel shells. Although the leading waves of Gloucesters and Berkshires had captured and swept over their front line trench objectives, the successive waves of supporting infantry were subject to this lethal fire.

Private James Groves – 10th Gloucesters:

> My brother Fred and I were in No. 3 Company and we hadn't got far across No Man's Land when a shell dropped amongst my section. The blast knocked me unconscious and shattered my rifle and entrenching tool but leaving me only scratched. When I came around it was late in the afternoon

Private Frederick Groves. Fred's home was at Stonehouse in Gloucestershire.

Lance Corporal Leonard John Freeman was a farm labourer, the youngest of the three brothers who enlisted in September 1914. The family home was at Fernbank Cottage, Churchdown near Gloucester. Leonard survived the Battle of Loos but lost his brother Arthur on September 25th 1915. Leonard was seriously wounded on May 25th 1916 by a trench mortar shell and suffered over thirty seperate wounds. Although he stoically spent many months in hospital he never fully recovered and died on December 3rd 1935 aged 39 years.

and I made my way forwards to find the rest of the battalion. Eventually I found them defending some captured trenches. Only three of my section were left and the battalion had lost so many men there was only one man every 20 yards of trench. I later learned that poor Fred was dead.

Lance Corporal Leonard Freeman:

> We must have lost thousands of men. I managed to get through it alright with Bill Collins. We dug ourselves in with our entrenching tools as we were both lost and did not know which direction to take as it was becoming dark. The next morning we found some of our fellows in a trench nearby and we stayed with them until we had a roll call. Our casualties were very heavy. I had the misfortune to lose my brother, and so was left by myself.

It was essential that the 10th's Maxim gun sections should get forward as soon as possible to occupy the captured positions and to repulse counter attacks. The War Diary notes:

One of our machine guns was put out of action on coming over the parapet, but two other guns reached a point in advance of Point 89 constructed later.

Private Walter Daffurn – 10th Gloucesters:

I was in one of the three machine gun sections. The first section was blown to pieces as they clambered out of the trench. The thing that sticks in my mind most was the weight of that gun with its water for cooling, tripod and boxes of ammunition. Somehow though, we made it across No Man's Land, through the wire and into their trenches, where we set up the gun.

Private Arthur Frederick Freeman, killed at Loos aged 23 years. Before the war he was assistant groundsman at Churchdown Golf Links.

Now totally exhausted and severely depleted in numbers, the New Army men were no longer an effective fighting force. French and Haig's decision to use them as leading shock troops had succeeded but the two battalions were all but destroyed.

Private Reginald Fennell:

I did not lose much blood but I knew right enough the moment I was hit, for the "pinging" pain was different to anything I have previously experienced. What hit me was no doubt some broken bits of metal contained in a shell from a field gun about 4in. in diameter, which on striking the ground bursts and whoever is in the neighbourhood has to look out. It came over my head sideways, I did not see it, but immediately on bursting I felt the twinge in my right side and on my left leg and foot. It travelled right through the thick of the leg, grazing the bone. Of course, I was done for as regards advancing because I could not keep up, and as there was no way of doing it, there was no chance cart passing that way, I had to walk absolutely alone. When I could not walk, I crawled and when I could not do that, I sat down and by perseverance and covering a distance of four miles, several hours later, I reached a dressing station. Because I could not carry them, being too done up, I left my rifle and kit in the field.

At this critical moment, the advance was revitalised when the men of the 1st Cameron Highlanders began to arrive amongst the disorganised survivors. But even the Camerons were not at full strength

Private Frederick Richard Hall from Eastington near Northleach, Gloucestershire, fell at Loos, aged 19 years.

Lance Corporal Ernest Harry Frowen, killed September 25th 1915. Ernest was from Woolaston near Lydney in the Forest of Dean, Gloucestershire.

having suffered heavily from enfilade machine gun fire from the enemy still resisting around Lone Tree as they crossed No Man's Land. Now encouraged by the battle hardened Scotsmen, the Gloucesters and Berkshires reorganised as best they could and continued the advance towards their objective, the village of Hulluch.

Crossing the La Bassée to Lens road, the rabble of British troops encountered the German second line of fortifications, which although were well wired did not seem to be effectively manned by the Germans. Worryingly, there seemed to be a total lack of support on either flank. To the left, the 2nd Gordons and 8th Devons of the 7th Division were only present in vastly depleted numbers and there was no sign of Green's Force and the 2nd Brigade to the right. A platoon of Camerons was sent into Hulluch where they remained for a number of hours until driven out by the enemy. Digging in with their entrenching tools, some 50 yards west of Hulluch, the surviving Gloucesters, Berkshires and Camerons took cover to await reinforcements.

The 8th Royal Berkshire's War Diary noted:

> Advanced and occupied the road west of Hulluch. We were unable to advance any further owing to our artillery fire, which was falling short. We then waited for our support to come up, in the meantime starting to dig ourselves in.

Private Frank Haile with his wife and two young daughters. Frank, who was from Lydney, Gloucestershire, died at Loos.

Private George Henry Hanks was killed on September 25th 1915 but his body was discovered buried on the battlefield in the 1920s. Henry now lies buried at Cabaret Rouge Military Cemetery with others of the 10th Gloucesters.

The time was now around 8.30am and they would wait a long time; something had gone disastrously wrong.

The 2nd Brigade – 2nd Royal Sussex, 1st Loyal North Lancashire,
          1st Northampton, 2nd King's Royal Rifle Corps.

The two leading assault battalions on this sector, the 2nd King's Royal Rifle Corps and the 1st Loyal North Lancashire, were unfortunate in having the longest stretch of No Man's Land to cross. Added to this, the German trenches were mainly out of sight beyond a slight rise. Consequently, despite the use of aeroplanes for directing the fall of artillery shells, these trenches had escaped the worst of the shelling.

Disaster befell the assault troops even before they were ordered to move forward. At 5.50am when the gas was released, it simply engulfed the British trenches. Such was the concentration of the gas, the gas/smoke helmets proved ineffective and the choking men were forced to run the risk of enemy fire and get out of their trenches to lie behind the parados where the gas was not so thick.

The King's Royal Rifle Corps War Diary stated:

> At 6am the gas blew back especially on 'B' Company. Gas helmets were used but 'B' Company was put out of action.

Each battalion suffered about 200 casualties from their own gas before the battle had begun. Mercifully, someone took the decision to turn the gas off, but at 6.20am a slight breeze sprang up and the gas was turned back on. This caused a delay as the troops waited for the fumes to drift away and so the 2nd Brigade's attack did not go in until 6.34am.

Protected in their deep trenches around Lone Tree, Captain Ritter and his men of the German 157th Infantry Regiment had suffered no casualties. The British artillery bombardment had not troubled them and the gas and smoke, for the most part, still blanketed No Man's Land. Their extensive wire entanglements were intact, the machine guns were well sited and provisioned with plenty of ammunition and the riflemen were at their posts. To the right and left heavy machine gun and rifle fire indicated that the British attack had already begun.

Faintly, in the depths of the fug, dark movements could be detected and then, startlingly, the movement developed into solid shapes as a line of British infantrymen burst from the murk and came on at a cracking pace, here and there the glint of a bayonet. The German soldiers were given the order to open fire and the first wave of khaki shapes collapsed out of sight into the rank grass. Nevertheless, groups of men swept on, now nearly to Lone Tree and the German wire. Almost suffocating in their gas helmets, the British infantry made a supreme effort to get amongst the Germans, but came up against the wire only to find it unbreached. Some men advanced straight into the blind entries, urgently intent on silencing the machine guns. Others, finding their continued progress barred, tried to cut their way through, or desperately searched for a gap, until shot down at point blank range.

Wave after wave of men rose from the British trenches and advanced into the gloom, unaware of the merciless slaughter up ahead around the Lone Tree.

A Brigade Staff Officer graphically described the horrors of an equally futile attack at the Battle of Neuve Chapelle in March 1915:

> **The line began to fall, moving from left to right, I did not realise how quickly people could be killed. Then the whole line hereabouts lay down. Some of them advanced again, but I do not think any of them reached the German trenches.**

Time after time, officers and NCOs rallied their shaken men, who unquestioningly rose from what meagre cover they could find, to rush forward and perish in front of the evil wire.

Chaos reigned in 2nd Brigade's trenches. Literally hundreds of men had been overwhelmed by gas poisoning and were feebly trying to make their way back from the front. Blood spattered wounded men crawled in from the slaughterhouse of No Man's Land, along with groups of dazed and leaderless troops.

At 7.30am, through this throng of misery and confusion, the Brigade's support battalion, the 2nd Royal Sussex, followed by the reserve battalion, the 1st Northamptons, were trying to move up and occupy the firing line trenches in preparation for their own advance. Despite sheltering in support trenches two hundred yards to the rear, men from both these battalions were badly affected by the gas and became casualties. 'A' Company of the 1st Northamptons was put out of action.

The Royal Sussex lost no time in supporting the two leading assault battalions by immediately launching their attack into the banks of smoke and gas. Their War Diary is brutally succinct:

We couldn't see how the advance had progressed. The battalion went straight into the attack and up to the enemy wire but the men were killed or wounded. The machine gun sections were shot down in front of Lone Tree. Major Willett went to Lone Tree for information but couldn't get beyond.

The Northamptons were next into the fray, going over the top at 9am. Again the enemy fire was accurate and merciless and the charge broke down leaving the survivors pinned down in No Man's Land amongst the bodies of their dead comrades. Four Victoria Crosses were won at Lone Tree, three posthumously.

Captain Anketell Moutray Read V.C. of the 1st Northamptonshire Regiment. He was originally gazetted into the Gloucestershire Regiment and served for three years in India. His family were from Cheltenham and he was a successful boxer, winning the Army and Navy heavy-weight championship three times. One of the judges said, "Read wins because he nver accepts defeat, and never knows when he is beaten."

Captain Read's grave at Dud Corner.

Captain Anketell Moutray Read was the youngest son of Colonel J. Moutray Read of Sandford Dene, Cheltenham. Serving with the 1st Northamptons, he distinguished himself when the battalion's attack withered in front of the German wire. His citation in the London Gazette reads:

> For most conspicuous bravery during the first attack near Hulluch on the morning of 25th September 1915. Although partially gassed, Captain Read

went out several times in order to rally parties of different units which were disorganised and retiring. He led them back into the firing line and utterly regardless of danger, moved freely about, encouraging them under a withering fire. He was mortally wounded while carrying out his gallant work. Captain Read had previously shown conspicuous bravery during digging operations on 29th, 30th and 31st August 1915 and on the night of 29th – 30th July he carried out of action an officer who was mortally wounded, under hot fire from rifles and grenades.

At only 18 years of age, Rifleman George Peachment of the 2nd King's Royal Rifle Corps went forward into the initial attack near Lone Tree and was caught up in the slaughter. The London Gazette recorded the following:

Rifleman George Peachment V.C.

For most conspicuous bravery near Hulluch on 25th September 1915. During very heavy fighting when our front line was compelled to retire to re-organise, Pte. Peachment, seeing his Company Commander, Captain Dubbs, lying wounded, crawled to assist him. The enemy's fire was intense, but although there was a shell hole quite close, in which a few men had taken cover, Pte. Peachment never thought of saving himself. He knelt in the open by his officer and tried to help him, but whilst doing this he was first wounded by a bomb and a minute later mortally wounded by a rifle bullet. He was one of the youngest men in his battalion and gave this splendid example of courage and self sacrifice.

Sergeant Harry Wells of the 2nd Royal Sussex was determined to lead his platoon forward:

When his Platoon Officer had been killed he took command and led his men forward to within fifteen yards of the German wire. Nearly half the platoon were killed or wounded, and the remainder were much shaken, but with the utmost coolness and bravery, Sergeant Wells rallied them and led them forward. Finally when very few men were left, he stood up and urged them forward once more, but while doing this he was killed. He gave a magnificent example of courage and determination.

Countless further acts of bravery and selflessness were never officially recognised as those involved perished in the monstrous gloom of the swirling smoke and gas, somewhere out there in front of the Lone Tree.

Attacking the German line immediately to the right of the 10th Gloucesters, the 1st Loyal North Lancashire were stopped by intact wire defences and murderous rifle and machine gun fire. Having made several attempts to penetrate the maze of wire, the battalion's survivors were forced back to their assault trench, leaving many of their dead and wounded in No Man's Land. In spite of the continued heavy enemy fire, Private Henry Kenny ventured out on six different occasions, each time bringing in a wounded man. Eventually Kenny was wounded in the neck and was unable to carry on. The wound was serious enough for him to be invalided home and his bravery was rewarded with the Victoria Cross. Henry Kenny recovered from his wound and lived to be 90 years of age.

Private Henry Kenny V.C.

Green's Force - 1/14th London (London Scottish), 1/9th King's (Liverpool).

Following zero hour, Major General Arthur Holland, commanding the 1st Division from Vermelles, was confronted with a confusing situation. By 8am he had been informed by Brigadier General Reddie, commanding the 1st Brigade, that, the 10th Gloucesters and 8th Royal Berkshires had broken through the German lines immediately north of Lone Tree. The news from the 2nd Brigade was less certain and it was not until 8.21am that he received a message stating that the leading assault battalions, the 2nd King's Royal Rifle Corps and the 1st Loyal North Lancashire had failed to get beyond the enemy wire. However, the message also contained the encouraging but erroneous information that the 2nd Royal Sussex had, **"got through into the German trenches."**

Meanwhile, at about 8am, in response to the 1st Brigade's success, but unaware of the breakdown of the 2nd Brigade's opening attack, Holland ordered Lieutenant Colonel Edgar Green, commanding Green's Force, to move up from Le Rutoire Farm to support the 2nd Brigade, as per the original plan. However, at 9.06am, Holland received a further message from 2nd Brigade stating that the 2nd Royal Sussex were not in the enemy's trenches but were actually held up on the enemy wire. This news dashed any hopes that the German line was breached around Lone Tree. It seems that at this point Holland began to re-evaluate the situation and to formulate a plan designed to outflank the resisting Germans around Lone Tree. At 9.10am he sent a message to Green stating:

> **"Sussexs are reported to be held up by wire in front of German trenches south of LONE TREE. Support with your two battalions attacking the Germans on flank if possible."**

At 10am Holland issued a further order directing Green's Force to assist the 2nd Brigade:

"Push in your attack on the German flank at once."

Unfortunately this order did not reach Green until 10.55am, due to three individual runners failing to get through.

Finally, Green's Force moved off, following their orders to approach the 2nd Brigade's positions in the open and not along the communication trenches, which were choked with wounded anyway. The enemy fire was still intense and consequently both battalions took casualties.

Private Alfred S. Dolden – 1/14th London (London Scottish)

> Bullets came flying round us from all directions, machine guns spat out their endless stream of lead, and shells came whizzing with a deafening roar. Everywhere showers of earth from the enemy barrage were thrown up.
>
> Our first casualty occurred when we had gone forward about ten yards and was a member of my Platoon. He fell shot through the arm. We walked over the ground from the reserve trench to the front line. At our second halt Savereux fell at my side with a wound in the back from shrapnel. We next ran into enfilading fire, and the place became very warm for the enemy's machine guns opened up on us. We had to advance over open country and the Germans had us at their mercy.
>
> During the next rush we lost more men. There was a trench in front of us and we were ordered to get into it. I made a furious dive into the trench, and just missed empaling myself on the upturned bayonet of a fellow who was sitting on the fire step.

Reaching the assault trenches, the two battalions found them so dangerous from the gas and choked with wounded and dead, that the men had to take cover from the veritable storm of enemy fire behind the scanty parados between the firing line and the support trench. Here they grimly awaited the long delayed order to attack.

Much controversy surrounds Green's interpretation of the order to support the 2nd Brigade with an **"attack on the German flank"** and accounts differ as to the actual time of the attack put in by Green's Force. Some accounts state 11.45am, others an hour later at 12.45pm, however, Green's two battalion's leapt over the British firing line and advanced immediately each side of Lone Tree against wire that was known to be uncut and with the enemy trenches fully manned. What chance did two battalions have when four others had failed before them?

It seems that Green was under the impression that his orders strictly meant that he was to attack on the immediate flanks of Lone Tree, rather than to try and outflank the Germans by deploying his battalions further to the north or south. One can speculate that Colonel Green possibly felt that further manoeuvring of his force largely in the open, under heavy fire and without the cover of smoke, was impractical and it was better to launch the attack from the position his battalions already held. In the event, the attack met the same fate as all the others and Green's Force ended up being pinned down in No Man's Land.

It is undoubtedly true that the utter confusion and massive casualties inflicted on the whole of the 2nd Brigade by their own gas and German fire, almost totally paralysed the capacity of the British to relay and receive accurate and up to date messages. Critically, by the time Green's Force had reached the front line from their original positions around Le Rutoire Farm, the Germans had already started to reoccupy the trenches passed over by the 1st Brigade and extended their flanks with enfilading machine guns. When Green's Force was finally in a position to attack, Holland's orders had been decisively compromised.

The 3rd Brigade – 1st South Wales Borderers, 1st Gloucester, 2nd Welsh,
                    2nd Royal Muster Fusiliers.

To the waiting support battalions of the 3rd Brigade positioned near Le Rutoire Farm, little could be seen of the attack, which was still concealed by banks of smoke and gas. By 8.30am this had cleared a little and from their assembly trenches the 1st Gloucesters could now see the diminutive figures of men charging forwards. Two hours had passed since the first waves had attacked; yet the waiting troops could not understand why there was still so much rifle fire.

The War Diary of the 2nd Welsh states:

> **No news was received until 11am when we were ordered up to Le Rutoire Farm. Whilst there, we saw a great number of wounded men moving back and an astonishing number suffering from gas and smoke. There were also some prisoners there.**

By 11am, Major General Holland was aware that the situation was now critical. His 1st Brigade had advanced successfully but the 2nd Brigade and Green's Force seemed to be unable to break the deadlock at Lone Tree. Concerned that the 1st Brigade was unsupported, he issued orders for the 2nd Royal Munster Fusiliers, the 2nd Welsh and the 1st South Wales Borderers to advance to Le Rutoire Farm in preparation to cross No Man's Land at La Haie, where the 8th Royal Berkshires had overrun the German front line.

Meanwhile, having successfully pinned down the whole of 2nd Brigade, the Germans began filtering northward to reoccupying their trenches already passed over by the 1st Brigade. They were able to reach as far as Bois Carré redoubt, where they repositioned a machine gun in the old redoubt that had been overrun by the 10th Gloucesters.

At 12.30pm the three battalions began their advance, but in the confusion of battle, the Munsters, who were leading, were pinned down by machine gun fire when they tried to cross No Man's Land close to Lone Tree.

The 2nd Welsh successfully navigated their way towards La Haie and in spite of being fired on from the enemy now in Bois Carré redoubt, crossed No Man's Land north of the Vermelles to Hulluch road and advanced towards Hulluch.

The 1st South Wales Borderers were not so lucky and were fired on by the same machine gun in Bois Carré redoubt. However, with the 1st Black Watch, who had been waiting patiently all morning opposite La Haie, the two battalions attacked and managed to clear the Germans from the redoubt.

They then advanced further, to get into the enemy main fire trench, working their way down it towards Lone Tree.

The 2nd Welsh had orders to support the 1st Brigade at Hulluch, however, such was the intensity of enemy fire now coming from Hulluch and to their surprise from the trenches around Lone Tree in their rear, that the battalion had to crawl into cover in a captured enemy trench known as Gun Trench. Correctly appraising the situation, Lieutenant Colonel Prothero, commanding the Welsh, detached elements of his battalion to threaten the Germans still resisting immediately to the rear and south west.

At 2.30pm this move paid dividends, for a white flag was shown from a portion of these trenches and 'C' Company accepted the surrender of five German officers and 160 men accompanied by a British officer with his wounds bound. The German's resistance at Lone Tree was nearly at an end.

'A' Company advanced a couple of hundred yards further south toward Lone Tree and at about 3.30pm Captain Ritter with 400 men, finding his position threatened from the rear and flank, surrendered to the Black Watch and the survivors of Green's Force, who rose from the slaughterhouse of No Man's Land and cut their way through the wire.

Private A.S. Dolden – 1/14th London (London Scottish):

> Our numbers were too few to rush across the ground to Lone Tree, for we would have been mown down before we got there. The tension was at its height when someone shouted "Look at the Lone Tree, they are taking prisoners." I looked up and to my utter astonishment and, needless to say, my unspeakable relief, saw the Germans coming out of their trenches with their hands up to give themselves up as prisoners.
>
> The scene that followed was the most remarkable that I have ever witnessed. At one moment there was an intense and nerve shattering struggle with death screaming through the air. Then, as if with the wave of a magic wand, all was changed; all over No Man's Land troops came out of trenches, or rose from the ground where they had been lying. Prisoners were everywhere.

The War Diary of the King's Royal Rifle Corps recorded:

> The Germans surrendered at about 3.30pm. The enemy front trench was protected by wire 10 yards wide, low and thick. Their front trench was in perfect condition, hardly touched by shellfire, wide and revetted and staked with wire netting to assist. The Germans used goggles and pad pattern respirators. There were no dead Germans in the trench.

For nine hours Captain Ritter and his men had held up the effective advance of a whole British Division. His machine guns had decimated the 2nd Brigade and Green's Force and also caused serious casualties to the 3rd Brigade and prevented them from assisting the savaged 1st Brigade in their efforts to capture Hulluch and secure a permanent breach in the German second line. The future consequences for the failure to capture Hulluch were very soon to prove catastrophic for the British Army.

By late afternoon, the mauled battalions of the 2nd and 3rd Brigades were able to limp eastward. Nearly all the battalions of the 1st Division had suffered very heavy casualties in capturing the enemy firing line and now they were not strong enough or organised enough to carry out their orders and advance against the German second line. The best they could do was to consolidate the line of the La Bassée to Lens road as stated in their original orders.

The 3rd Brigade eventually arrived to support the remnants of the 1st Brigade, still clinging to their half dug trenches on the outskirts of Hulluch. The 2nd Brigade advanced to the Chalk Pit, Chalk Pit Wood and Puits 14Bis, which fortunately had been evacuated by the Germans due to the presence of the 15th Scottish Division who were now desperately fighting to retain possession of nearby Hill 70 and Chalet Wood. The Brigade was able to link up with the Scots and also to occupy the western portion of Bois Hugo.

The London Scottish Regimental Gazette described the Chalk Pit as follows:

> **It proved to be a most uninviting place for a bivouac. It was about forty feet deep, with steep sides of wet chalk and a lot of water in the bottom of it. If a German counter attack came in the night, the Chalk Pit would be a trap.**

Green's Force extended the British line northward along the La Bassée to Lens road. The two battalions were severely depleted in numbers and the exhausted soldiers had to dig trenches from scratch alongside the road. In the confused situation they failed to extend their left flank far enough along the road to link up with the troops of the 1st and 3rd Brigades to the west of Hulluch. Likewise the troops opposite Hulluch did not link their right flank with Green's Force. The result was that as night approached, a thousand yard gap in the British line existed that nobody seemed aware of.

Despite the enormous casualties, there was great relief that an advance was now under way. An officer of the 1st Gloucesters recorded:

> **For some time there was no sign of war, a lull having set in over the neighbouring battlefield. It was rather exciting to advance over coarse autumn grass of fields that had been neither cultivated or grazed since the war began and had for so long been in German territory.**

The battle had now swept on over Lone Tree Ridge and down into the shallow Loos valley. In its wake, amidst the ruin of the battlefield, beside La Haie, Bois Carré, Lone Tree and the Northern Sap, lay the swathes of dead and dying. The 1st Division's cynical and proud Regulars, the bright optimistic New Army men and Territorials, united in pain and death. The total horror of battle graphically displayed, vivid and brutal enough to turn the stomachs of those who thought War to be, "a marvellous game."

To the north and south of Lone Tree, beside the La Bassée Canal, amidst the shambles of the Hohenzollern Redoubt, Loos and the Double Crassier, the carnage was equally shocking.

Men were still fighting and dying and there was always the threat of an enemy counter attack. Field Artillery was being rushed forward and supporting troops, together with Royal Engineers,

The hunched forms of dead British soldiers lie in No Man's Land at Loos.

Signallers and Royal Army Medical Corps, were picking their way through the bloody, frightful scenes littering the former No Man's Land. They stared, grim and disbelieving at the grisly sight of the endless numbers of dead who lay strewn everywhere in awful unnatural, leaden poses. Were they to share in this miserable, inhuman fate?

Captain Wyllie – Royal Scots Fusiliers, 9th Division:

> From our new position we watched the 18pdr batteries galloping up the Hulloch Road, which was situated on our right. The guns wheeled round in circles at full gallop and took up positions in the open, the guns coming into action almost as soon as the gun trails hit the ground. I do not remember how many batteries were involved, but it was a wonderful sight to see these guns coming into action and also the gun limbers galloping down the road for more ammunition.

W.J. Kemp - No. 59 Siege Battery, Royal Garrison Artillery:

> I was employed as a runner that day to repair the telephone lines between the battery and our OP. The first I saw was the battery with all four guns, horse drawn in No Man's Land that was coming into action. I was very near to them and the first thing I saw in No Man's Land was that it was full of dead, dying and wounded, we carried some of them out on to the road as some waved to us when they saw we were going to open fire. They had not got far out of their front line trenches before being struck down and all this after four days of bombardment.

At 5pm on the afternoon of September 25th, the mixed up collection of battalions from the 1st Division's 1st and 3rd brigades were still trying to dig in on the outskirts of Hulluch. The window of opportunity to capture the village was now closed and the Germans had long since rushed in reinforcements to adequately occupy Hulluch and to defend their formerly abandoned second line.

As early as 3.30pm, when the supporting 3rd Brigade was still occupied taking the surrender of Captain Ritter at Lone Tree, the Germans had mounted a counter attack from Hulluch.

The 8th Royal Berkshire's War Diary noted:

> At 3.30pm the Germans counter attacked driving in our flanks and as the support had not yet arrived we were compelled to retire, holding a position about 100yds west of the road. The Berks numbers were reduced to about half. On receiving news that the supports were coming up, we again advanced to the road, which we proceeded to place in a state of defence.

By 6pm on the evening of September 25th, the ever-growing counter fire from the Germans occupying Hulluch was causing serious problems for the British soldiers crouched in their inadequate scrapes along the La Bassée to Lens road.

Corporal Albert Carter:

> I was lucky really. I got into the German trenches unscathed with the few survivors of the battalion. The Germans had made off to a village not far away called Hulluch. We were ordered to dig in and repulse any attacks the Germans might make, but at about 6pm I felt my rifle fall from my fingers. I looked down and to my amazement saw that I had been shot through the hand. Strangely I didn't feel a thing at the time.

The men were ordered to fall back on Gun Trench, a more easily defended position some 500 yards to the rear. However, it appears that some men, including a number of the surviving Berkshires, remained positioned along the road.

At 11.30pm, under cover of darkness, the Germans again counter attacked with about 300 soldiers trying to infiltrate the British positions. Those British troops still holding their positions on the La Bassée to Lens road found themselves in trouble. The Berkshire's War Diary records:

> The Germans again counter attacked in large numbers, driving in our right flank. We retired to the position we had before held in the afternoon. The Germans continued to push the counter attack. Our support line then opened fire and we were caught between the two fires. We then made our way as well as possible to our supporting line. Only six of the Berkshires returned safely.

The recorded history of the South Wales Borderers states that after dark an enemy counter attack developed but was quickly repulsed by the battalion's machine gunners, but interestingly goes on to say:

> Notwithstanding this, a much stronger force approached the trenches, calling out, "Don't shoot; we are the Welch," Colonel Gwynne and his men were not to be taken in and with admirable coolness reserved their fire until the enemy were quite close to the parapet. Then a sudden burst of rapid fire swept the approaching Germans down, hardly any escaping.

The night was wet and stormy, the few remaining officers of the 10th Gloucesters gathered together only 60 exhausted survivors of the battalion. The rest were scattered, wounded or dead. A counter attack from the enemy was expected so a redoubt was constructed at Point 89 on the army maps. Point 89 was christened Keep 89 and was garrisoned overnight by 40 men with three machine guns under the command of newly promoted Lieutenant Royds.

In the meantime, now that the German resistance around Lone Tree and the Grenay Ridge was over, medical orderlies could freely search for survivors amongst the shell craters, sapheads, tall grass and tangles of barbed wire. Moving between each crumpled body, they would kneel momentarily beside the thousands who were beyond human assistance. The machine guns and shrapnel shells had done their grisly butcher's work well. Haig's initial analysis of the chances of success had proved ironically accurate. The battlefront was indeed, impossible, fire swept ground. It was only the

A contemporary artist's depiction of a stretcher bearer party removing wounded British soldiers from a captured trench.

unsurpassable, naive courage of the New Army men that had carried them into the enemy redoubts and trenches.

Amongst the thousands who lay still and glassy eyed were 163 men and officers of the 10th Gloucesters. Their bodies lay in No Man's Land, amongst the wire and in the almost intact enemy positions. A further 275 were wounded and gassed with 20 dying of their wounds in the next few days. The 10th's War Diary pays tribute to their incredible courage:

> The officers fell as the position of their bodies showed, leading their men,
> fourteen out of twenty one were lost. The bodies of our dead indicated how
> they died, with their faces to the enemy.

The 8th Royal Berkshires suffered similarly, losing 181 killed with many more wounded and gassed. The 2nd Brigade and Green's Force were also very badly mauled with the 2nd Royal Sussex suffering particularly badly.

All along the battlefront, the frightful scenes were repeated. Some lay in neat rows, caught by the machine guns, others were reduced to little more than bloody rags. A Staff Officer, who visited the captured Lens Road Redoubt where the 9th Black Watch of the 15th Scottish Division had advanced, recorded:

> In front of the Lens Road Redoubt, the dead Highlanders in Black Watch
> tartan lay very thick. In one place, about 40 yards square, on the very crest

of the ridge and just in front of the enemy's wire, they were so close that it was difficult to step between them. Nevertheless the survivors swept on and through the German lines. As I looked on the smashed and riven ground, I was amazed when I thought of the unconquerable spirit, which these men of the New Armies must possess, to enable them to continue their advance after sustaining such losses.

For now, with the struggle still continuing, there was no time to bury the dead and they were left to lie where they had fallen.

Dishevelled groups of mud caked, dazed walking wounded, clutching bloody, hastily bound wounds, pushed their painful way back along crowded communication trenches. Although the long communication trench known as Le Rutoire Alley had been reserved for the passage of the wounded to the advanced bearer's post at the farm, their sheer numbers caused severe difficulties. The situation was made worse by the throngs of troops loaded down with equipment, moving forwards to support the assaulting infantry. Enemy artillery, anticipating the advance of reinforcements,

Wounded British soldiers return from the battlefield. The man in the foreground is still wearing his gas/smoke helmet.

continued to hurl shrapnel shells over Lone Tree ridge, forcing much movement to be conducted along the packed trenches.

Private William Jennings:

> I made my way back along some crowded communication trenches to a field dressing station where I was told to hold my wounded hand in a bowl of antiseptic water. Later I was given some soup and had my uniform taken from me. My boots and puttees had to be cut off; they were covered in chalky mud and had set on me like cement. Eventually I was sent back to England to a hospital near Weymouth, but because my trigger finger had gone I never went back to the front, but spent some time at R.F.C. Cranwell, where I did batman duties.

In the forward British trenches, grubby, pathetic knots of badly wounded men crouched, sheltering from the cart wheeling shards of steel unleashed by the German barrage. Some whimpered and slobbered, clawing jaggedly at their mouths with dirt encrusted fingers, their eyes bulging with helpless fear. These were the victims of shell shock. Others lay still, their breathing shallow, as their lifeblood welled into livid, crimson pools in the trench bottoms.

Many more were victims of the gas, wheezing and vomiting as they desperately tried to fill their tortured, scorched lungs with the still tainted air. Even the brass buttons on their tunics had turned a strange green colour from exposure to the gas.

One soldier, both his arms wrapped in cotton wool and his face the colour of an orange from the effects of gas, managed to whisper to a group of wide-eyed soldiers moving up:

> **Buck up boys there's no more gas up there, we have swallowed it all.**

Letters sent home by British soldiers were censored and those reproduced in Gloucestershire newspapers were typically vague when mentioning gas. Corporal Charles Hautin's letter, reproduced in the press, merely stated:

> **I have got a bullet wound in the head and am suffering from gas. It is awful stuff if you get much of it, but still I am going on very well.**

Sergeant Herbert Algernon Vale wrote home with a splendid account of his part in the battle, but mentions nothing of the origins of the gas that hospitalised him:

> **Just a few lines to let you know I am safe and well. As you know there has been a great battle and we have come out on top. We had all been in the trenches three days waiting for the attack but on Friday night we were told that in the morning we should go over the parapet, so you can tell we were feeling just about wound up when Saturday morning came. Our guns started telling them a few tales, it was just like thunder, but our fellows did not go on for long before the Bosches started giving us gip, and unfortunately a good number of our chaps got hit.**
>
> **At five past six we went over the top, it was a grand sight to see how they did it. You may say that the good old 10th maintained the Gloucester's reputation. Our battalion and the 8th Berks led the attack of the first brigade and did it splendidly. Our orders were to take three lines of trenches, two more battalions would come through and go on.**
>
> **I was gassed after going to their trenches and had to have oxygen pumped into me, but I am going on first rate now and shall soon be back again.**
>
> **I think this is the beginning of the end and it won't last much longer now. The Germans must have lost terribly.**

Chlorine gas was a crude weapon, but despite its potentially traumatic effects, most men who caught just a 'whiff' of it were able to carry on without medical attention. Even those who inhaled fair quantities were often able to recover and were sent back to the front.

Lance Corporal Edmund Lord pictured second left, during the 10th Gloucester's early days in Cheltenham.

Lance Corporal Edmund Lord and Private Albert Edward Agg were both victims of the gas, however, they were able to return to the battalion a few days later, following treatment. The ultimate fates of these two men were quite different.

Edmund, who was originally from Hexthorpe near Doncaster in Yorkshire, had moved to Birmingham in the early 1900s. Following Loos and for much of 1916, Edmund suffered bouts of fever, which eventually invalided him from the battalion to which he did not return until 1917. He was eventually captured in the Kaiser's Offensive of 1918 and survived the war in Dulmen prisoner of war camp at Munster.

Albert, who was from Alderton near Tewkesbury in Gloucestershire, also survived the war but was wounded on the Somme on September 3rd 1916 when 'C' and 'D' Companies were detached to the 1st Black Watch for an assault on High Wood. The assault, which was to be supported by the explosion of a number of mines and the use of liquid fire, was initially successful with 400 prisoners taken, but the

Private Albert Edward Agg of Alderton near Tewkesbury, Gloucestershire.

Gloucesters, Black Watch and Camerons were forced out by shellfire during the night with very heavy casualties.

Even as the struggle at Loos raged, scientists of both sides were experimenting with new, even more noxious gasses and chemicals. The much deadlier and odourless phosgene gas would soon replace chlorine gas. It produced no immediate effects, allowing enemy troops to breathe in large quantities, with deadly effect.

Out in No Man's Land, amongst the shell holes, jumbles of rusty barbed wire and littered equipment, the battalion stretcher-bearers were swamped by the task of tending to the hundreds of wounded men. Those capable of walking were sent back to find their own way to the advanced dressing stations, but too often the bearers came upon groups of men thrown down, their bodies torn to shreds by bursting shells. Also rows of prone soldiers riddled with machine gun fire. Some would stir, still clinging to life, but there was little to be done for such mutilated men. A morphine tablet placed under the tongue would ease the misery into merciful unconsciousness.

The large number of men still wearing their gas/smoke helmets made the job of the bearers more difficult.

Lance Corporal Clifford – 10th Gloucesters:

> At Loos, I acted as a medical orderly and stretcher-bearer. On the battlefield we had a terrible time telling whether a man was dead or just unconscious. You see, most of them were wearing their gas helmets and we couldn't see their faces, so we had to go to each one and take off these gas helmets. Many were dead, and we marked their bodies by sticking their rifles, butts upwards, in the ground at their side. I think most of the casualties were caused by the machine guns.

Strecher bearers of the 10th Gloucesters.

Patrick MacGill, a stretcher-bearer serving with the London Irish in the 47th Division, recorded this graphic account:

> Another soldier came crawling towards us on his belly, looking for all the world like a gigantic lobster which had escaped from its basket. His lower lip was cut clean to the chin and hanging apart, blood welled through the muddy khaki trousers where they covered the hips . . . men and pieces of men were lying all over the place. A leg, an arm, there again a leg, cut off at the hip. A finely formed leg, the latter gracefully puttee'd.

Amazingly, amidst these harrowing scenes, some were able to find a streak of black humour in the situation.

Private Alfred Ernest Wildsmith dashed unscathed across No Man's Land but was checked by the German wire. There appeared to be no way through so he set to work with his wire cutters and began snipping at the strands. Bullets 'zinged' off the wire and the cutters fell from his hands. A bullet had passed through both his arms. Taking cover in a shell hole he found another soldier from the 10th who had been shot through both heels. Enemy bullets were still tearing overhead so they both hugged the earth praying for the nightmare to end. Eventually the cacophony of gunfire died down and it became apparent that the Germans had fled their trenches.

The soldier wounded in the heels complained bitterly to Alf that he could not walk and begged not to be left alone. At length two stretcher-bearers approached, pausing beside each sprawled body. As they drew closer, up jumped the heel casualty and stumbled to the bearers, leaving Alf Wildsmith to ponder the perverseness of the incident.

Private Alfred Ernest Wildsmith lived in Cheltenham. He was shot through both arms whilst trying to cut a path through enemy wire.

Plucked from the battlefield by stretcher-bearers, the seriously wounded were carried back to regimental aid posts situated at Le Rutoire Farm and dugouts in Le Rutoire Alley and Le Rutoire Keep. Here they received rudimentary attention before being loaded by bearers onto a horse drawn wagon or a motor transport and moved along uneven, shell-cratered roads to the advanced dressing station at Philosophe, a mining settlement two and a half miles behind the British lines.

Philosophe's strategic importance lay in its rail link to the main casualty clearing stations. The wounded were placed onto the platform on long lines of stretchers. Some lay quiet and motionless, neatly blanketed up to their necks, others thrashed in their agony crying out in pain and delirium, casting back the covers that concealed their mutilated bodies.

Corporal Wallace Grey from Minchinhampton in Gloucestershire was wounded on September 26th 1915 and died at Lillers the following day.

Private David Hail, originally a collier from the Forest of Dean, Gloucestershire. David died of wounds at Chocques near Béthune on October 9th 1915.

At length, a train would draw into the station, its great clanking and hissing drowning the pitiful moans of pain and anguish as each stretcher and its occupant was placed in the carriages. Their destination was the No.1 Casualty Clearing Station situated at Chocques near Béthune, some eleven miles from Philosophe. Hopelessly wounded and receiving only the basic attention of overburdened orderlies, many never survived to reach Chocques alive and sadly expired on these trains of misery.

Among the scores of wounded men of the 10th Gloucesters destined for Chocques, was David Hail, formerly a collier from the Forest of Dean. Seriously wounded, David clung to life until October 9th when he mercifully died and was buried in the nearby military cemetery, which was rapidly filling with casualties from Loos.

Literally thousands of wounded soldiers arrived at Chocques. Many, whose wounds were not considered immediately life threatening, continued their rail journey to Etaples on the Channel coast where they were treated in the concentration of military hospitals located there. Surviving long enough to reach Etaples did not guarantee recovery and the nearby Etaples Military cemetery expanded to become the largest British war graves cemetery in France.

Wounded on September 25th in the Gloucester's attack, was Private Ernest Albert Young. Ernest died of his wounds on October 1st 1915 at St. John's Hospital at Etaples and was buried in Etaples Military cemetery in Plot 1V where many other soldiers wounded at Loos now lie.

Having been treated at Etaples, wounded soldiers were repatriated to various hospitals in Britain via the French ports of Le Havre and Boulogne. Private Walter Edward Littlefield never made it across the Channel. Aged just 17 years, he died in one of Boulogne's hospitals on October 3rd and was buried in Boulogne Eastern Military Cemetery. Major W. R. Paterson, who was shot in the foot, was luckier and eventually recovered in a Dublin hospital.

Private Ernest Albert Young died of wounds received at Loos. His home was at Stow-on-the-Wold in Gloucestershire.

Private Richard Hubert Hanks.

Private Richard Hanks spent five weeks being treated in France before being brought home to England. His wounded leg had refused to heal and so it was amputated in Nottingham Hospital. Sadly complications set in and he died eleven days later on December 4th 1915. Richard's body was brought home to Painswick near Gloucester, where, at a funeral service attended by hundreds of local people, his coffin, draped in a Union Flag and bearing his Fire Brigade helmet, tunic and belt, was conveyed on a fire engine from the church to the cemetery on Painswick Hill. At the graveside, firemen and members of the Training Corps and the Boy's Brigade formed in a circle whilst Reverend W.H. Seddon recited the last rites. Richard Hanks was 25 years old and left a widow and two young children. Today his Commonwealth War Grave headstone stands in a quiet corner of the pretty hillside cemetery at Painswick, surrounded in the spring by myriads of wild primroses.

Sixteen year old Joseph King, the young lad who in happier days had worked on W.H. Smith's bookstall at

An unknown soldier of the Gloucestershire Regiment who has paid a terrible price.

the Midland Road rail station in Cheltenham, had fallen, seriously wounded in the advance. He was speedily brought to England but tragically died of his wounds in the Royal Victoria Military Hospital at Netley, Southampton, on October 8th 1915. The boy soldier's funeral took place in Cheltenham Cemetery at Prestbury, and to this day his headstone stands beneath Cleeve Hill where the sublime comradeship of 'The Fighting Tenth' was forged all those years ago.

Many wounded soldiers did eventually recover sufficiently to return to the front. Private Reginald Fennell was sent to the Gray's Inn Road Hospital in London, where his wounded leg healed well. All his relatives and friends wrote to their relatives and friends in London so he did not lack visitors or presents. Indeed, he recalled that he had so many pretty girls visiting that his fellow patients nicknamed him 'The Sheik of Araby.'

On the 8th of January 1916, having recovered sufficiently from his wound, Reg was posted to the Gloucester's 11th (Reserve) Battalion stationed at Seaford near Eastbourne in East Sussex, here he met up with many more of the 10th Gloucester's men who had also recovered from wounds.

Private Joseph Sidney King died of wounds on October 8th 1915, aged just 16 years. He lived at 6, Brunswick Buildings, Cheltenham.

Young Joseph's grave beneath Cleeve Hill, Cheltenham.

Private Frederick George Hale, 11th Gloucesters, was the youngest son of Mr. and Mrs. C. Hale of 2, Brevit Terrace, Charlton Kings, Cheltenham. His death on January 15th 1916 was officially recorded as being due to bronchitis. Frederick is buried at Seaford, East Sussex.

Private Walter Edward Littlefield, wounded at Loos on September 25th 1915. He sadly died in hospital at Boulogne on October 3rd 1915 where he lies today in Boulogne Eastern Military Cemetery.

At Seaford Reg resumed his acquaintance with Ernest Chadband, the teenage soldier who had almost certainly cheated death by being evacuated with pleurisy just before the Battle of Loos.

Sergeant Ernest Chadband:

> I was sent to Seaford, Sussex to join the 11th Training Reserve Battalion. On the first pay parade I was called into the Orderly Room in front of Major Hewitson who told me I was being put through for a stripe. I told him I did not wish it as I wanted to go back to the 10th Battalion, but he took no notice and put my name

through. I was soon put on the square with two Sergeant Majors, ex Metropolitan Policemen, drilling recruits.

Now some of the 10th were returning and those who had been slightly wounded and recovered were sent to the 11th where they were not very happy. The Commanding Officer was Lieutenant Colonel Hale, we were told he had been Governor of Gloucester Gaol and one of his favourite expressions was, "Get your hair cut." The Colonel paraded with a draft of men back to the front which consisted of mainly old 10th men. The Colonel went to the station with the draft after giving them a lecture and telling them that few of them would be returning. He even had a guard to parade them to the station. The men were treated more like convicts than volunteer soldiers but on this occasion he overstepped the mark. As the troops were in the train and the doors locked, he went along the train offering to shake hands with them, when a fellow from the Forest of Dean by the name of Collins told him to, "Go and get your hair cut you slack jowled old bastard; I only shake hands with a man!" and as the train was moving out there was little he could do about it but returned to camp in a fury.

Reg Fennell was equally disgruntled, referring contemptuously to this battalion as the "**Shiney 11th**" and he railed at the inhuman way the men were treated by the NCOs.

Went to the funeral of a chap who stayed in this hut. He asked to fall out sick while on march. NCOs and the officer would not let him. He died in hospital next day. The way he was treated was disgraceful. In my opinion the NCOs and officer ought to be charged with furthering his death. In face of this, the government say "Your King and Country need you" at the same time allow you to drop dead in the road like a dog. I think the NCOs here are the worst I have ever met; they are afraid of their own shadows and nearly drop dead with fright at the sight of the Colonel. When the lad's mother arrived here they have the sauce to tell her they did the best for her son. Ah well! It's a sad world after all.

As a seasoned soldier who had experienced and survived the full horror of the battlefield, Reg and the other recovered men of the 10th understandably resented the 'bull' of a reserve battalion.

Went on bayonet fighting in the afternoon. Us 10th chaps were sneered and snubbed by all on parade. I should like to meet some NCOs in civil life.

Following medical inspections on January 18th and 25th, Reg was passed fully fit for duty and on February 20th he was warned that he was to join an overseas draft destined for the 8th Gloucesters. Understandably he was disappointed not to be sent back to the 10th Gloucesters, however his salvation arrived in the form of the 10th Gloucester's Major Kirkwood, who had been posted to Seaford having recovered from wounds also received at Loos. Major Kirkwood immediately pulled a few strings. Reg recorded in his diary:

Adjutant tells me he has got me out of the draft to the 8th Gloucesters. To proceed to the 10th by the first draft that goes.

Corporal Albert Carter also found himself at Seaford and was sent on a draft to the 9th Gloucesters where he served abroad in Salonika. After the war he rose through the ranks of the Gloucestershire Constabulary to become Assistant Chief Constable.

Private Alfred Ernest Wildsmith was just one of many who never totally recovered from his wounds. Initially posted to the Royal Scots Fusiliers, he was discharged on 7th September 1917, having been pronounced, **"No longer physically fit for war service."**

Despite such stringent planning and attention to detail, the first day of the battle had only achieved limited success. Even though vastly outnumbered, the Germans had resisted stoutly and extremely effectively. Captain Ritter's stand at Lone Tree was an outstanding example of their cool and co-ordinated defence strategy. Their artillery and machine guns had taken such a huge toll of the assaulting troops that the British were fought to a standstill, or were too weak in numbers to press home any advantage that presented itself. Only at Hulluch had the second German line been briefly penetrated by the 1st Brigade.

To the south of the 1st Division, on the extreme right of the British Army, the 47th London Division had successfully secured the right flank, allowing the 15th Scottish Division to advance through Loos and to capture the dominating position of Hill 70. However, the Germans quickly rallied and drove the Scots, who were far from effective artillery support, off the summit where they were forced to entrench in exposed positions on the lower slopes.

Immediately to the north of the 1st Division, the 7th and 9th Divisions respectively, suffered truly massive casualties in capturing the formidable enemy positions known as the Quarries, the Hohenzollern Redoubt, the Dump and Fosse 8. They were fought to a similar standstill and the Germans lost no time in organising counter attacks that put enormous pressure on the exhausted British troops trying to consolidate the captured ground.

Further north still, straddling the La Bassée canal, the 2nd Division met with total disaster when their gas blew back. It had to be turned off and the attacking troops were mostly shot down by machine gun fire as they cleared their own wire. North of the canal, a brigade did manage to capture the enemy fire trench, but was soon forced out by the enemy who overwhelmed them with copious supplies of grenades.

To the south, the French, who had not used gas, but relied instead on a short but powerful artillery bombardment, had made little headway below the formidable heights of Vimy Ridge. Without the support of a huge, decisive breakthrough by the French, a sustainable smaller scale advance by the British at Loos had virtually no chance of success.

For the battle-fatigued survivors of the 1st Division, a long, cold, wet and uncomfortable night lay ahead.

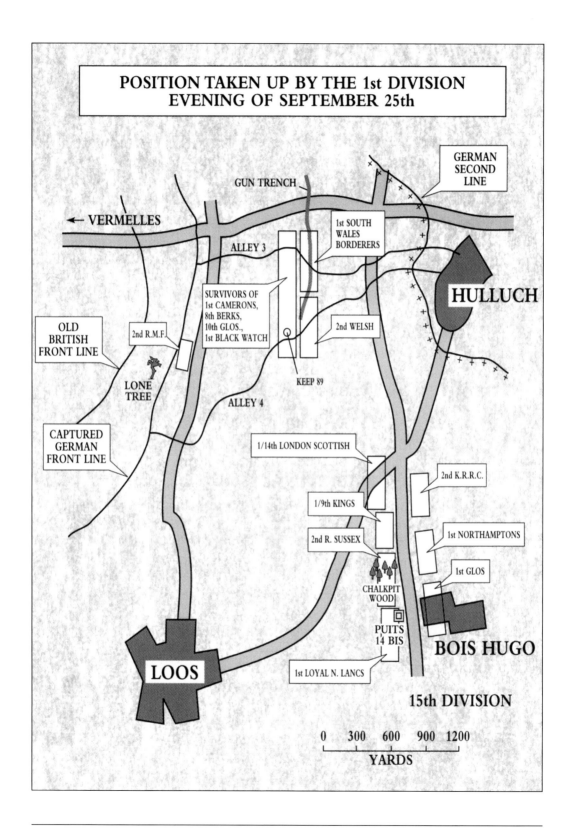

POSITION TAKEN UP BY THE 1st DIVISION
EVENING OF SEPTEMBER 25th

GERMAN SECOND LINE

GUN TRENCH

← VERMELLES

1st SOUTH WALES BORDERERS

ALLEY 3

HULLUCH

SURVIVORS OF
1st CAMERONS,
8th BERKS,
10th GLOS.,
1st BLACK WATCH

OLD BRITISH FRONT LINE

2nd R.M.F.

2nd WELSH

LONE TREE

KEEP 89

ALLEY 4

CAPTURED GERMAN FRONT LINE

1/14th LONDON SCOTTISH

2nd K.R.R.C.

1/9th KINGS

1st NORTHAMPTONS

2nd R. SUSSEX

1st GLOS

CHALKPIT WOOD

PUITS 14 BIS

BOIS HUGO

LOOS

1st LOYAL N. LANCS

15th DIVISION

0   300   600   900   1200

YARDS

CHAPTER IV

The Second Day

**The nimble gunner with linstock now the devilish cannon touches
And down goes all before them**

King Henry V. Act II, Scene IV

During the hours of darkness, enemy patrols probed forward in a determined attempt to establish contact with the British and to identify the exact extent of their advance. In the dark confusion of the night, the inevitable close quarter clashes cost the lives of many German soldiers who were surprised and shot down. In the eerie depths of Bois Hugo, the 1st Gloucesters repulsed several attempts to infiltrate their positions. Nevertheless, by dawn these costly encounters had provided vital information indicating the strength and deployment of the British troops.

As the first day of battle had progressed, General Haig, ensconced in a chateau far behind the battlefront at Hinges, north of Béthune, had been receiving encouraging reports. It was true that the 2nd Division had been repulsed, but to the south all the other divisions had eventually overrun the enemy forward trenches on a front of over three miles, a considerable achievement when measured against all previous offensives. The town of Loos was in British hands and the dominating feature of Hill 70 and its redoubt had been captured. Further north, the tough nut of the Hohenzollern Redoubt had been cracked and it was believed that the 1st Division had breached the German's second line of defences at Hulluch. In light of this latest information, General Haig asked Sir John French to release the reserve formations into his command.

The reserve force consisted of the elite Guards Division and two Kitchener Army divisions, namely the 21st and 24th. Both the Kitchener divisions had been in France for less than four weeks and were completely untried with absolutely no battle experience. Sir John French was acutely aware of this factor and considered that they should only be ordered into action once the Germans were forced to abandon their trench lines and were in full retreat. However, as the situation seemed favourable, Sir John agreed to release these reserves to Haig, but it was not until late in the afternoon of September 25th that orders were issued for the two divisions to advance to the captured line of the La Bassée to Lens road, between Loos and Hulluch. The Guards Division, which was moving up to the front from the direction of Lillers, was to form up in the positions vacated by the 21st Division, around the town of Noeux-les-Mines, more than six miles behind the front.

Dusk was already falling as the two 'green' Kitchener divisions began to march for the battlefront, now spectacularly illuminated by star shells and the flashes of artillery fire. As the men marched along the narrow, tree lined and roughly cobbled French roads, they found their progress seriously impeded by motor and wagon transports removing the wounded to the rear. True, the darkness concealed their approach to the front but the interminable stops and starts reduced their movement to a fitful crawl. On top of this, the heavens opened and the troops were soaked.

Now that the reserves were finally on the move, General Haig began issuing orders for a swift and decisive resumption of the battle. By late evening on September 25th a much clearer picture of the situation was emerging.

Still with the objective of securing the canal crossing at Pont à Vendin firmly in mind, Haig planned to exploit the considerable breach in the German front. In his implacably optimistic manner, he was firmly of the opinion that the Germans had taken such a mauling that their second line was now sparsely manned and would fall to a swift and determined attack. However, by this time Haig had now been updated with the disturbing news that the 1st Division had not broken the German second line at Hulluch and that Hill 70 and its redoubt was back under enemy control. He also knew that the ground gained by the 9th Scottish Division on the left flank, in the vicinity of the Hohenzollern Redoubt, Fosse 8 and the Dump, was seriously under threat from very determined enemy counter attacks. The good news was that the 47th Division, holding the right flank immediately to the south of Loos, was standing firm.

Haig's plan was therefore to order a massed advance of the 21st and 24th divisions to overwhelmingly force open the German second line between Hill 70 and Hulluch. The hard pressed Germans would give way and the vital canal crossing could be captured. But before these two divisions could be committed to battle, Haig needed to make some adjustments to help improve the chances of success.

The 21st and 24th Divisions each contained three brigades consisting of four infantry battalions in each, and to aid the hard pressed 9th Scottish Division, the 24th Division's 73rd Brigade was to be detached to help stabilise the left flank where they were to defend Fosse 8 and the Dump. The Division's remaining two brigades, the 71st and 72nd, were to advance against the German second line immediately south of Hulluch.

Hill 70 was rightly identified as the key to the success of this advance. It not only dominated the town of Loos, but gave an uninterrupted view and field of fire as far north as Hulluch. Clearly Hill 70 would have to be captured before the advance could begin. To assist in the planned capture of Hill 70, the 21st Division's 62nd Brigade was detached to support the exhausted 15th Scottish Division, which was precariously entrenched just below the summit of the hill. The 21st Division's other two Brigades, the 63rd and 64th, were to relieve the battle weary 2nd Brigade of the 1st Division, currently occupying positions in and around Bois Hugo. From here they would launch their attack on the morning of September 26th in conjunction with the 71st and 72nd brigades of the 24th Division.

The village of Hulluch would also have to be captured to avoid the Germans from firing into the left flank of the advance. The job of capturing this important village was given to the tired and savaged 3rd Brigade of the 1st Division, currently manning trenches just to the west of the village. For good measure, the 7th Division was ordered to capture the village of Cité St. Elie, situated just 1,000 yards north of Hulluch.

It was not until the very early hours of September 26th that the brigades of the 21st Division began to reach the former British assault trenches north of Loos. Here in the inky blackness, the officers were faced with the daunting task of manoeuvring thousands of men over unfamiliar, cratered ground ridden with a maze of tumbled, blasted trenches and intersected with belts of hidden wire. Hundreds of fallen soldiers, many still wounded, lay in their path. There were few recognizable features by which to navigate and progress by compass bearing was painfully slow towards the new and uncharted British front line. In many places this line existed only in the form of unconnected,

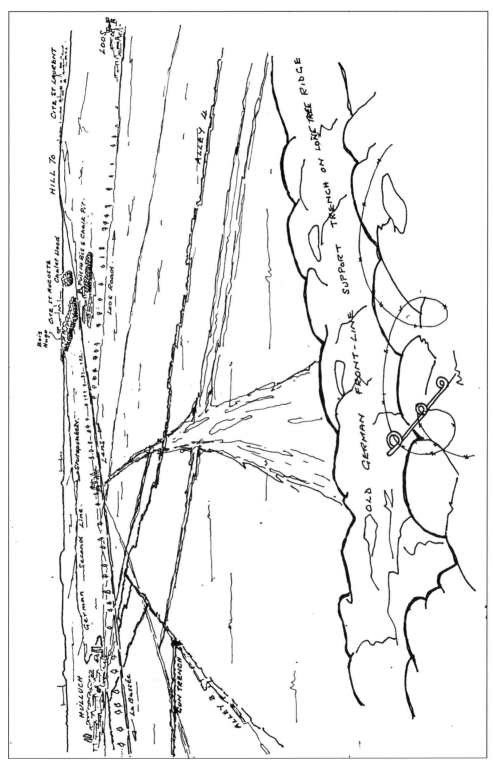

The shallow Loos Valley immediately to the east of Lone Tree Ridge. Here in front of Hulluch the advance of the 1st Brigade was checked and where on September 26th the slaughter of the 21st and 24th Divisions took place. The front line soon stabilised along the Lens to La Bassée road. After a sketch by an officer of the London Scottish.

shallow and exposed trenches with no wire protection.

The enemy artillery was still very active, vigorously shelling all known approaches to try and disrupt the British from bringing up reinforcements and supplies. Reliable information regarding the disposition of the enemy could only be gleaned from the tired British troops that they were about to relieve or reinforce.

Despite the exhausting march and horrific revelations of the battlefield, the men's spirits were not dimmed and they were eager to continue the advance. Indeed, their officers were initially expecting to be able to hotly pursue the Germans, who they had been led to believe were now on the run.

Finally at about 3am on the morning of September 26th, the 63rd Brigade was able to begin relieving the 1st Division's 2nd Brigade, along with Green's Force and the 1st Gloucesters, from their positions around Puits 14Bis, the western end of Bois Hugo, Chalk

A dramatic depiction of British troops attacking an enemy trench.

Pit Wood, the Chalk Pit and a short stretch of trench line bordering the La Bassée to Lens road, northward towards Hulluch. The 64th Brigade took up support positions in captured enemy trenches approximately 500 yards to the rear.

The 1st Gloucesters, together with other relieved battalions, made their way back to the old British front lines between Lone Tree and Le Rutoire Farm, losing a number of men to enemy shellfire on the way. An officer of the 1st Gloucesters recorded dispassionately:

> It was a fine, fresh morning, and moving by the way of the Lone Tree, one watched with interest the various activities which were going on in connection with the clearing of the flotsam of the battlefield.

Private A.S, Dolden – 1/14th London (London Scottish):

> Just as dawn was breaking we filed out of the chalk pit, and formed up on top. The German snipers were busy, and they 'bagged' two of our men, one

of whom was quite close to me. We marched back to the reserve position and in doing so had to pass the ground over which the battle had raged the previous day. We had ample time to take everything in, and the sight was truly appalling. The dead were lying everywhere, some across the enemy's barbed wire. One could see limbs that had been wrenched off by shells and some of the wounds were truly ghastly. Many of the wounded men were still lying out there, and some had done so for thirty-six hours.

Doing their best to improve their newly occupied positions, the men of the 63rd and 64th brigades struggled to excavate the hard chalky soil with their entrenching tools. Their divisional transports carrying much of their equipment, including picks, shovels and barbed wire, had been left far behind in the snarl up on the approach roads.

The 62nd Brigade, more by luck than expert guidance, managed to pick their way through the still burning ruins of Loos to liase with troops of the 15th Scottish Division who they were to support in the forthcoming attack on Hill 70.

Slogging along the muddy, rutted and traffic choked roads, the battalions of the 24th Division were equally exhausted as just before midnight on September 25th they reached the area of Le Rutoire Farm. Scouting patrols were sent out across the battlefield to make contact with the advanced British troops. These patrols soon came under fire from Hulluch, which they had expected to find in British hands. Instead, they fell in with the dishevelled remnants of the 1st and 3rd brigades, which included the 10th Gloucesters, manning positions in Gun Trench, Alley 4 and Keep 89. From these tired men they learned of the 1st Division's ordeal and something of the confused and desperate situation to be faced at daybreak.

The 24th Division's three brigades were therefore deployed in accordance with General Haig's orders. The 72nd Brigade formed up in the old German front line on Lone Tree Ridge with the 71st Brigade acting as support in the old British front line west of Lone Tree. The 73rd Brigade was detached to assist the 9th Scottish Division in their defence of the left flank around Fosse 8 and the Dump.

Confused, soaked through and hungry, the 24th Division's battalions found themselves having to shelter in battered trenches still reeking of gas and ankle deep in water. All about in the gloom lay the sad crumpled forms of dead men, their white faces illuminated momentarily by flashes of gunfire and the blaze of Very lights.

As dawn broke on September 26th, a thick mist hovered in the Loos valley, blotting from view the village of Hulluch and the surrounding German positions. However, the mist soon cleared revealing the fine, fresh morning described by the 1st Gloucester's officer. The scene was now set for what General Haig hoped would be a spectacular thrust deep into enemy held territory.

Perched in the captured enemy positions on the hillside to the west of Hulluch, the 10th Gloucester's survivors were ideally placed to witness the disturbing events that were about to unfold.

In Keep 89, Private William Collins was one of the 10th Gloucester's 60 survivors:

That night we manned the captured trenches but in the morning it must have got light suddenly because as I was messing about at something on the trench parapet, a sniper put a bullet through the front of my kneecap.

General Haig's plan was based on the information then at his disposal and by his conviction that the enemy were not yet present in sufficient force to effectively oppose his troops. On paper it was logically presented and apparently endowed with a reasonable chance of achieving success. Hill 70 was to be assaulted and captured at 9.30am, followed at 11am by a mass advance of the remaining brigades of the 21st and 24th Divisions. The 1st Division's under strength 3rd Brigade would lend support by advancing at the same time to capture and neutralise the enemy bastion of Hulluch village. All well and good, but unfortunately factors of a dramatic nature were already at work, conspiring to confound even the best laid plans. Poor intelligence and woefully inadequate communications would also play their part, but it was the swift response of a well organised and resilient enemy that would prove decisive.

Haig's assessment that the Germans were short of reserves seems to have been based almost entirely on wishful thinking rather than on any concrete intelligence. Indeed, under cover of darkness, the Germans had been hard at work stringing out belts of additional barbed wire and enough reserves had been rushed in to adequately reinforce their positions. This resulted in their former second line now being at least as strong as the original one that faced the British at the outset of the battle. Even more critically, the Germans had reacted much more swiftly than the British and had amassed enough troops to launch an attack that would effectively trump Haig's hastily prepared plan.

The British artillery was supposed to provide an hour-long bombardment of the enemy positions on Hill 70 and northward to Hulluch and Cité St. Elie. However, many of the guns were moved up during the night, and as dawn broke and the mist cleared, it was discovered too late that some of the batteries had been positioned in view of the enemy and these were subsequently destroyed by enemy counter artillery fire. To top this, the old problem of insufficient supplies of artillery shells came into play and the British artillery barrage would turn out to be a hopelessly inadequate and puny affair.

 As for his assault troops, General Haig would have been fully aware that the battalions of the 15th Division that he was directing against Hill 70 and those of the 1st Division ordered to capture Hulluch, had been in constant action since the evening of September 24th. None of these units were at full strength, having suffered serious casualties in the initial advance. Furthermore, in the ruins of Loos and in hastily prepared forward positions, enduring constant enemy small arms and artillery fire, the men had not received the benefit of sleep or a hot meal. That Haig was prepared to gamble on the effectiveness of these exhausted men reflected the urgency which he rightly placed on continuing the battle, but which also highlighted the lack of suitable numbers of fresh and experienced reserves.

As we have already seen, the 21st and 24th divisions arrived on the battlefield in total darkness, tired, hungry and wet, having endured a long, fraught march to the battlefront. The officers and men had no experience of combat and although their morale was high, they were now being ordered into the very situation that Sir John French had deemed them unsuitable to handle.

At 9am on September 26th, the Germans crucially seized the initiative and struck devastatingly. Using the cover of Bois Hugo and Chalet Wood, they filtered forward and overran the 8th Lincolns who had taken over the positions vacated by the 1st Gloucesters. Many of the Lincolns were killed, wounded or captured, including their commanding officer, and the survivors were forced to retreat across the La Bassée to Lens road. Temporarily detached to support the Lincolns, Second Lieutenant George Egerton Clairmonte, commanding the 1st Gloucester's machine gun section, perished with several of his men.

Utter slaughter. The bodies of dozens of British soldiers and their equipment litter the ground in front of the German parapet at Loos.

Promptly at 9.30am, soldiers of the 15th Scottish Division left their shallow trenches just below the crest of Hill 70 and advanced against the redoubt. Some managed to enter the earthworks but the Germans were too strong and soon forced them out again. Now it was the turn of the 21st Division's 62nd Brigade.

In Harry Fellows' famous account of the attack, one cannot fail to be struck by the horrifyingly surreal way that the men calmly formed up and jostled together in the assault trench, before obediently surging forward in long regular lines onto that bald, open hillside, to advance without question into the cruel embrace of utter oblivion:

> As I walked along the parados I could plainly see that events had been moving during the time I had been away. All the men crowded together, along with those of our men in the trench, were standing with bayonets fixed. It was useless trying to get into the trench as it was so solidly packed. Then our lads began to climb out and go forward as fast as their cumbersome equipment would allow. The men at the back dropped into the places which had been vacated and then climbed forward. Suddenly realising the Captain must have gone forward, but not comprehending that the message I had for him was now out of date, I scrambled across, still intent on finding him. The whole slope in front of me and as far away to the left as one could see was crowded with cheering men moving forward as fast as they could. And still the enemy had not fired a shot. It seemed like they had gone home.
>
> The leading men would have been about 100 yards from the German wire, and I was about the same distance from my starting point when all hell was let loose. As if from some predetermined signal the enemy machine guns opened up with a murderous fire, both from the front and enfilading fire from some buildings which had been out of sight behind some trees. Men began to stumble and fall, then began to go down like standing corn before a scythe. The cap from the head of the lad in front of me flew from his head and he fell – I stumbled over him – and even to this day I feel no shame when I say that I stayed where I was, my face buried in the grass, and never had the good earth smelled so sweet. I was 19 years old and no hero – just a scared teenager who had no wish to die and, after seeing all that devastation in front of my eyes, I was frightened. The firing seemed to go on for hours. I afterwards learned that it was not even ten minutes.

General Haig's plan was already starting to unravel and the situation would soon become much, much worse.

Having secured most of Bois Hugo, the Germans were able to concentrate troops within the cover of the trees for an attack against Puits 14Bis and Chalk Pit Wood. This attack was to be supported by more troops advancing to the line of the La Bassée to Lens road from Stutzpunkt III and Stutzpunkt IV in their second line.

At 10am masses of German troops issued from Stutzpunkt IV and advanced against troops of the 63rd Brigade who were dug in along the La Bassée to Lens road, just to the north of Chalk Pit

Wood. This attack was quickly stopped by heavy fire from rifles and Lewis light machine guns. The 3rd Brigade also stopped the enemy advance from Stutzpunkt III. However, the Germans were far from finished and very soon after surprised the British troops dug in immediately to the north of Bois Hugo by opening up flanking fire from the wood. At the same time they struck against Puits 14Bis and Chalk Pit Wood. Although this attack stalled temporarily when the British artillery managed to land five heavy shells amongst them, such was the confusion amongst the ranks of the inexperienced troops of the 63rd Brigade that they began to fall back from Puits 14Bis and the line of the La Bassée to Lens road.

It is fair to say that the retreat became a rout and the men falling back were even fired upon by a battalion of the 64th Brigade, who, whilst moving up to give support, mistook them for advancing Germans.

Not all the men of the 63rd Brigade ran. Two companies of the 8th Somerset Light Infantry held on to Chalk Pit Wood and the Chalk Pit until they were eventually isolated and had to fall back. Many other groups of men fought on until they were overrun and killed or captured. Unfortunately the result was that the Germans captured Puits 14Bis, Chalk Pit Wood and a stretch of trench line running northwards along the La Bassée to Lens road. Meanwhile the officers of the 63rd and 64th Brigades managed to halt the rout and stabilised the British line just to the west of Puits 14Bis and Chalk Pit Wood. Even so, the 1st Cameron Highlander's War Diary records with contempt that the battalion later collected up five wagonloads of equipment thrown down by these panic-stricken men.

Haig's plan had now completely jumped the rails. Hill 70 had not been captured and the 21st Division was locked in a desperate struggle for its own survival. The battalions of the 24th Division were now preparing to advance into a huge, open pocket of ground that was now flanked on three sides by the enemy. It is likely that even if Haig had been aware of the dangerous situation into which that Division was about to enter, there was not sufficient time for the orders to be countermanded.

Meanwhile at 11am, 'A' and 'C' companies and then 'B' and 'D' companies of the 2nd Welsh climbed from their trenches and advanced towards the La Bassée to Lens road and the village of Hulluch just beyond. Last minute orders postponing the attack until noon had failed to reach their commanding officer and the battalion advanced alone and unsupported by the 1st Black Watch and 1st South Wales Borderers. Hardly had the men emerged into the open before a deadly concentration of machine gun and rifle fire cut them down. The Welsh, who were already reduced to half strength, lost 100 men as casualties within minutes. Pinned down and in full view of the enemy, their position appeared hopeless. However, at that moment and to their great amazement, tiny figures of the massed battalions of the 24th Division appeared behind them on the crest of Lone Tree Ridge and marched in extended order down into the Loos valley.

This amazing spectacle was truly astonishing and heart stirring. Here were thousands of men advancing, their company officers mounted on horseback steadying the men. The entire scene was reminiscent of the massed advances of the Crimean War, sixty years before.

It was now the turn of the German infantry, who had previously advanced to the line of the La Bassée to Lens road, to bolt back to the safety of their trench lines. On came the Kitchener battalions, now enthusiastically cheered by the 10th Gloucesters and their comrades as the lines of infantry passed through their positions. Here was the moment they had spent long months training for, their chance to face the Germans in combat. Now spurred forward by this seemingly irresistible wave of men, the 2nd Welsh rose from No Man's Land and renewed their efforts to break into Hulluch.

The serried ranks of the 24th Division swept across the La Bassée to Lens road on a broad front between Hulluch and Bois Hugo, straight into the jaws of a huge trap. As the British soldiers drew level with Hulluch and Bois Hugo, a veritable hail of enfilade fire swept their ranks. Caught in a huge pocket of open ground, literally thousands of men fell victim to the deadly crossfire. However, such was their steadiness and resolve that groups of men managed to advance right to the wire protecting the enemy trenches in front of Stutzpunkt III and IV.

These German redoubts were immensely strong, being deeply dug and bolstered with concrete covered machine gun positions and protected by thick belts of wire. The inadequacies of the British artillery meant that these defences had not been sufficiently 'softened up' and that the wire was uncut. By consequence, the British infantry had absolutely no realistic chance of success.

Eventually, the British infantry could sustain the ordeal no longer. Fired on from three sides they began to fall back across the La Bassée to Lens road, leaving thousands of dead and wounded in their wake. Meanwhile, the 2nd Welsh had actually managed to penetrate the web of enemy trench systems protecting Hulluch, but without further support were unable to exploit this meagre success and had to fall back as well.

By 2pm the rout was complete, and in awe at the huge number of casualties that their machine gun, artillery and rifle fire had inflicted, the Germans sent out stretcher bearers and medical orderlies to tend the wounded British soldiers lying near their wire. Those who were able to walk or crawl were allowed to return to the British lines, others more seriously wounded were treated and taken into captivity. Shocked by the magnitude of their bloody repulse, the British were overwhelmed by the huge numbers of casualties and struggled to rally the shocked and leaderless troops who were returning from the massacre.

For their part, the Germans did not attempt to press their advantage other than to strengthen their hold on Hulluch, Chalk Pit Wood, Bois Hugo, Puits 14Bis and Hill 70.

Lance Corporal Edward John Farrell seated with two fellow British prisoners at Hammelburg.

Shot in the leg whilst advancing with his platoon, Lance Corporal Edward Farrell of the 9th East Surrey regiment lay in the meagre cover of a shell crater. All around lay the bodies of his comrades. In spite of the earlier show of compassion from the Germans, snipers were now active, shooting at those who stirred amongst the heaps of dead.

Darkness was beginning to fall before Farrell judged it was safe to attempt to get back to the British lines. Crawling from cover, his movements were spotted by an enemy sniper who promptly fired a round which bowled him over but fortunately only grazed the back of his head. Later that night he was discovered by a German patrol that took him and a number of other wounded men into the safety of their lines and where their wounds were dressed.

Edward Farrell recovered from his injuries and was sent to a large prisoner of war camp at Hammelburg in Bavaria. Here he spent the remainder of the war with other allied prisoners in deprived but bearable conditions.

After darkness fell, the British sent out their own stretcher bearers who brought in many more wounded men. Sadly, the bodies of those who were killed could not be recovered and remained on the battlefield until blown apart by shellfire, or were buried at a later date by the Germans.

One of those lucky enough to be rescued by his own side was Private Albert Yemm of the 8th Royal West Kent Regiment. His mother was greatly relieved to receive the following letter from Reverend Cecil Money-Kyrle, an Army Chaplain serving with the 3rd Infantry Brigade, 1st Division:

> **October 10th 1915. Dear Mrs. Yemm. I heard yesterday that a British soldier was in the French hospital at Les Brebis, so I called to see him, and found it was your son. He gave me your address and asked me to write you a line. He was wounded on September 26th in the battle of Loos, and unfortunately it was some time before he could be brought into hospital, as he fell between the two firing lines, so he suffered from exposure as well as his wounds in the leg and back. Now he is very comfortable and everything possible is being done for him, and though seriously ill, I hope, please God, he will pull through. I am going to see him again today and take him English papers, and hope to find him improved. When better he will be moved to an English hospital, as it is hard for him to be amongst strangers where only French is spoken, but the nurses are Sisters of Charity and more than kind, so you may rest assured that he gets every attention. Curiously my home is quite close to Cinderford, at Much Marcle, about seven miles from Ross, where my brother is Rector, so I could talk to your son about the Forest, which I know well. I'll write again in a day or two and hope to be able to give a good account.**

Albert Yemm was indeed lucky to survive. As he lay wounded and helpless, an enemy soldier bayoneted him in the back and left him for dead. Later, another German soldier, noticing he was still alive, took pity on him and gave him a drink of water. Never able to fully recover from his wounds, Albert Yemm was discharged from the army in 1917 and died in 1932 aged 52 years.

At General Haig's headquarters, news of the disastrous rout was met with complete disbelief. How was it possible for two whole divisions to be defeated in a matter of hours? The suspicion that the news was the result of scare mongering was eventually dashed when a staff officer reported back having confirmed the awful truth.

The near destruction of these two divisions is one of the most harrowing features of the Battle of Loos. The casualties sustained by the 21st and 24th divisions on September 26th amounted to a staggering 4,051 and 4,178 men respectively. The Germans, who moved forward to occupy much of the contested ground, christened it the **"Leichenfeld von Loos" – Corpse Field of Loos.**

Allied prisoners assemble for roll call at Hammelburg, Bavaria.

CHAPTER V

The Awful Shell Strewn Ground

**For husbands, fathers and betrothed lovers
That shall be swallowed in this controversy**

King Henry V. Act II, Scene IV

For the time being the position of the British between Hill 70 and the Dump was extremely precarious. All along this front, crude, makeshift trenches, often without wire protection, were being held by the disorganised survivors of the 21st and 24th divisions, along with the battered remnants of the initial assault divisions that had been in constant action since the evening of September 24th.

In Keep 89, the pitifully few remaining Gloucesters resigned themselves to yet another cold, uncomfortable night without their greatcoats, which had been left at Vaudricourt. However, in the early hours of September 27th, the 1st Guards Brigade finally arrived on the battlefield to relieve them from their positions.

Beneath the gleams of a fitful moon, Lieutenant Colonel Pritchard led the remnant of his battalion back over the eerie battlefield, through the captured German trenches and strong points, and past the, sinister avenues of barbed wire where his dead men still lay thickly.

Dreadful, harrowing scenes met the tired gaze of the returning troops. In the heat of the battle these men had obeyed their instructions not to halt their advance to aid those who had fallen. Now with their job completed and the Germans finally wrenched off the Lone Tree Ridge, not even the inky darkness could conceal the ghastly, pale, bloodless features of the dear friends, brothers, fathers and sons that had fallen in their wake.

The strain of command was weighing heavily upon Pritchard. He and his battalion had been under constant fire for two whole days, during which time they had been sustained only by what was in their water bottles and contained in their iron rations. The Colonel had witnessed the mass slaughter of thousands, and now his beloved battalion had almost ceased to exist. Treading the battlefield that night, the frightful scene of scores of his men lying dead in rows shocked him to the core. Lance Corporal Clifford recalled that the trauma of his ordeal caused the Colonel's hair to literally stand on end.

Later, after the war, Lieutenant Colonel Pritchard wrote the following letter to Sergeant Alphonse Meulbrouck. It amply describes the complete anguish of a man genuinely proud of his men and broken by the loss of so many:

> I cannot tell you how great an honour I felt to have had the fortune, through God's providence, to have collected together, brought into one camp, trained into one body, such a battalion of men of our race. How proud we can all be to think that we rushed to their rescue and leaped on the shores of France and away to the enemy, whom the regiment drove back and sent flying out

of his positions, until we stood there with only a small band of our men left, (about 60 strong), winning that foremost position opposite Hulluch, which was kept then and kept afterwards and never lost again. But the glorious deeds of our men was at the cost of the practical loss of the greater part of my dearly loved regiment.

When those of us who remained alive were ordered back to Les Brebis to re-organise and to evacuate our lines, I well remember crossing over the battlefield, seeing our men in rows, dead, with their faces turned towards the enemy, their faces lighted up by the pale and tender gleams of moonlight struggling thro' storm clouds. Through these unforgettable scenes we passed, as we traced our way through the lines of our heroic men. It was my fate I should never again lead such men. I was stricken with grief, stricken with the strain of those few days of such intense effort, and a morning or two afterwards I discovered myself on a stretcher, being carried away, until I was landed in a hospital at home in the old country.

Sergeant Frederick Ewart Bridgeman. Killed in action September 25th 1915. Before the war he worked as a clerk in Cheltenham.

In Cheltenham, Canon Cox received this letter from Mrs. Pritchard:

My husband is here at Brighton suffering from shock and severe nerve strain. What you have heard of the battalion is true; they suffered heavily but fought magnificently. Had a letter from the Adjutant today, the Tenth have made a name for themselves. They have performed magnificently and have added further laurels to the traditions of the Gloucester Regiment. The praise of the 8th Berkshires and ourselves is everywhere unstinted. My husband too, tells me the regiment did nobly, he had nothing but praise for them. How I wish I could convey this knowledge to the relatives of the men who have fallen. I thought perhaps you, who may know so many of them, will be able to do so.

Fittingly, it fell to the 1st Gloucesters to begin burying the vast numbers of dead still lying about the old German front line where the 10th had forced their way through. Private John Bayliss wrote home to a friend in Cheltenham:

Just a line to let you know I found this little photo (of a young woman) on a dead body which is that of Sergeant F.E. Bridgeman 13335, No.3 Company, 10th Gloucesters. I am sorry to say that he lay by a trench and from what I can see he was one of the first to get to the enemy trench.

The editor of the Dean Forest Mercury received the following letter:

Dear Sir, am sending you photos found on the battlefield when we were burying the dead, but as our searchers had taken away all their identifications there was nothing to tell whom they belonged to, only a Cinderford photographer's address. There was a cigarette case by it marked 'B.T., a present from Blackpool 1915'. If anyone recognises this inscription I shall be only too pleased to send it to them as anyone likes something in remembrance. Trusting the rightful owner will get same, yours sincerely, Private A.H. Jordan, 1st Gloucesters, D Company, 13th Platoon.

A young man appearing on one of the photographs was recognised as Theophilus Gabb, serving with the 13th Gloucesters (The Forest of Dean Pioneers) at Aldershot. However, it was quickly ascertained that his younger brother Dennis was with the 10th. The fears of his worried parents were sadly realised when Private William Bannister, who as one of the mumps cases had missed the battle, wrote home to his parents at Cinderford in the Forest of Dean:

Private Dennis Gabb. Killed in action September 25th 1915, aged 17. His brother Theophilus was killed to the north of Loos in 1916 and is buried in Cabaret Rouge Cemetery near Vimy Ridge, seven miles south of Loos.

Bugler Theophilus Gabb of the 13th Gloucesters.

> I daresay you know that poor Denny is killed and Jack Arkell. I was not in
> the fight or else I should have seen dear Denny die.

Private 16196 Albert Henry Jordan was himself a Kitchener volunteer and was drafted into the 1st Gloucesters to replace the battalion's enormous casualties sustained in 1914. Albert was also from the Forest of Dean, his home being at Primrose Hill in Lydney. Sadly, Albert did not survive the Great War and died in 1918, being buried far from his native Gloucestershire in Mikra British Cemetery, Kalamaria, Greece, where he was then serving with the 2nd Gloucesters.

Another soldier of the 1st Gloucesters, Lance Corporal W.E. Herbert, sent home this description of the battle:

> I have got through once again, we have had some stirring times lately and there is better news than on 9th May. (Aubers Ridge) We were in the reserve when the attack was made. Some of our side soon broke through and we went into the front line, but there was a keep with about fourteen machine guns in it that held us up for a long time. At last our men outflanked them and about 200 Germans surrendered to the Gloucesters. Then we crossed their trenches and made an advance. We must have advanced three miles. There were scouts out in front of us to see if there were any Germans about. We went through a wood and came to a railway and then had orders to dig ourselves in. It did not take us long to get some head cover, for the Germans were just in front of us and opened fire.
>
> We held the position until morning and were then relieved, for which we were not sorry as it had been raining and we were all wet through. We came back to what had been the German's front line. I don't know how true it is, but our fellows say the Germans pulled some of the 10th into the trench and shot them, but anyhow when we came back to the trench there were several of the 10th Gloucesters dead in it. The Germans were comfortable, for in the dug out we occupied they had a bed, a stove, a table and chairs, and oilcloth for the floor. They even had a bookshelf there, so it came in just right for us, and we were glad at the time they had such places.
>
> Through the day we could hear our fellows making an attack in different places, of the Germans counter attacking, but the Germans were repulsed everywhere. If our men had to retire from a position they soon retook it, and they were still pushing on. We were relieved from the trenches, but I don't know for how long,

On the captured German parapet the bodies of Lieutenant Symons and his platoon were discovered. The 10th's Adjutant, Captain Stanley Stephenson, wrote to Symons' parents:

> As you know, the Army carried out an assault on the 25th ult., and to the 10th Gloucesters was assigned a line of front in the very van of the battle, No.2 Company being in the first line. Gloriously they performed, and the ultimate success obtained was in no little measure due to the heroic way in which the officers led their men. This was particularly the case with your son.

I saw and I know. When with the Headquarters party, I came across the awful shell strewn ground, I found your son at the head of his platoon. He had managed to get through the wire entanglements only to pay the price on the other side. He was shot through the head so death must have been instantaneous. Behind him were the men of his platoon, hung on the wire, nobly following this splendid example and leadership. We have lost a number of fine, brave officers we could ill spare, but we honour his deed, and are proud of the sacrifice he made. He was buried with other officers of the 10th who fell in the assault, by the side of a much battered copse known as the Bois Carré, which is an easily recognised spot in a huge field which now seems a mass of graves and all the hideous effects of war.

Lieutenant Colonel Pritchard found time to write:

Your son's bravery and leading were spoken of soon after the battle on September 25th last, by those who survived the assault, in terms of unstinted admiration and loving praise. I cannot omit also to record that he was not only devoted to his duty, but was a particularly efficient young officer, and his buoyant spirits inspired his men and secured his whole hearted affection, so they would follow him anywhere. Our consolation is that he and others like him have added to the glory and honour of the Gloucestershire Regiment.

Even now the 10th's ordeal was not yet over. Far from being marched out of the line and back to well-deserved, dry, warm billets, they were ordered to occupy the devastated Y1 trenches from which their attack had been launched on September 25th. Strewn with mangled bodies, the whole area was a ghastly, unhealthy place. Whilst occupying these trenches, the men of the 10th took the opportunity to help bury some of the corpses.

Private William Sidney Charles Hart from Longdon near Tewkesbury was killed on September 25th 1915. Aged 18 years, his father Sidney was also serving with the 10th Gloucesters.

On September 29th, George Coppard, a young Private serving with The Queen's Regiment, was moving up to the front along a freshly dug communication trench that now connected the former British fire trench with the captured enemy front line. Here, on each side of the Vermelles to Hulluch road, the 2nd Gordons of the 7th Division had attacked on September 25th, with the 8th Royal Berkshires and 10th Gloucesters to their right. George later wrote:

Private Cecil Delaney from Cheltenham was killed in action on September 25th 1915, aged 18 years.

Sergeant Frank Maurice Driscoll from Cheltenham was killed in action on September 25th 1915, aged 20. His body was discovered in the captured German positions. Before the war he worked for Messrs. Norman Bros., printers.

Going up the communication trench at a snail's pace, the battalion suffered casualties from shrapnel fire. As many troops were coming away from the front line as were going up. Stretcher bearers with the wounded, fatigues parties, telephone linesmen, runners and parties of relieved troops wended their way to the rear, jamming the narrow trench. The trench was parallel to the Vermelles – Hulluch road and was only a few yards from it. Bordered with tree

Private Frank Charles Wyniatt from Didbrook near Winchcombe, Gloucestershire, was reported missing in action on September 25th 1915. His body was never identified and his name is recorded on the Dud Corner Memorial.

stumps, it ran due east straight to the village of Hulluch, which was just behind the German lines.

At last we reached the top of the slope where the German front line had been before the attack. And there, stretching for several hundred yards on the right of the road lay masses of British dead, struck down by machine gun and rifle fire. Shells from the enemy field batteries had been pitching into the bodies, flinging some about into dreadful postures. Being mostly of Highland regiments, there was a fantastic display of colour from their kilts, glengarries and bonnets, and also from the bloody wounds on their bare limbs. The warm weather had darkened their faces and, shrouded as they were with the sickly odour of death, it was repulsive to be near them. Hundreds of rifles lay about, some stuck in the ground on the bayonet, as though impaled at the very moment of the soldier's death, as he fell forward.

Literally thousands of bodies lay along Lone Tree Ridge, presenting a veritable tide of death. Amongst this unbelievable carnage, heavy hearted, battle weary Gloucesters searched for missing relatives and comrades, praying that those for whom they searched had somehow survived and were now in the safety of a field hospital. Hundreds were indeed wounded or suffering from gas poisoning, but 163 of those who had proudly posed for photographers at Codford and in Lansdown Crescent now lay with sightless eyes, cold and stiff on the field of battle.

Private William Hawkins had witnessed the death of his brother Francis. With a heavy heart, William undertook the unpleasant task of writing home with the sad news:

Just a few lines to let you know I am still alive and well. We are back again for a rest. Should have written before, but we were not allowed to as we have been in the firing line. We were in that charge on Saturday morning, September 25th. I might as well tell you that Francis was killed. I know you would rather know from me. He was knocked over with a piece of shell. I got through all right.

Death was no respecter of youth and the young gardener Frank Gapper had fallen, never again to tend an earthly garden. The Tewkesbury schoolchildren who had so thoughtfully sent a parcel to their former schoolmaster, Arthur Harrison, would soon be heartbroken to hear of his death.

George Evans, the Forest of Dean collier who had defied his wife to enlist, also lay dead. It was officially reported that his body was buried at Lone Tree. However, in common with many of those killed at Loos, his remains were never identified when the battlefields were cleared after the war and his name appears on the Dud Corner Memorial to the Missing, just outside Loos. Of the 10th Gloucester's 163 officers and men who fell on September 25th, only 34 have identified graves.

There are a number of reasons why so many of those who died at Loos do not have identified graves. On the evidence of Private Jordan's letter, stating that the 'searchers' had taken the identifications of the dead, some bodies were buried without being fully identified. At the time of Loos, soldiers were issued with a single circular aluminium identity disc threaded with a cord and worn around the neck. On the disc was impressed the soldier's service number, name, religious denomination and regiment. It would seem that the 'searchers' had removed the disc from each

Private Francis Clare Hawkins was formerly a collier from Cinderford in the Forest of Dean, where he was in charge of a haulage engine at the Eastern United Colliery. His grave at St. Mary's Advanced Dressing Station Cemetery near Hulluch is one of the very few Gloucestershire Regiment graves that bears a name.

Private Ernest Holford of The Ferns, Quedgley, Gloucester, fell on September 25th 1915, aged 23 years. He has no known grave and is honoured at Dud Corner.

body, along with the dead man's pay book. The term 'searchers' implies soldiers of front line units detailed to assist the Graves Registration Commission staff.

It was not until August 1916 that a new form of double identity disc made of compressed fibre was issued. A neck cord was threaded through a green lozenge shaped 'disc' stamped with the soldier's details and a second red circular disc with the same information was suspended from the first. The red disc only was to be removed if the soldier was killed, whilst the green disc remained with the body.

Private Charles Murrell was formerly a collier from Littledean in the Forest of Dean. For many weeks his fate was uncertain having last been seen lying seriously wounded on a stretcher. Charlie must have died soon after, for his grave can be found in Dud Corner Cemetery.

Captain Ivan Richard Gibbs. Killed in action September 25th 1915, aged 24. He was educated at Cheltenham Grammar School, afterwards proceeding to Jesus College, Oxford.

A small plot in the far corner of St. Mary's Advanced Dressing Station Cemetery contains the token headstones dedicated to Captain Gibbs, Captain Tongue, Captain Sale, Lieutenant Leary, Lieutenant Robinson, Lieutenant Whiffin and Second Lieutenant Field.

Lieutenant Geffrey Wathen Robinson. Killed in action on September 25th 1915, aged 23 years. He lived at Sandford Dene, Prestbury, Cheltenham, and was manager of the Bath Road branch of the leather firm B. Robinson.

Lieutenant George Godfrey W. Leary.

Captain John William Collis Tongue.

Captain Edward Hanson Sale.

The very open and fire swept nature of the Loos battlefield made it extremely difficult and dangerous to recover and safely bury the huge numbers of bodies. Although the British had captured a pocket of territory on a frontage of 3½ miles by up to 2 miles deep, all of it was under observation by the Germans and subject to accurate artillery fire and its periphery to machine gun and sniper fire. By necessity, some bodies had to be left where they lay and were often destroyed by shellfire.

By the middle of October, when the Battle of Loos finally fizzled out, many of the fallen British soldiers now lay in territory won back by the Germans who eventually collected the bodies and buried them in mass graves. Some of these graves may still remain undiscovered to this day.

During and in the years following the Battle of Loos, the landscape was subject to bouts of intensive shellfire, and the explosion of dozens of mines formed huge crater fields. Many established graves and their markers were literally obliterated, or simply flattened by the passage of troops, guns and transports.

A fine portrait of Private Albert Edward Higgins of Painswick, Gloucestershire. Albert has no known grave and is honoured on the Dud Corner Memorial to the missing.

CHAPTER VI

The Final Throes

Once more unto the breach, dear friends, once more
Or close the wall up with our English dead

King Henry V. Act III, Scene I

Filthy, unshaven, hungry and utterly exhausted, Lieutenant Colonel Pritchard and his men were finally relieved at 11.35pm on September 29th by a battalion of the Guards Brigade. The 10th Gloucester's numbers had now swelled to 130 as men who had become separated from the battalion during the confused fighting returned. They were marched to billets in the nearby town of Les Brebis.

It was here at Les Brebis, at 6am on the following morning, that Lieutenant Colonel Pritchard finally collapsed from extreme nerve strain and exhaustion. The 10th Gloucester's War Diary recorded:

> **Here at 6am Lt. Col. Pritchard left under orders from the GOC 1st Infantry Brigade to be evacuated. Under the stress of the continuous shelling his health had given way and the M.O. reported that in his opinion he was no longer able to carry on.**

Interestingly, the original document reveals that someone attempted to obliterate the last three words of the first sentence and the entire last sentence with a blue crayon.

The battalion's second in command, Major Kirkwood, had been wounded and evacuated and so Major H. Sutherland of the Black Watch was appointed to the command.

On September 30th, the battalion, along with others of the 1st Brigade, marched the short distance to Noeux-les-Mines. Here, in spite of the Brigade's vastly reduced numbers, the men had trouble occupying their allotted billets when it was discovered, to their disgust, that the billets were being used to accommodate staff horses.

Whilst at Noeux-les-Mines, the remaining officers of the 10th were able to complete a roll call that revealed the ration strength to be 11 officers and 373 men. The fighting strength, exclusive of the 95 mumps cases still at Gosnay, was just 276 men.

Apart from those seen dead on the battlefield, the fate of many was unknown and these men were officially reported as missing. A good number were known to be wounded, but some died at advanced dressing stations or at casualty clearing stations.

The difficult task of writing to the families of the men known to be dead fell to the surviving officers and senior NCOs. Their intentions were to console the bereaved, but the contents of some letters reflect the patriotic, 'stiff upper lip' attitudes of the time, attitudes that today we would find amusing.

The mother of Private William Rivers learned of her son's death from his platoon officer:

Private William Rivers was killed by a shellburst whilst helping a wounded comrade. His home was in Cheltenham.

> He was helping a comrade who had been wounded in the ankle when a shell killed them both. Death was practically instantaneous. I knew your son to be a good soldier and I sympathise with you in this great trial. But do not grieve too much, rather temper your sorrow with pride in the fact that he was murdered in the act of protecting from the ravages of the Huns the homes, lives and honour of the women of France and England.

Eventually it was established that between September 24th and September 29th the 10th Gloucesters suffered 459 casualties, killed, wounded and gassed. The 8th Royal Berkshires lost a similar number.

From October 1st, the Brigade was now at 'General Rest' in the safety of Noeux-les-Mines. The men and officers were able to get a much-needed bath in a local brewery. The Corps Commander, Lieutenant-General Sir Henry Rawlinson and the General Officer Commanding 1st Division, Major-General Holland, congratulated the Division on what was termed as their **"Brilliant Success."**

During this rest period the soldiers were allowed to write home to their families. Private William Ireland of Painswick near Gloucester was serving in the 10th Gloucesters with his two younger brothers Frederick and Jack. He wrote home to their parents, Arthur and Fanny:

> Dear Mother and all. No doubt you have heard we have been in battle and no doubt you will see in the papers we were the Regiment in the first line to make the charge last Saturday morning at half past six. I can tell you it was hell upon earth, with the shells, guns, machine fire, rifle fire, hand bombs, and I don't know what else, but we got to their first trench, and those who did not get away were killed or taken prisoner. On we went and took their next trench, and then up came a Scotch Regiment, and they took it up for a bit. The Germans made a counter attack but they were simply mown down. We were praised for the fine charge we made and no doubt you will see in the papers the 10th Gloucesters broke their line. I am sorry to say H. Hanks is wounded in the leg or thigh, but I don't think it's very bad and he must think himself very lucky it is not. I have not seen him and I did not do so when he was hit for you had as much as you could do to

look after yourself. Our Jack and Fred were not out there as some of their Company had the mumps and they were isolated with them. We hope soon for a rest, for I have had one wash in a fortnight and have just had a shave. But I don't mind, it won't last for ever. We have lost a lot of men and officers. I shall never forget it as long as I live, nor the rest of us who are left. I expect it was the biggest battle ever known.

But, such was the critical situation faced by the British on the Loos front that even these mauled battalions could not be spared from the line for long. On October 5th, the 10th Gloucesters were ordered to occupy trenches in the old German front line opposite Le Rutoire Farm. Whilst here, beside the many fresh graves of their comrades, Corporal Albert Harding of the machine gun section was killed by a British shell that fell short.

Meanwhile, the Germans had been very active in trying to recover the ground they had lost on September 25th. Following the utterly disastrous attempts by the 21st and 24th divisions to follow up that initial success, the Guards Division was thrown into the fray on September 27th. Their orders were to recapture the vitally strategic positions of Chalk Pit Wood, Puits 14Bis and Hill 70. An officer of the 23rd London Regiment witnessed their advance:

Corporal Albert Harding. Killed October 5th 1915. He was originally from Prestbury, Cheltenham.

More came over the crest by platoons in artillery formation, and the intensity of the shelling increased. Quite quickly the opposite slope took on the appearance of a gigantic moving chessboard as the platoons approached with intervals between them. So inspiring was the sight that scores of 23rd men of their own accord clambered out of their trenches, and under machine gun fire, pulled aside wire entanglements and threw duckboard bridges over the ditches to facilitate the way for the Guards when it was seen that they had to pass through their lines.

Advancing with the 1st Grenadier Guards were two brothers, Privates William and Reginald Tuffley from Soudley in the Forest of Dean. William wrote home:

I am in the best of health in spite of having to rough it out here. I dare say you have seen what has happened out here. I am pleased to say I did my little bit in the great attack. The cannonading for just an hour before the

Taken on September 14th 1915, this interesting aerial photograph reveals the area surrounding Puits 14 Bis and Bois Hugo which are situated centrally either side of the La Bassée to Lens road. Chalk Pit Wood and the Chalk Pit are at top left and Chalet Wood is bottom right. Hill 70 and its redoubt are just out of shot at bottom centre.

By the late afternoon of September 25th nearly all this ground was captured by battalions of the 1st Division and 15th Scottish Division. At dawn on September 26th the Germans effectively counter attacked through Bois Hugo and Chalet Wood to recover Puits 14 Bis and Chalk Pit Wood. It was in the vicinity of Puits 14 Bis that John Kipling of the Irish Guards was last seen alive during the recapture of Chalk Pit Wood on September 27th.

The Tuffley brothers
William Tuffley | *Reginald Tuffley* | *Percy Tuffley*
1st Grenadier Guards | *1st Grenadier Guards* | *10th Gloucesters*

general advance was sounded like hell. We shelled the enemy trenches until there were no trenches left, and got the best of them. We took a great many prisoners. My brother Reginald was also in it, but I never saw him at all. I hope he came through alright. We are now back from the firing line, taking a rest. I am enclosing a German bullet which fell into our trench the last day I was there. It fell harmlessly right by my side. I hope you will keep it in memory of me and the war.

William and Reginald were later to discover that a third brother, Percy, was happily one of the 10th Gloucester's survivors.

Despite the resolute and ordered advance by the Guards, which took them through Chalk Pit Wood and into the heavily defended colliery buildings of Puits 14Bis, they could make no further progress and were forced back into Chalk Pit Wood, which they managed to hold on to. During this attack, John Kipling, the eighteen-year-old son of Rudyard Kipling, was seen to fall wounded. John Kipling was never seen again and due to the furious fighting that continued to rage around Puits 14Bis his body was never identified. In 1992, a grave to an unknown Lieutenant of the Irish Guards, situated in St Mary's Advanced Dressing Station Cemetery near Hulluch, was identified as John Kipling's and renamed accordingly. Controversy still continues today over whether this grave really is John Kipling's last resting place.

The loss of Chalk Pit Wood was a minor setback for the Germans, who were determined to recapture all they had lost. With ruthless efficiency, their troops bombed their way into the warren of trenches around their former positions at Fosse 8, the Dump, the Hohenzollern Redoubt and the Quarries. In spite of extremely costly attempts by units of the 7th Division, 24th Division, 2nd Division and the 28th Division to stop them, the Germans had won back all these positions by October 8th.

British soldiers defend a crude front line trench.

The hand to hand fighting was murderously brutal, and even short stretches of the ruined trenches were taken, lost, and then retaken by suicidal bayonet assaults from soldiers of both sides. Taking full advantage of superior tactics employed against the willing but mainly inexperienced British troops, and with a very efficient supply of hand grenades with a longer range than the newly issued British Mills bomb, the Germans prevailed.

Further to the south, the Germans still held the summit of Hill 70. Between Bois Hugo and Hulluch they erected strong belts of barbed wire and constructed a new trench system following the line of the La Bassée to Lens road. The buildings surrounding Puits 14Bis were turned into a series of formidable strong points and the entire area now presented a deadly wilderness of barbed wire, tumbled trenches and unburied corpses.

In early October, French intelligence reports warned that the Germans were planning an assault on Chalk Pit Wood. This information proved to be uncannily accurate.

On October 8th, at 11am, a terrific artillery bombardment enveloped the British trenches in and around the wood. Due to the fire swept nature of the terrain, these trenches were poorly constructed with no accommodation or shelter. The British wire entanglements were described as "**sparse.**" Finally, at about 4.10pm, the shelling lifted and a mass of German infantry advanced from trenches in and around Bois Hugo.

Occupying the British firing line were the 1st Gloucesters, the 1/9th King's and the 2nd Royal Munster Fusiliers. Despite suffering serious casualties from artillery fire, these three battalions were able to line their trenches and direct a withering fire into the advancing enemy ranks. Within fifteen minutes it was over. The enemy retired leaving between 400 and 500 dead in their wake. It was now the turn of the surviving Germans, pinned down in No Man's Land, to lie low until darkness arrived.

One German soldier actually reached the Gloucester's parapet where he was promptly captured. He claimed to be a former sailor and didn't care for land fighting.

The 1st Gloucesters suffered 123 killed and wounded. Among these were Privates Harry Mills and Tom Hart. Private B. Brooks wrote home to Harry's aunt in Harrow:

> Just a few lines of sympathy for you, letting you know that Harry Mills was killed on October 8th. He was very happy when he got hit, and I can tell you he accounted for three or four Germans. He died doing his duty well, and I am very sorry myself to have lost my chum. We buried him alright. Harry was a brave chap and he was always wanting to have a pop at the Germans. I hope you will take it lightly, but I know it is a great loss. The boys in his platoon send their greatest sympathy to you and his parents.

The father of Tom Hart, who was from Ruspidge in the Forest of Dean, received this moving letter:

> No.2 Stationery Hospital, Advanced Base, BEF, France. Oct. 29th 1915.
> Dear Mr. Hart, I regret to tell you that your son, (I believe it was), passed away yesterday. From the time that he was admitted he never spoke or seemed conscious. I do not think he suffered, but the wound to the head is so often curable that we never gave up hope. However, he quietly passed away, and we may now believe he is in Paradise. He gave his life for his friends and no one can do more. May God comfort and support you in this trouble and draw you nearer to Himself. I buried him this morning in Abbeville Cemetery on a hill overlooking the town. English ladies tend the graves, and an oak cross with name marks each. With sincere sympathy, yours ever truly, (Rev.) H.J. Watney, C.F.

Private Tom Hart served with the 1st Gloucesters but was formerly a collier from Lower Ruspidge in the Forest of Dean. He was employed at the Lightmoor Colliery and played football with Francis Hawkins for Ruspidge.

Caught up in the thick of the fighting were two Tewkesbury brothers, Sergeant Tom New and Lance Corporal Ernest New. Tom was mortally wounded and died on the battlefield the following day. He has no known grave. Ernest, who was later wounded in the face by shrapnel, wrote home to their parents:

Tom Hart's grave on the hill above Abbeville.

> **He was shot with a rifle bullet through the lungs, he got excited and got up
> on top of the trench so that he could play more havoc with them and that
> is how he was hit having exposed himself too much.**

Meanwhile, the 10th Gloucesters were employed turning the captured German positions, west of Hulluch, into adequate support and communication trenches. Two companies also manned the firing line here, but it was a perilously exposed, fire swept position and three men, Private William Barnfield, Corporal Bernard Mossop and Corporal William White were killed during these operations.

At several places along the new British front, it was feared that the Germans were busy tunnelling underneath with the intention of detonating large mines. On October 10th, officers of the 2nd Welsh occupying forward trenches opposite Hulluch were convinced they could hear the faint sounds of digging beneath their positions. A mining expert was hastily summoned and directed to the dugout from beneath which the suspicious sounds could be heard. Their War Diary records somewhat laconically:

> **The expert arrived around midnight, but promptly went to sleep. Nothing
> further heard.**

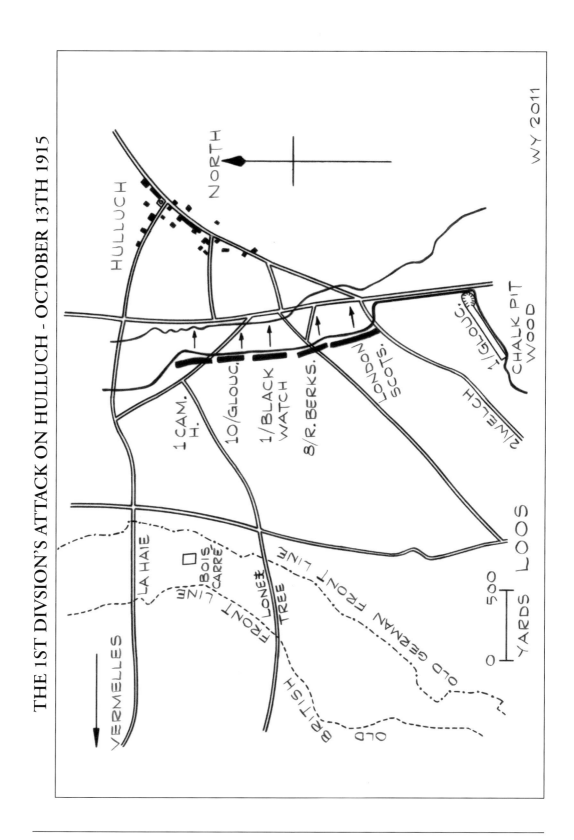

THE 1ST DIVSION'S ATTACK ON HULLUCH - OCTOBER 13TH 1915

To help replace the 10th Gloucester's very heavy casualties, a fresh draft of men arrived from England in early October. No doubt these men were shocked to discover exactly how badly the battalion had suffered. Sadly, within ten days, many of these 'green' soldiers would also be dead.

On October 13th, General Haig launched a new attack designed to recover the ground lost in the vicinity of the Hohenzollern Redoubt. It was also his intention to penetrate the enemy's second line at Cité St. Elie and Hulluch. Once more gas and smoke was to be released prior to the infantry assault. The task of breaking into Hulluch and capturing the enemy trenches southward along the La Bassée to Lens road was given to the 1st Division's 1st Brigade.

The 12th Eastern Division, a New Army formation, was to retake the Quarries and capture Cité St. Elie, whilst the 46th North Midland Division (Territorial) was tasked with the capture of Fosse 8, the Dump and the Hohenzollern Redoubt.

The following Operation Orders are taken from the 8th Royal Berkshire's War Diary:

> Operation Order No 2
> by
> Major C.F.N. Bartlett, Commanding
> 8th Batt Royal Berks Regt.
>
> Reference.   Place.   G 24 b. 1. 8
>   Date.   12.10.15.
>
> The Battalion will attack the German line at 0.p.m. the objective being the 1st line German trenches from above CROSS ROADS (exclusive) to H 19 A 7 5. The Black Watch will be operating on our left and the London Scottish on out right.
> "A" Coy & "B" Coy will be operating the firing line, "D" Coy and "C" Coy the support line, in the positions already allocated.
> At the signal for the attack 2 Platoons of "A" Coy and 2 Platoon of "B" Coy will advance extended to four paces. One Platoon of each Company will be told off for wire cutting and Fumite Bomb throwing. The remaining halves of these companies will leave our trench as soon as the first line reaches German wire, each man carrying a pick and shovel.
> "C" & "D" Coy will support the front lines as occasion requires.
> All companies will be in Battle Positions by 12 midnight tonight.
> The following Officers will join the 1st Line of Transport tonight.
>
> > CAPT.D.TOSETTI
> > LIEUT ROBINSON
> > 2nd LIEUT WATSON
> > 2nd LIEUT WILLIAMSON
>
> They will join the Battalion the morning after the attack unless otherwise ordered.

Operation Order No 3
by
Major C.F.N.Bartlett, Commanding
8th Royal Berks Regt.

Place. G 24 b. 1. 8
Reference FRANCE 1/10000 Date. 12.10.15.

GAS — During the period that the gas is turned on all troops in the front and support trenches on the gas front will wear their gas helmets, care being taken to ensure that the ends are well tucked in. These can be raised for the assault itself, but not removed from the head.

CONSOLIDATION — As soon as the German trenches along the main road have been captured, they must be consolidated at once and connected with our own trenches. One connecting trench should be made near point 8.0. Wire must be erected along the EAST of the captured trench by Brigade wire workers.

FLAGS — Only one class of flag will be used to show the position of our bombers and will consist of a red flag 1 foot by 1 foot with a white vertical strip.

RATIONS — An iron ration will be carried by each man, and in the event of rations carts not being able to reach the troops on the night after the attack will be eaten.
Water will be stored in petrol tins probably at G 24 b. 1. 8.

(Sgd) C.S. Cloake
Lieut & A/Adj.

8th Berks.

4.0.p.m 12.10.15.

Operation Order No 4
by
Major C.F.N. Bartlett, Commdg
8th Royal Berks Regt.

Place G 24 b. 1. 8
Reference FRANCE 1/10000 Date 13.10.15.

ZERO — ZERO has now been fixed for 1.0.p.m.today.
WIRE — At 0.50 (i.e. 1.50.p.m.) our own wire will be cut or removed by Battalion wire cutters, under cover of the smoke.

SMOKE BOMBS   SMOKE BOMBS will be thrown provided that the wind is blowing from such a quarter that the smoke will be carried in any direction except straight back on our own trenches.

SMOKE CANDLES will be used during consolidation.

All movement of supporting troops must be made over the open.

Waterproof sheets will be carried. Bayonets will not be fixed after dawn until 0.30.p.m. (i.e. 1.30.p.m.)

Greatcoats will not be worn. Smoke helmets will not be put on until Zero (i.e. 1.0.p.m.)

During the consolidation of captured position one in three men will be told off to keep down enemy's fire and look out for a counter attack. If the field of fire from captured trenches is bad "T" heads should be constructed.

Reports every half hour in addition to special messages.

In the event of it being decided not to turn on the gas the Infantry attack will take place as already ordered.

Operation Order No 5

Time Table of Gas and Smoke Discharge

Date 13.10.15.

To: O.C.

0 to 0.5	5 minutes gas (4 cylinders)
0.30 to 0.33	3 minutes gas (1 cylinder)
0.37 to 0.40	3 minutes gas (1 cylinder)
0.45 to 0.50	3 minutes gas (4 cylinders)

SMOKE   The smoke grenades will be thrown out from the front parapet as follows :-

One "P" grenade for every 3 yards at following times :-

0.0	0.30	0.50
0.15	0.40	0.55

The grenades will be distributed to the men along the front line and will be thrown out by them under supervision of section commanders. When section commanders have not got watches of their own they should take the time from the sections on their flanks or judge when the smoke is getting thin and requires thickening.

No "Fumite" Bombs are available so wire cutters will carry ordinary "P" Grenades.

(Sgd) C.S. Cloake.   Lieut & "Adj"
8th Berks.

10.a.m. 13.10.15.

At 11.30pm on the evening of October 12th and under the cover of darkness, the assault battalions of the 1st Brigade left their reserve trenches and filed along communication trenches to take up their battle positions in the firing line. To these soldiers tasked with capturing Hulluch, the operation did indeed present a daunting prospect. Dominated by cleverly camouflaged enemy redoubts, many of which were dug into ruined houses, the ground over which they were expected to attack was totally exposed. Now liberally sewn with thickets of barbed wire, the patches of rank grass barely concealed the bloated corpses of hundreds killed weeks earlier.

At noon, a relatively puny artillery bombardment was directed on the German lines and at 1pm clouds of smoke and chlorine gas were released from the British lines. This time the gas and smoke carried well, but critically it also obscured the effectiveness of the artillery in the final attempt to destroy the enemy wire. Worryingly, the gas did not seem to have any effect on some of the enemy machine gun crews who kept up a constant hail of fire during the whole time of the gas and smoke discharge.

Manning trenches to the south, in the vicinity of Chalk Pit Wood, the 1st Gloucesters and 2nd Royal Munster Fusiliers of the 3rd Brigade, were not required to attack but created a diversion by throwing smoke bombs and directing heavy machine gun and rifle fire on the enemy trenches. This drew a storm of retaliatory artillery fire, which caused considerable casualties to these two battalions.

At 1.50pm the gas was turned off and under cover of a continued release of smoke, parties of men left the British trenches with the task of making sure that the wire was thoroughly cut.

The 10th Gloucesters occupied a battle frontage of 200 yards, opposite the southern tip of Hulluch, with No.1 Company on the right and No.3 Company on the left. No.2 and No.4 Companies were kept in support. The German trenches were barely 200 yards distant down a gentle slope and bordering the western side of the La Bassée to Lens road. To the Gloucester's left were the 1st Cameron Highlanders and to their right the 1st Black Watch, 8th Royal Berkshires and 1/14th London (London Scottish) respectively.

Punctually at 2pm the British troops left their trenches and began the assault.

Private James Groves:

The wire was unbreached and it was the job of the bombing section of No.3 Company to crawl up and cut it. The Germans laid down such a continuous

fire that we could do nothing but lie still until dark when we crawled all the way back to our trenches.

Private Walter Daffurn:

It was far worse than on the 25th. The Germans were waiting for us. They held their fire until we were almost on their wire then cut us down.

Lance Corporal Leonard Freeman:

Over the top we went, once again the fire from the German machine guns was terrible and we were literally mown down and eventually beaten back again. I however, managed to get through without a scratch. After this there were but very little of the old battalion left. We were relieved from here and went back out of the trenches for a rest to a town called Lillers.

Mills grenades had very recently been issued to the 1st Division, with each bomber carrying eight grenades in bandoliers and the riflemen carrying two each in their pockets. These new grenades were infinitely more effective and reliable than the old cricket ball bombs, but were still in short supply. Using these to good effect, a small number of Camerons and Black Watch bombed their way down some old communication trenches and into the German line, using scaling ladders to get over blocking barricades. The enemy responded with vigorous counter bombing which drove the Scots back. The Scottish soldiers found it was virtually impossible to dislodge the Germans, who skilfully defended their positions with their bombers secreted in narrow cuts made in the side of their trenches.

In reserve were the 1st Northamptons and 2nd Royal Sussex of the 2nd Brigade. Both battalions were heavily shelled in their assembly trenches before each committing a company to the attack. 'A' Company of the Northamptons and 'A' company of the Royal Sussex were mown down by machine gun fire before they even got to their own front line.

A short distance to the north, the 12th Division suffered severe casualties whilst vainly trying to capture the Quarries, a series of heavily fortified chalk workings. This Division's only gains were a dangerously exposed section of enemy trench on the northwestern edge of the Quarries and known as the Hairpin, also a small section of Gun Trench, north of the Vermelles to Hulluch road.

The 46th Division suffered very badly from their own gas and were then heavily shelled in their assault trenches. Immediately the men climbed into the open they were shot down by machine gun and rifle fire. Nevertheless, some managed to enter the warren of trenches that formed the Hohenzollern Redoubt and became engaged in a deadly grenade and bayonet fight with the enemy. The Germans again proved that they were very determined trench fighters and gradually gained the upper hand, leaving the British with just a toehold in the extreme western perimeter of the redoubt.

Retaining mastery over the battlefield, the German infantry and machine gun crews dealt mercilessly with every attempt to penetrate their lines. The attack achieved very little and only added thousands more bodies to those already putrefying across the riven landscape.

The entire area surrounding the Hohenzollern Redoubt was so fire swept and dangerous that its reputation as an abominable "Hellhole" endured for years until the Germans finally withdrew in

Private Frederick Bowkett of Little London near Longhope, Gloucestershire. Killed October 13th 1915.

Private John Barnes lived at Tibberton near Gloucester. Killed October 13th 1915.

Private John Ireland.

Private Frederick Ireland. Brothers John and Frederick were both killed together on October 13th 1915.

No._____   Army Form B. 104—82A.

(If replying, please quote above No.)

Infantry RECORD OFFICE,

Warwick STATION,

11 Sept 191*6*

SIR,

It is my painful duty to inform you that no further news having been received relative to (No.) *1604* (Rank) *Pte* (Name) *F. Bowkett* (Regiment) GLOUCESTERSHIRE REGT. who has been missing since *13.10.15*, the Army Council have been regretfully constrained to conclude that he is dead, and that his death took place on the *13.10.15* (or since).

I am to express to you the sympathy of the Army Council with you in your loss.

Any articles of private property left by missing soldiers which are found are forwarded to this Office, but they cannot be disposed of until authority is received from the War Office.

Application regarding the disposal of any such personal effects, or of any amount that may eventually be found to be due to the late soldier's estate, should be addressed to "The Secretary, War Office, London, S.W.," and marked outside, "Effects."

I am,

SIR,

Your obedient Servant,

Major, for Colonel,

Officer in Charge of Records.

1918. To this day, the scrub covered craters and mounds that mark the redoubt's location undoubtedly conceal the remains of untold numbers of men, both British and German.

The 10th Gloucester's casualties were very severe and amounted to 150 killed wounded and missing. Nearly all those unaccounted for were in fact dead; shot down in the anonymity of the gas and smoke cloud, their bodies lying within the arc of the German machine guns, never to be recovered in an identifiable state. The 8th Royal Berkshires lost 153 officers and men. Their Adjutant baldly recorded in the War Diary:

I attribute the failure of the attack to the inability of our artillery to silence the German machine guns, and the complete absence of support.

The families of the men officially posted as missing, clung to the faint hope that their loved ones had been taken prisoner. Eventually, nearly a year later, such hopes were dashed when relatives of the missing began to receive Army Form B104-82A, officially notifying them that the men were now presumed to be dead.

The family of Frederick Bowkett of Little London, Longhope, near Gloucester, received their form in September 1916. In this manner too, the deaths of many others were made official.

Private William Ireland had once again survived the slaughter but discovered that his two younger brothers had both been killed. He wrote home to his sisters Lily and Amy:

Private Albert Lockey of Lower Harford, Naunton, Gloucestershire, fell on October 13th 1915, aged 20 years.

Private Frank Allen Shilham came from Rodborough near Stroud, Gloucestershire. His body was discovered and identified after the war and he lies buried at Rue Petillon near Laventie, north of Loos.

Have you heard the sad news about Jack and Fred, for I got the Quartermaster of their Company to write Mr. Seddon and break the news at home? What a blow it must be for you all and I don't know how mother will stand the terrible news. The poor boys never suffered any pain. I hope you will try and bear this great strain for war is a terrible thing. Your broken hearted brother, Will.

Also among the dead was Lieutenant Frederick Carnegy, recently returned from Gosnay with the contingent of mumps cases. Killed too, was Lieutenant Harley Russell who had been posted to the 10th Gloucesters from the 1st Gloucesters on October 1st. Neither officer has a known grave, along with 58 out of 60 of their men who died that day. Their names instead appear on the Loos Memorial to the Missing at Dud Corner.

That evening, during the hours of darkness, the 10th were withdrawn to the relative safety of the British fourth line behind Lone Tree Ridge. Their position in the firing line was handed over to the 1st Northamptons.

History records that the Battle of Loos finally ended with the failure of the British attack on October 13th; however, the War Diary of the Northamptons reveals how close the action came to being continued the following day.

Now occupying the firing line in front of Hulluch, the 2nd Brigade received orders to capture Hulluch "at all costs." The renewed attack was to be made at 4am under the cover of darkness on October 14th. Unprepared, it was 5.20am before the Brigade was in a position to launch the

Second Lieutenant Frederick Alexander Carnegy. He was left in charge of the mumps cases and so was spared the opening day of the Loos battle. He did not survive the assault of October 13th 1915.

attack. Concealed by a heavy mist, the tired, cold men wearily climbed from their trenches and lay in front of the parapet in preparation to advance. Just as the leading companies had actually begun to move forward, the attack was cancelled. Advanced patrols had reported that the enemy wire was still uncut. Someone had finally realised the utter futility of continuing the battle.

Having suffered 1,200 casualties in the attack of October 13th, the 1st Division was withdrawn from the front line on October 14th and then sent by train for a well-deserved rest at Lillers.

The cessation of the Battle of Loos drew to a conclusion the British effort to comply with General Joffre's demands to support the French in their offensive in the Artois and Champagne regions. The anticipated British breakthrough to the Haute Deule Canal, which the cavalry were expected to exploit, was never achieved. At an enormous cost in human life, the formidable enemy strongholds of Fosse 8, the Dump, the Hohenzollern Redoubt, the Quarries, Puits 14Bis and Hill 70 were heroically captured but then lost. The town of Loos with its famous Tower Bridge landmark remained in British hands.

The Battle of Loos has been described as the "**Unwanted Battle**" and indeed it is easy to understand why Field Marshal Sir John French and General Sir Douglas Haig initially resisted Joffre's plan. Following the very heavy losses sustained in battle earlier in 1915, the British Army was simply not yet strong enough or adequately supplied to prosecute and sustain a battle of such relatively large proportions. Eventually, having been forced by Lord Kitchener into accepting Joffre's plan, French and Haig had to consider their available options.

On the manpower front, it was true that thousands of fresh British troops were beginning to arrive on the Western Front in the form of Kitchener battalions, mostly arranged into New Army Divisions. But the vast majority of these men, and their officers, had been civilians less than a year previously. Like the men of the 10th Gloucesters, they were totally inexperienced and had received very little musketry training. Furthermore, they were drilled in tactics that had already proved suicidal against entrenched enemy positions defended with machine guns and registered artillery. Even the ranks of the Regular Army battalions were now heavily bolstered with drafts of volunteers who had received even less training than those in the New Army battalions.

The unexpected availability of gas, and in large quantities, seemed to provide a timely answer to the problem. In theory its mass use would conveniently make up for the limitations of the shell-starved artillery, which could not deliver enough shells to adequately destroy the enemy wire, knock out enough enemy machine guns and support a breakthrough by damaging the German second line of defences.

Relying on the effectiveness of the gas cloud therefore represented a massive gamble by French and Haig. Dramatically encouraged by its potential, they gambled spectacularly, attacking on a six-mile front using six divisions of infantry with a very high proportion of inexperienced but highly motivated New Army battalions spearheading the attack. Indeed, the Battle of Loos became the biggest offensive yet mounted by the British Army. In the event, the crude way in which the gas was used resulted in a tragic own goal. This disaster, along with the inability of the artillery to comprehensively destroy the enemy wire, silence the machine guns and to effectively support the troops that did break through, resulted in the bloody slaughter of British soldiers on an as yet unprecedented scale.

The cynical expectation that the raw enthusiasm of the New Army soldiers would make them effective assault troops proved to be correct. The undimmed courage and self-belief possessed by these men sustained their discipline in the terrifying gas cloud as they waited to advance against an enemy steadily raking their parapet with machine gun fire. But once in No Man's Land, sheer courage was all they could muster against a hail of flying steel. Too many of these brave men paid the ultimate price on the exposed, fire swept terrain in front of the enemy's first and second lines of defence and the resolute Germans seriously blunted the effectiveness of the British advance.

The story of the Battle of Loos is littered with 'what ifs'? What if the gas cloud had asphyxiated the enemy in their fire and support trenches? What if the artillery had been more effective against the wire and against portions of the German second line of defences? What if the reserves had been fresh, experienced and immediately to hand? What if communications hadn't broken down so badly? What if the French Army to the south had managed to advance on a wide front?

I suspect that the answer is that very little more would or could have been achieved. The British Army would possibly have penetrated the German second line at Hulluch and perhaps at Cité St. Elie. An advance would have been made, with the cavalry as its spearhead, producing a large bulging salient from Cité St. Elie in the north to Cité St. Auguste in the south. The advance would quickly run out of steam as inadequate numbers of inexperienced soldiers were forced to defend the flanks from determined enemy attacks. Poorly supplied with grenades, machine guns, ammunition, and barbed wire, and crippled by a too fragile communications system, the British infantry would have been unable to hold the ground. The shell-starved artillery would have had little opportunity to support the infantry, resulting in a costly retreat to existing trench systems.

The cold and depressing truth was that in spite of the massive effort and high hopes for the offensive, the infrastructure and capacity of the British Army in 1915 was simply not advanced enough to achieve more.

In terms of tactics, communications and armament, the British infantry at Loos shared more in common with the pike men of the English Civil War than with the well equipped and supported men of the British Army that achieved victory in 1918. Against machine guns, artillery, barbed wire and entrenched positions, they advanced in waves, line abreast with their rifles and bayonets at high port. Contrast this scene with the later terrifying mass deliveries of mustard gas, high explosive and liquid fire, rained down on the enemy by the artillery, mortars and Livens projectors. Concentrated machine gun and creeping artillery barrages, wire and strong point busting tanks, preceding steel helmeted snakes of infantry heavily armed with dozens of Lewis guns, stokes mortars, hand and rifle grenades. The whole, supported from the air by armoured trench strafing fighters and artillery spotter planes carrying radio equipment.

It is tragic but true, the Battle of Loos merely served as part of a huge learning curve that eventually moulded the British Army into the formidable fighting force that finished the war. General Haig and his staff did learn many lessons from Loos, but sadly it took the truly abominable casualties sustained during the Battle of the Somme to ram many of them home.

Unwanted and hastily conceived from the outset, the harrowing tragedy of Loos lies in the unnecessary sacrifice of thousands of Britain's finest young men merely to satisfy the political expediency of complying with the impossible timetable dictated by General Joffre and acquiesced to by Lord Kitchener.

At Loos more than 50,000 British soldiers became casualties. Dozens of battalions were all but wiped out. Field Marshal Sir John French paid for these appalling casualties with his job, but over 15,000 Britons paid with their lives. Ironically it was General Sir Douglas Haig who became his successor.

The Star Shell

A star shell holds the sky beyond
Shell shivered Loos, and drops
In million sparkles on a pond
That lies by Hulluch copse.

A moment's brightness in the sky,
To vanish at a breath
And die away, as soldiers die
Upon the wastes of death.

Patrick MacGill

These 10th Gloucesters survived Loos. "Not a man lacked courage."

CHAPTER VII

Ordeal in The Loos Trenches

Like sacrifices, by their watchful fires
Sit patiently and inly ruminate
The morning's danger: and their gesture sad
Investing lank – lean cheeks and war torn coats
Presenting them unto the gazing moon
So many horrid ghosts

King Henry V. Act III, Scene II

At 5pm on October 14th, the 10th Gloucester's exhausted survivors finally made their way from the field of battle, passing through Le Rutoire Farm and Philosophe to Sailly La Bourse where they entrained for Lillers, a small town west of Béthune. Utterly exhausted, the battalion arrived at 1am the following day and were shown to billets in the Rue Du Bourg D'Aval and Rue De Contrainne. Here they were soon to be joined by the remainder of the 1st Division, which had been relieved in the trenches by the 47th London Division. Each and every man was heartily glad to escape from the evil, raw, festering landscape where too many good friends and comrades lay in shallow, hastily prepared graves, or still hung like grisly scarecrows amidst the tangles of rusting barbed wire.

Whilst at Lillers, the 10th Gloucesters experienced a period of sorely needed recuperation and reorganisation. New drafts of officers and men arrived along with 19 men who had recovered from wounds and gas poisoning. The battalion was to be reconstructed with fresh drafts, but never again would its officers and men go into action with such a spirit of dash and enthusiasm. Their brutal baptism of fire had dispelled any naïve illusion of warfare's perceived glory. Gone were those recent cocky Cheltenham smiles, now replaced with grim, careworn stares from eyes that had witnessed unspeakable suffering. To the end of their days the lurid, nightmare visions of death and mutilation at Loos would haunt those few who eventually survived the Great War.

On October 28th, a wet, miserable day, 208 picked NCOs and men of the battalion formed up alongside others of the 1st Division in a field near Hesdigneul just south of Béthune. Here, they were inspected by King George V who rode past on a chestnut mare. The Berkshire's War Diary states:

> H.M. seemed very pleased with what he saw. It was just after this that his horse slipped.

Lance Corporal Leonard Freeman:

> We had to march about 15 to 20 miles for the King's inspection, it was a miserable day. We arrived at this place, Louvener, and were placed in a

> position in this ploughed field with mud over our boot tops. At last the King came along with his staff on horseback, all the men were at attention presenting arms. However, after passing our Division something happened, for the King fell off his horse and was hastily took away by car. I don't think he was seriously hurt.

Startled by patriotic cheers, the mare reared up in fright and toppled over pinning His Majesty to the ground. Later, it transpired that the King had suffered a fractured pelvis and cracked ribs. The painful effects of these injuries remained with him until his death.

Later that day, the 10th were marched to the village of Houchin near Noeux-les-Mines, but had to leave 85 men at Lillers suffering from a mild form of diphtheria.

It was not until November 14th that the battalion was sufficiently rested and re-equipped to again take its place in the trenches. Between November 17th and 19th, Privates Henry Wilcox and George Bedwell were killed whilst the battalion occupied forward positions near Loos.

Near Mazingarbe on November 25th, Sir John French addressed the 1st Brigade and acknowledged the bravery shown by the 1st Division, paying particular tribute to the officers and men of 10th Gloucesters and the 8th Royal Berkshires. Sir John went on to add:

> In future generations it will not be forgotten that you worked hard for your country.

Through the bitter winter of 1915/16 and the following spring and early summer, the 1st Division remained to fight on the Loos - Hulluch sector. Each battalion forced to endure the day-to-day misery of life and death conducted in the filth and squalor of sodden, rat infested trenches. The enemy remained aggressively active, their artillery and trench mortars claiming victims daily, many of them men of the 10th Gloucesters.

Lance Corporal George Nash from Lydney in the Forest of Dean was killed on December 19th 1915, during an enemy artillery bombardment. George's parents learned of their son's death when they received a letter from Lieutenant Royds, written on Christmas day 1915.

Lance Corporal George Harold Nash. Killed in action December 19th 1916.

> It is with very deep feeling of grief and sympathy that I write to report to you the death of your son L/Cpl. Nash, killed on December 19th whilst nobly doing his duty for his country. He was killed near his gun in our front line trenches by a German shell and it may be perhaps of some small comfort for you to know that his death was

instantaneous. Your son will be a great loss to me and the machine-gun section, and his comrades have asked me to join their names to mine in expressing our very deep sympathy and sorrow for you and yours in this bereavement.

On March 29th 1916, several soldiers were wounded when a box of grenades exploded accidentally. Three soldiers from 'B' Company, Privates Charles Fryer, Frederick Griffiths and Charles Kingstone were killed on April 4th whilst with a work party at the 'Embankment', just behind the British front line opposite the twin slag heaps of the Double Crassier, south west of Loos. Corporal Willie Pegler wrote to the wife of Charles Fryer who lived at Slimbridge near Gloucester:

Private Charles William Fryer. Killed in action April 4th 1916.

> It is with my deepest regret that I have to write and tell you the sad news about your husband who was killed while at work repairing a trench on the night of Tuesday April 4th. There were also two other men killed at the same time and it all happened in a few moments. We were all hard at work when all of a sudden there was a flash and a report, and the shell dropped right on the spot where your husband was at work. We immediately had the stretcher-bearers attending to them, but alas, it was no good – all three of them died instantaneously. Our poor comrades were buried the next day in a cemetery (but I am not allowed to tell you where). They were buried by fellow mates from the same platoon, the Brigade Chaplain officiating. Your husband was a fine fellow, cheerful and always ready to help another. I wish to say that your husband died doing his duty for King and Country, and no soldier could

KILLED IN ACTION.

The parents of Corpl. Willie Pegler, 17375, of Coaley, have this week received the official notification from the Army authorities to the effect that their son was killed in action on August 19. The deceased soldier, who is much regretted, was in the Gloucesters, and would have been 21 next Dec. His untimely death was reported in last week's Gazette.

do more than that. I hope you and your children will be comforted from above.

Twenty year old Willie Pegler who was from Coaley near Gloucester, had less than six months to live himself, for he was killed on August 19th 1916 when the battalion attacked a strongly held German trench known as the Intermediate Line near High Wood on the Somme. His name appears on the Thiepval Memorial.

Officers were equally at risk. On April 19th 1916, Second Lieutenant Hubert William Corke was struck in the lung by a shell splinter as he stood by the entrance to a dugout in a trench named 'Regent Street' just south of Loos. His injury was serious and he soon expired from the wound.

Lance Corporal Leonard Freeman:

> One morning a shell dropped, or I presume it was a shell, in the trench close by me. Of course I received the full contents of it but I didn't remember any more until I found myself in hospital at Calais on the coast, which was a few days' journey from where we were. When I did come round I found myself in a nice condition I can tell you. I was covered in bandages from head to foot as I had over thirty wounds, so you see I was really very lucky to escape as I did. From what I could gather from comrades, we came down the river on barges fitted up as hospital boats.

Second Lieutenant Hubert William Corke. Killed in action April 19th 1916. He was 22 years of age and son of the Rev. H. A. Corke, vicar of Holy Apostles' in Cheltenham.

Enemy snipers were very active on this sector and took the lives of Second Lieutenant Ralph Albert Negus on April 18th in 'Copse Lane', and Second Lieutenant Stanley Percival Darch on April 22nd in 'Vigo Street'.

Ralph Negus was originally a Lance Corporal with the 14th Gloucesters. However, he successfully applied for a commission and was eventually posted to the 10th Gloucesters. His mother lived at Bon Marché, Suffolk Road, Cheltenham.

Stanley Darch had originally gone to war in 1914 as a Private in the 7th Dragoon Guards, but in early 1915 was commissioned and was sent to the 10th Gloucesters in France on October 15th 1915. His home was at 33, Tredworth Road, Gloucester.

Second Lieutenant Ralph Albert Negus. His home was at Cheltenham.

Maroc Cemetery near Loos.

Second Lieutenant Stanley Percival Darch. His family lived in Tredworth Road, Gloucester.

Sniper Private William Henry Taylor. Killed in action May 11th 1916.

Snipers did not have it all their own way and if detected could find themselves the target of concentrated artillery or trench mortar fire. Unfortunately it was a sniper from the 10th, Private William Taylor, who on May 11th 1916 picked off a German soldier but was in turn killed by a retaliatory bombardment from an enemy trench mortar. William Taylor was from Clearwell in the Forest of Dean. A collier in civilian life, he was well known locally as being an excellent shot. On enlistment he was sent to Gallipoli where he volunteered for sniping duties and accounted for several Turkish soldiers before being wounded and sent back to England. Having recovered he was posted to the 10th Gloucesters.

Even at extreme ranges, stray bullets could easily provide an unexpected death. Private Thomas Page from Swindon was killed in this manner on June 12th, near the village of Maroc, a little distance behind the British front line near Loos.

In the spring of 1916, the village of Maroc was perilously close to the front line; however, it still held attractions for the troops. A soldier of the 10th, weary of the threat of sudden death in the muddy, dangerous trenches, sensitively describes the place:

> Now that the days are longer, the time seems to slip by more quickly, and the day is almost gone before one can look round. It is true that in the trenches the time seems to hang a bit, but at present we are in a village a short way behind the firing line and there is somewhat more to attract one's attention. This is a pretty little place, one of the many small colliery towns one comes across in France. The flowers in the one-time gardens are in bloom, including lilies, pansies, forget-me-nots, etc., and it is a pleasure to see nature alive once more. The fruit trees also are in bloom; but there will only be 'Tommy' to pick the fruit this year. It is so lovely out here just now that one cannot help being in good spirits.
>
> No doubt you have heard of the death of two Cheltenham officers who were in this battalion – Second Lieutenants Corke and Negus, and a Gloucester officer, Mr. Darch. They met their death when last the battalion were in the trenches. Two of them I believe were killed by sniper's bullets, and the third by a piece of shell. During the last twelve days we were in the line our casualties were rather severe, so you can see we are in a fairly warm shop.

The bodies of Darch, Corke, Negus and their men, now rest in the neat military cemetery in Maroc, known to the troops in that far off spring as, "**The Garden City.**"

As if a violent death from a sniper's bullet or cartwheeling shards of red hot metal was not enough, the awful cold, damp conditions the troops were forced to endure claimed the lives of many. Pneumonia struck down hundreds of young men. Even the tough colliers from the Forest of Dean were not immune. Private Fred Harris from Joyford Hill near Coleford succumbed on March 23rd 1916. His father was able to cross the Channel and was present at his funeral, which took place at Rouen with full military honours.

Privates Alfred and George Lovell, from Wickwar north of Bristol, survived the fighting in September and October 1915. Sadly, 30 year old Alfred was taken ill in the trenches with pneumonia and only lived for three days before dying in hospital at St. Omer on May 2nd 1916. He left a widow and two young children. His elder brother George survived until April 20th 1918 when he died of wounds at Gorre near Béthune, having been transferred to the 1st Gloucesters. George was 40 years old.

British offensive operations around Loos at that time were largely confined to tunnelling under the German positions with the object of planting large amounts of high explosives to be detonated at a pre determined time. Both sides made extensive use of this tactic which produced crater fields that were often connected by saps to their respective forward trenches and fortified by the opposing troops of each side. The 10th Gloucesters assisted the Royal Engineers by forming a company of men, consisting largely of former Forest of Dean miners, whose experience was to prove invaluable during the risky tunnelling operations.

Private Frederick Harris from Joyford Hill, near Coleford in Gloucestershire's Forest of Dean, died of pneumonia on March 22nd 1916. His grave is at Rouen near Amiens.

Sergeant Ernest Chadband:

> Our Engineers used to tunnel under Jerry's trenches and blow them up and of course he did the same and we had to get the sandbags out and tip them. On this particular night the Berkshires, who were holding the line, decided to do some wiring and had a party out. Jerry was waiting for them and there was a real little scrap and the Gloucesters were called out from the tunnel. I was first in the tunnel so I was last out.
>
> Jerry had got into the trench and I had no rifle as we dumped our rifles as we went in, but I managed to pick up one from the trench and after some time managed to get the bolt to move. I think it had belonged to a sapper. Anyway I joined the party and Jerry was in the trench alright and I can remember one of my platoon, who was a stretcher bearer with us, I believe he was from Cheltenham, name of Gillman, (Pte. 12418 Ernest Gillman killed Le Hamel, Somme 4.4.18) kneeling on the parapet throwing Mills bombs straight at them. I found my pal, Sgt. Dowle; he had been in the 7th Battalion in the Dardanelles stunt and had the scars to show it. He shouted to me, "Look quick Ern, you wanted an officers helmet" and I got him but not before he shot our sentry at the end of the sap. I carried the helmet round until I got tired of it. Dowle took his revolver and after getting the wounded back to the trench and sorting out the dead, and there were quite a lot, we straggled back to the battalion who were standing to. A poor looking lot we must have been, covered in blood,

The 10th Gloucesters Mining Company.

smoke and chalk etc. The whole Division were standing to as they thought a big attack was coming off, so our lads told us when we got back.

We were praised by the Colonel of the Berks and General Rawlinson – another night to remember.

Not only was Ernest Chadband involved in risking his life by helping to constructing the tunnels, he was expected to fight for the resulting mine craters.

Our company was billeted in Les Brebis when Lord Kitchener was drowned. We had quite a cushy time, apart from a few raids as each side kept blowing up mines and we had to prevent each other taking the craters which blew up. I was in charge of a post in a 'T' shaped sap head which was only occupied at night, near the Double Crests (Double Crassier) two huge mounds of waste from the pits. The Germans were on one side and we were opposite. It was a weird place to be at night as the rats scampered around and brought all sorts of things rolling down and anyone a bit timid was scared stiff.

On this particular night we were told a mine was going up and we were to see that Jerry didn't occupy the crater. My squad had got a bit windy before this

Photographed in May 1916, these 10th Gloucesters men enjoyed boxing, football and rugby when out of the line. Arthur Chandler is seated far right in the middle row and Frederick Chandler has the football.

Many of the front line trenches at Loos were crude and primitive affairs.

was due to go up but a chap called Len Landalls was on sentry duty, a cool customer, and he told them "Its rats you fools."

I was fool enough to volunteer for this party under Colonel Patsy Fagan, whose name was well known in the Gloucesters. He always wore a Private's uniform and carried a rifle and, of course, his revolver in his holster and he was afraid of nothing and nobody, as I found out that night. This was a special big one, and of course there were Germans and Gloucesters trying to capture it. It was called Gloster Crater afterwards, but I don't think it would have been if it had not been for Patsy. He looked as if he was shooting rats and was calling "Come on Glosters." Of course being dressed as a Private made all the difference as the Germans didn't know where the orders were coming from, but we did and I was so glad when we got more men on the crater and the raiding party was relieved. We lost a lot of men but it's a night I shall never forget as it was the first time I had been hand to hand, but we were all excused duty for a long time as we were all being briefed for the Somme.

The dangers and rewards of patrolling No Man's Land are also eloquently described by Ernest Chadband.

One night that sticks in my memory was when I was detailed to take out a patrol and I could pick my own men. It was always safer not to take too many men as you had to be quick and quiet. I had no trouble getting two volunteers. We had to get through our wire and get to Jerry's wire to see the strength of it and what was going on as much as possible.

We did not have long to wait as he had a party out wiring and we found out how many and their position of the line. With this information I decided we had done enough and we started to make our way back to our lines but had some difficulty in finding the gaps in our wire. Jerry must have heard us and put up some Very Lights and opened up machine gun fire and we had to lie as flat as we could, expecting every minute to get riddled. After what seemed an eternity they ceased firing and we got back to where our company was standing to.

It had been raining and we were soaked with wet crawling about, so we reported to the Captain's dugout and he said to the Sergeant Major, "they had better have a drink" whereupon he produced a whisky bottle, a thing unknown to other ranks. So, fortified, we made our way to our little shack; we didn't even have a dugout, just a little shelter scooped out of the side of the trench. On the way we came across some of our chaps with Lt. Street revetting. I jumped up on to the parapet and told them, "That's not the way to lay sandbags, whereupon Lt. Street told me to go and lie down for a while. Then the Sergeant produced our rum ration and after this I was soon asleep. The next thing I knew was the Sergeant kicking me to rouse up. I said, "I'm not standing to I've been out all night." He said, "You've been here 2 hours and the relief has arrived. "Oh" I said, "that's different" and soon began preparations to leave.

On May 6th 1916, Reginald Fennell noted in his diary that the 10th Gloucesters were issued with the new steel helmets, and on the 29th:

Turned trousers into "knicks" - some style.

On July 3rd 1916, the 10th Gloucesters were relieved by the 12th South Wales Borderers and marched to billets in the nearby town of Barlin. The battalion's hideous ordeal on the flat, murderous sweep of the Loos sector was finally at an end. Instead they were destined for a new Hell, the undulating, chalky uplands of the Somme, where nearly 20,000 British soldiers already lay dead, killed on just one day, July 1st 1916.

At Loos, the poor, mangled, metal riddled bodies of their fallen comrades remained on the battlefield, buried in shallow graves, or lying, decomposing amongst the barbed wire in No Man's Land. Sadly, all but a handful would be denied a final resting place beneath a stone bearing the proud legend of their earthly identity. The static nature of the battlefront during 1916, 1917 and much of 1918 ensured that thousands of graves would be lost by the constant churning of shellfire. At the finish of the war, the Imperial War Graves workers were left with the often impossible task of locating huge numbers of unmarked graves and collecting the scattered remains.

To this day, the cemeteries at Loos contain row after row of neatly maintained graves dedicated to unknown soldiers. Yet, here lie all those missing Gloucesters, and their fine comrades. They lie in the dignified and peaceful military cemeteries and in the rich soil where the original Lone Tree once stood and this book will help ensure that their sacrifice is never forgotten.

Matey

Not comin' back tonight, Matey,
And reliefs are coming through
We're all goin' out all right, Matey,
Only we're leavin' you.
Gawd! it's a bloody sin, Matey,
Now that we've finished the fight,
We go when reliefs come in, Matey,
But you're stayin' here tonight.

Over the top is cold, Matey,
You lie in the field alone,
Didn't I love you of old, Matey,
Dearer than blood of my own?
You were my dearest chum, Matey,
(Gawd! but your face is white)
But now, though reliefs 'ave come, Matey,
I'm goin' alone tonight.

I'd sooner the bullet was mine, Matey,
Goin' out on my own,
Leavin' you 'ere in the line, Matey,
All by yourself, alone.
Chum o' mine and you're dead, Matey,
And this is the way we part,
The bullet went through your 'ead, Matey,
But Gawd! it went through my 'eart.

Patrick MacGill.

CHAPTER VIII

The Present Day

**Thus far with rough and all-unable pen,
Our bending author hath pursu'd the story**

King Henry V. Act V, Scene II

For those who are inspired to explore the landscape of the tragedy that was the Battle of Loos, the town of Loos, or more correctly Loos-en-Gohelle, is but a swift, hour long car journey from Calais. Take the A26 motorway southward and head for Arras and Paris. Before reaching the Arras exit, take Exit 6.1 onto the A21 for Lievin – Bully Les Mines - Lens, and then after 4 miles take Exit 8 signposted Lens – Ouest and onto the N43 where you will quickly approach a roundabout signposted - Vermelles and Béthune. On the roundabout take the exit at 9 o'clock towards Vermelles and Mazingarbe, you will immediately be presented with a long straight road dipping through the built up outskirt of Loos and then rapidly rising to open farmland on the Grenay Ridge.

Continue along the N43 in the direction of the Grenay Ridge, bypassing the town of Loos. Loos is now little more than a suburb of Lens and was almost totally destroyed during the Great War but has now been rebuilt very much in its original style. The famous Tower Bridge did not survive the ravages of the war and only the discreet military cemeteries provide an obvious reminder of those sad years.

Progressing up onto the Grenay Ridge, beside the road you will soon become aware of a large high walled structure graced with a number of domes dominating the skyline. Here is the Dud Corner Memorial honouring the British soldiers killed on the Loos sector who have no known graves. Within its confines is the Dud Corner Military Cemetery. There is a parking area at the open roadside entrance to the memorial, but take care as the road is often very busy and the traffic passes at speed.

Dud Corner gained its unusual name from the astonishing number of dud British shells that littered the ground here following the capture of the German Lens Road Redoubt by the 15th Scottish Division. The graves of 1,785 officers and men are contained within its high walls, which support large memorial panels inscribed with the names of nearly 21,000 British soldiers. It is here, on panels 60 to 64 in one of the alcoves at the far end of the memorial that the names of all but a handful of the men and boys of the 1st and 10th Gloucesters are remembered. Among the names of the honoured dead are my Great Uncle, Sergeant Reginald Betteridge, Privates John and Frederick Ireland - the brothers from Painswick, Lt Clement Symons, who fell on the enemy's parapet, Corporal William Ingles DCM and Private William John Williams whose brave and vivid letter opens the narrative of this book.

Here too, amongst the many neat rows of graves, can be found those of the 10th Gloucesters whose bodies were identified when the battlefields were cleared in the years following the Great War. Sergeant Ernest Artus, the Boer War veteran, Private Charlie Murrell, the teenage collier, Sergeant

Ernest Betteridge, the Cheltenham Town footballer and Lance Corporal Arthur Harrison, the 45 year old assistant school master. Also here are the graves of the VC winners, Captain Anketell Moutray Read of the 1st Northamptons and Sergeant Harry Wells of the 2nd Royal Sussex. Private George Peachment of the 2nd King's Royal Rifle Corps is commemorated on panel 102.

To the left of the entrance to the memorial a set of steps leads up to an excellent viewing platform and here is provided a wonderful view over a large swathe of the old battlefield. Where once the clear country air was fouled with the insidious stench of chlorine gas and terrifyingly rent with the 'whooping' and 'screeching' of shells, the sweet songs of skylarks and the 'jangling' of corn buntings, have soothed away the dark shadows of that nightmare. Long gone are the murderous, rusting avenues of barbed wire; and the raw, chalky, shell scarred expanses of rank untended farmland has nearly all been levelled and ploughed. Now, graceful hen harriers and kestrels skim low over neat ordered crops, in pursuit of unwary partridge chicks.

Although the contours of the land remain little altered since 1915 and many of the features mentioned in the narrative are still recognisable, obvious visible signs of the great drama played out here are few. The vista is wide and far reaching, but if you look along and past the wall of the memorial below, you are looking to the north east and directly down the low Grenay Ridge on which the Germans chose to establish their formidable defences. The open ground laid before you is where the 15th Scottish Division and the 1st Division beyond, advanced across No Man's Land from left to right against storms of machine gun and artillery fire.

Turn to face the other way and across the road is a massive slag tip sporting twin conical peaks. These are often mistakenly identified as 'The Double Crassier', but are in fact of fairly modern vintage. They do, however, occupy the former position of the Double Crassier, which was buried amongst the terraces of slag that extends out to the right at the foot of these peaks. Recently, much of this slag was removed revealing plenty of evidence of the war years. Between your position and these tips, the right wing of the 15th Scottish Division advanced into Loos and onto Hill 70, and beyond, the 47th London Division secured the right flank of the attack at the Double Crassier.

Leaving Dud Corner, continue along the N43 which will quickly take you through the outskirts of Mazingarbe. Turn right at the roundabout where the Lidl supermarket is situated and onto the single-track road, which takes you out past a local cemetery and into the fields. Continue for about 1 mile and on the right, just before joining the D39 Vermelles to Hulluch road, you will find Le Rutoire Hamlet. The original Le Rutoire Farm is in fact the last farmhouse on your right, with a tall opening into a large square, enclosed farmyard. Long since rebuilt, its red brick walls conceal the vaulted cellars and underground connecting passageways once so appreciated by the British soldiers.

Forming the foundations of an outhouse is a concrete British blockhouse dating from 1917/18. A narrow tunnel running under the courtyard connects it with a second, more obvious pillbox situated some distance away on the edge of a field behind the farm.

Approximately 50 yards short of the junction with the D39, a small metalled road leads off on the right into the open fields. Leave your transport here, being careful not to block access, and put on a good pair of walking boots, for the road soon becomes a rutted and uneven farm track.

As you take to this road you are immediately passing over the British support trench known as Fosse Way which ran alongside the road from Le Rutoire Farm. From this trench Private Dolden of the London Scottish advanced with Green's Force to assist the 2nd Brigade at Lone Tree.

Stride on out along this road into the wide-open plain and you will soon be approaching the former location of the British trenches occupied by the 1st Division at 'Zero Hour' on September

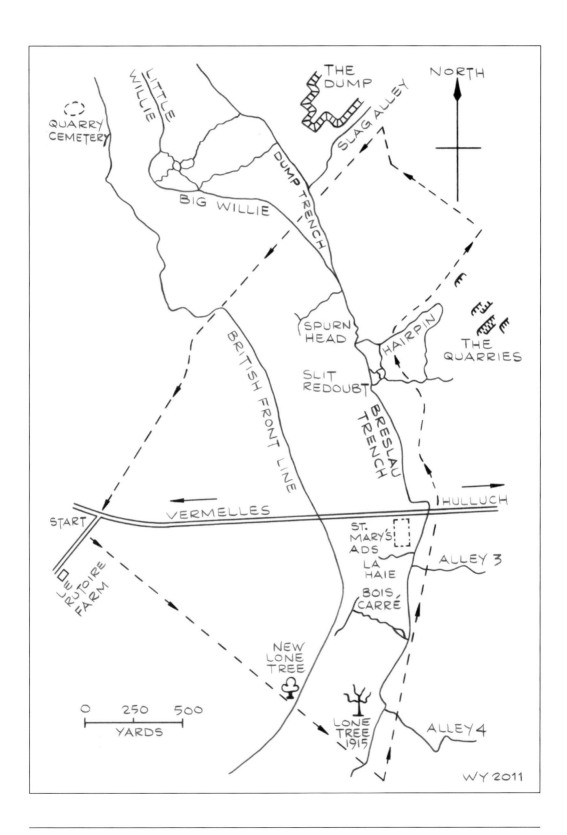

25th. If the track is muddy and the going difficult remember that the soldiers of 1915 were forced to cover the same ground along tortuous communication trenches carrying the enormous gas cylinders, or, like Green's Force and the 3rd Brigade, 'over the top' through banks of swirling gas, smoke and raking enemy machine gun and artillery fire.

Those with keen eyesight will be the first to spot a single tree growing beside the track some distance ahead. On drawing closer it will be recognised as a cherry tree and at its base a bronze plaque bearing the following dedication in English, French and German:

LONE TREE
REPLANTED IN MEMORY OF ALL
THOSE SOLDIERS WHO LOST THEIR LIVES
AT THE BATTLE OF LOOS 1915

This tree was planted on September 25th 1995, through the dedicated efforts of my late father John Christian and Wayne and Michelle Young and also with the vital help of the Fouquenelle family at Le Rutoire Farm. The new tree is representative of the original Lone Tree, however due to the local French agricultural boundary complexities and for reasons of continued good will and security, this new tree was planted at a spot, which is exactly where the British assault trench faced into No Man's Land at the time of the Loos battle. The original Lone Tree was positioned approximately 300 yards directly to the east. Such is the ordinary peacefulness of the setting that one would never guess that such terrible slaughter was once inflicted here.

The 1915 Lone Tree was eventually cut down because it provided the German artillery observers with a convenient reference point. It certainly vanishes from the trench maps of 1916. Indeed, to the British troops, the Lone Tree was so closely identified with the terrible events at Loos that slices of it, some containing bullets, exist to this day in various Regimental Museums and in private hands. One piece can be found in the excellent South Wales Borderers Regimental Museum in Brecon.

Private Albert Swaine - Army Cyclist Corps:

> **My next visit to the Lone Tree was with several others, to cut it down and**
> **drag it back behind our lines. We were told H.Q. wanted it cut up for them**
> **for souvenirs so I cut two chunks off it for myself.**

A compellingly romantic tale, which persists to this day, describes how the ruined tree survived and in 1920 blossomed once again, symbolising the triumph of life over the spectre of death and destruction.

If you are lucky enough to stand beside the tree when the area has been ploughed, look to the north; great pale, chalky stripes in the rich earth reveal the location of the forward British trench systems. Exactly mirroring the trench maps and aerial photographs of 1915, it is possible to identify precisely where the 10th Gloucesters and 8th Royal Berkshires waited patiently for the whistles signalling them over the top.

Continue along the track beyond Lone Tree, you are now entering what was No Man's Land, which after the battle the 10th Gloucester's Adjutant described as **"A huge field which now seems a mass of graves and all the hideous effects of war."**

Dud Corner Memorial and Cemetery.

From Dud Corner there is a fine view to the north east and along the Grenay Ridge.

The site of the Double Crassier at the base of the left hand, more recent, conical slag heap.

Here the bodies of literally hundreds of men were eventually buried in the days following the initial assault. In 1919, efforts to recover the bodies were begun; however most were never positively identified other than by regimental shoulder titles attached to the remnants of their tunics. Most were reburied at Dud Corner or at nearby St. Mary's Advanced Dressing Station Cemetery. Further bodies were regularly being discovered until the late 1920s, after the local cemeteries had been closed to new burials. This explains why a number of the 10th Gloucesters are buried several miles to the south at Cabaret Rouge and Private Frank Shilham is buried at Rue Petillon near Laventie, several miles north of Loos.

Careful scrutiny of the surrounding soil will reveal chunks of shrapnel, cartridge cases, live rounds, shrapnel balls, tunic buttons and even the occasional cricket ball bomb. Constant ploughing regularly unearths relics of the battle and many local people have private collections containing cap badges, shoulder titles, water bottles, rifles and bayonets.

The track soon leads you onto the Grenay Ridge where it meets another track running north to south. Turn left and follow this track to the north in the direction of the two battlefield cemeteries known as Bois Carré Cemetery and Ninth Avenue Cemetery respectively. At this point, running on a parallel course in the field immediately to your left and approximately 150 yards distant, ran the deep, well prepared German front line trench, with its support trenches slightly closer to you. From this position you will also be able to turn and look to the southwest where the Dud Corner Memorial can be seen dominating the horizon. To the south you are looking downhill into a valley in which the town of Loos stands and to the northeast is the village of Hulluch. *(see sketch on page 123)*

Immediately to the east, the busy La Bassée to Lens road crosses in front of Hulluch and continues south to sweep past a group of buildings that today mark the original position of the Chalk Pit, Chalk Pit Wood and Puits 14Bis. Behind these buildings, the wooded area is all that remains of Bois Hugo. The road continues and rises slightly over the brow of Hill 70, now covered in buildings.

Around Hulluch, little has altered over the years and it requires small imagination to picture the muddy, disordered remnants of the 1st Division advancing down the gentle slope towards the village, girded by enemy trench systems and thick belts of wire. Also too, the massed ranks of the 24th Division advancing in waves from the direction of Lone Tree and over the Grenay Ridge into the jaws of the trap that doomed their assault against the distant German second line.

Bois Carré Cemetery mainly contains the graves of men killed in 1916 and belonging to battalions of the 16th Irish Division who were then holding the line on this sector. However, these graves were placed around the existing battlefield graves of officers and men of the 8th Royal Berkshires who fell in the initial assault on September 25th. The irregular arrangement of some of the graves, in particular those of 8th Royal Berkshire officers Haynes and Keable, identify it as an original battlefield cemetery, rather than a neat concentration cemetery constructed after the war. The cemetery is named after the copse known as Bois Carré, which was situated 300 yards to the southwest. The position of this cemetery is on the original German front line trench.

Return to the main track and continue to the Ninth Avenue Cemetery. This tiny battlefield cemetery is named after a communication trench which was dug by the British after the nearby enemy fire trench was captured. It is, in fact, a mass grave containing the bodies of 42 soldiers of the 1st Cameron Highlanders, nearly all of which are recorded as being killed on September 28th 1915. Private Thomas Young of the 10th Gloucesters is also buried here.

Returning to the main track, continue the short distance to the D39 and being mindful of the traffic, which is not inclined to slow down for pedestrians, turn left and enter the nearby St. Mary's

Advanced Dressing Station Cemetery. This is a large concentration cemetery constructed immediately after the war. It is situated in the former No Man's Land, just forward of the German front line and contains almost 2,000 burials of bodies nearly all originally recovered from the immediate farmland. Only 218 of these burials are to soldiers identified by name, although many others are identified solely by their regiment or merely as **"A Soldier Of The Great War Known Unto God."** Here one will see complete rows of unidentified Gloucesters, Royal Berkshires, Royal Sussex and men from numerous other regiments, all recovered in groups from mass graves or from single burials scattered across the local terrain. The reason for the large numbers of unidentified bodies has been outlined in the narrative.

To the rear of the cemetery is a row of token headstones dedicated to seven of the 10th Gloucester's officers who fell at Loos. None of these officers have known graves and the headstones proclaim that they are: **"Believed To Be Buried In This Cemetery."**

Retrace your steps to where the track met the D39 and cross the road to continue along the track that runs towards the wooded area. You are now entering the battlefield just behind the German front line, which encompasses the ground assaulted and captured by the 7th and 9th Divisions on September 25th. It was also further fought over by the 28th Division on September 28th and the 12th and 46th Divisions on October 13th.

Follow the track around the wood, which is bordered by a concrete wall and continue, keeping to the track that skirts left around an area of hawthorn scrub.

In the field to your left are two isolated areas of scrub. These are the remnants of old dumps where the local population piled the detritus of the battlefield when they finally returned to reclaim the former farmland after the war. They conveniently mark the position of the German fire trench

The new Lone Tree pictured in 2009.

Three cemeteries stand today in the rich farmland that was once No Man's Land on the 1st Division's front. In the foreground is the Bois Carré Cemetery, beyond to the left is the smaller Ninth Avenue Cemetery and distantly is St. Mary's Advanced Dressing Station Cemetery.

on September 25th, and if you visit in early April you will be able to see the chalky stripe of Breslau Trench etched in the ploughed soil.

To your right, amongst the scrub, you will be able to see that the chalky soil is unevenly heaped, still retaining the ravaged, shell scarred and trench ridden terrain that existed in 1915. This is the enemy position known to the British as the Slit. The 8th (Service) Battalion, The Devonshire Regiment advanced to capture this area on September 25th. Like the 10th Gloucesters, the battalion encountered enemy wire that was not properly cut and lost a staggering total of 619 men and officers with nearly 300 killed. All around in the soil you will see great lumps of shrapnel, spent cartridge cases, dud and unexploded shells, and bent screw pickets, testimony to the ferociousness of the fighting that raged here in 1915 and beyond.

Continue a short distance along the track and you will draw level with a small, square concrete observation post situated out in the field to your left. At this point you are standing on the former location of the Hairpin, a feature captured by the British on September 25th. The Hairpin was part of a former German communication trench that formed a narrow, elongated loop and now connected the new British and German firing lines across an insignificant stretch of No Man's Land. Its extremely dangerous and exposed position became the focus of some very vicious trench fighting following its loss and subsequent recapture by the 12th Division on October 13th 1915. Here, during the fighting, the acclaimed poet, Charles Sorley of the 7th (Service) Battalion, The Suffolk Regiment, was killed at the age of 20 years. Captain Charles Hamilton Sorley is commemorated on the Dud Corner Memorial, Panels 37-38.

On the afternoon of December 30th 1915, the Germans exploded five mines under the Hairpin, which was occupied by the 22nd London Regiment. The resulting crater field became a common feature of the Loos battlefield of late 1915 and into 1916. Indeed the vestiges of these explosions

One of a number of slices of the Lone Tree that still exist today.

Courtesy Andrew Tatham.

can be discerned amongst the scrub today. Unfortunately, the area is currently used by the local population to dump building and household waste and is very untidy.

At this point the track passes beyond the scrub and to your right is a large modern slag tip that slopes down towards you. Here, under the near edge of the tip and extending into the farmland, is the former enemy strongpoint of the Quarries. Captured by the 1st South Staffs of the 7th Division on September 25th, the position was lost to a German counter attack during the early hours of September 26th in which the General Officer Commanding the 27th Brigade, Brigadier Bruce, was captured.

As you look northwestward towards Cité Madagascar, the bare, unrelieved nature of the battlefield is striking. Here, the terrain gently slopes away and then rises to a significant swell in the farmland, topped by a mass of scrubby trees from which a number of large electricity pylons protrude. This feature marks the site of the infamous German Hohenzollern Redoubt. Originally captured by the 7th Seaforth Highlanders and 5th Cameron Highlanders of the 9th Scottish Division, it was the scene of incredible violence and unprecedented slaughter during and following the Loos battle.

Today, when the fields surrounding the former redoubt are ploughed, a circlet of white chalky soil graphically reveals the extent to which the terrain has been deeply disturbed by the explosions of numerous mines, continuous trench digging and concentrated shell and mortar fire.

Both sides launched near suicidal attacks and counter attacks, with bomb and bayonet, to cling tenaciously to even the smallest stretches of trench line. For those wounded in this fighting, there was little chance of rescue and survival. The 46th North Midland Division lost over 3,500 men trying to retake the redoubt on October 13th, and in the days following.

A short distance to the northeast the equally formidable former enemy position known as the Dump still dominates the skyline. In 1915 it was approximately 30 feet high and flat topped, containing the spoil from the nearby pit known as Fosse 8. Like the Hohenzollern Redoubt, it was successfully stormed on September 25th and marked the northern extremity of the British success on the opening day of Loos. Like the Quarries, it was quickly lost and was back in German hands by September 27th. Today, part of it is still used for dumping building rubble, but the Dump's southern contour is still instantly recognisable.

Continuing along the track for a short distance, turn left where the footpath marker directs you in the direction of the Dump. Take the second track to the left, just before you reach the Dump perimeter.

Running in the lee of the Dump and parallel with your track, was the German communication trench known as Slag Alley, and after approximately 400 yards, just as you reach the pylon beside the track, you are crossing Dump Trench, which continued to the southward to connect with Quarry Trench and Breslau Trench at the enemy position known as the Window, thus forming the German firing line to the south on September 25th.

In the early hours of September 28th, the 1st Battalion, The Royal Berkshire Regiment, was part of a force cobbled together to try and retake the Dump and Fosse 8. Unfortunately it was a moonlit night and the Germans spotted the force approaching and opened up a very heavy fire, forcing the British troops to take cover in Dump Trench. The Germans immediately pressed their advantage and issued in force down Slag Alley and into Dump Trench. A furious grenade contest ensued in which Second Lieutenant Alexander Buller Turner, with "**dash and determination,**" drove back the Germans for 150 yards by counter bombing. His actions won him a Victoria Cross, but sadly he

The new memorial to the 46th North Midland Division near to the site of the Hohenzollern Redoubt.

was hit in the stomach by a rifle bullet and died at No.1 Casualty Clearing Station at Chocques on October 1st. He lies buried at Chocques in Plot 1, Row B, Grave 2.

Continue for 150 yards and you will be crossing the position of Big Willie Trench, which was the German front line position at this spot on September 25th.

On October 29th, the Germans once again tried to capture Dump Trench from their positions on the Dump and from a section of Big Willie that was in their hands. The 1st Battalion Yorks and Lancs of the 28th Division were defending Dump Trench, as well as their part of Big Willie, but they began to run out of grenades. Private 8273 Samuel Harvey crossed back and forwards in the open between Big Willie and the old British front line, bringing up 30 boxes of grenades over a period of 13 hours. He was eventually wounded in the head but was awarded the Victoria Cross for his bravery.

Keeping to the track, you are now entering the former No Man's Land of September 25th. Attacking towards you on that day was the 2nd Battalion, The Royal Warwickshire Regiment of the 7th Division. On reaching the enemy wire the assaulting troops found that it was uncut. Private 3719 Arthur Vickers disregarded the enemy fire to cut two gaps in the wire allowing his company to enter the enemy trenches and continue their advance beyond the Quarries. Arthur Vickers survived the battle to be awarded the Victoria Cross for his cool courage.

Continue for a further 300 yards and the track will cross the 7th Division's assault trenches, which were dug just prior to the initial assault. The track will return you to your vehicle.

Back with your car, turn left onto the D39 and head towards Vermelles. At the roadside on your left, just as you enter Vermelles, there is a memorial in the shape of a white cross on a plinth, dedicated to the 46th North Midland Division.

When the main carriageway takes a sharp left hand turn, bear right and follow the road out into the farmland towards Cité Madagascar and Auchy. Very shortly you will encounter on your right a Commonwealth War Graves sign directing you to the Quarry Cemetery. This cemetery is unusually situated below the level of the farmland in a quarry that in 1915 was just behind the British front line. This is a true 'battlefield' cemetery, evidenced by the haphazard positioning of many of the graves. Its close proximity to the Hohenzollern Redoubt meant that it was regularly under fire from enemy artillery and mortars, resulting in the destruction of a number of graves. By consequence, some graves bear the legend: **"Known To Be Buried In This Cemetery."**

Five hundred yards to the east, one can see the scrubby area revealing the position of the Hohenzollern Redoubt. The British assault trenches of September 25th were situated mid way between Quarry Cemetery and the redoubt.

By September 27th, the Germans were closing in on their former positions in the redoubt and subjecting the inexperienced defending battalions of the 24th Division's 73rd Brigade to a torrid time. At 10am on September 27th a mixed force of 5th Battalion Cameron Highlanders and 8th Battalion Black Watch was sent to support the defenders. Corporal 12087 James Dalgleish Pollock of the Camerons won a Victoria Cross. **"With the utmost coolness and disregard of danger"** he climbed from the cover of his trench and worked his way along the parapet of the enemy held Little Willie Trench, hurling grenades into the attacking Germans. He remained unscathed until the moment he jumped back into the British held trench when he was wounded in the arm.

The following day, the Germans had managed to infiltrate parts of the redoubt and were once more pressing down Little Willie Trench to try and complete the job. Their bombers forced men of the 2nd East Surrey Regiment to retreat over a trench barricade and back into the West Face of the redoubt. Here, the Surreys made a stand behind a second barrier.

On the afternoon of September 29th, following thirty-six hours of constant fighting, their spirited defence was beginning to crumble when the supply of bombs began to run out. The situation was saved with the arrival of Second Lieutenant Alfred James Terrence Fleming-Sandes and a party off men from the East Surreys. Bringing a fresh supply of bombs, Fleming-Sandes took the initiative and repeated Pollock's feat by climbing onto the trench parapet and bombing the Germans from above. Although a rifle bullet broke his right arm, he continued to throw bombs with his left arm and succeeded in driving the enemy back. Eventually he was shot in the face and was evacuated from the redoubt. Fleming-Sandes survived and was awarded a Victoria Cross for his bravery that day.

By October 13th, the Germans had regained control of the redoubt. The 46th North Midland Division attacked this day to try and recover the position. As on September 25th, chlorine gas was released from the British trenches. Corporal James Lennox Dawson of the 187th Field Company Royal Engineers won a Victoria Cross for preventing the gassing of troops waiting to go over the top. Three cylinders were found to be leaking, which Dawson rolled away under heavy enemy fire to a distance of 16 yards. He then fired bullets into them, safely releasing the gas. In a strange twist of fate, Corporal Dawson was the cousin of Corporal Pollock.

The local population of Cité Madagascar and Auchy are well aware of the immense historical significance of the area and particularly of the fact that the battlefield has a Royal connection. During the fighting on September 27th, Captain Fergus Bowes-Lyon of the 8th Black Watch and elder brother of the future Queen Mother, was killed in the vicinity of the Hohenzollern Redoubt. His body was never recovered and his name is therefore recorded on the Dud Corner Memorial.

Leaving the Quarry Cemetery, turn right towards Cité Madagascar and take the first road on your right into the houses. Continue straight on, keeping to the right at the next junction. You will quickly come to a crossroads with a large set of farm buildings ahead of you and slightly to the right. Here you will find a sign directing you to the right towards a new 46th Division memorial. Turn right and park at the roadside. The road quickly becomes a farm track, which you need to follow on foot. Just beyond the farm buildings and behind a screen of evergreen trees, you will find a second, more recent memorial to the 46th North Midland Division, honouring the astonishing number of 3,583 men who became casualties in and around the Hohenzollern Redoubt between October 13th and 15th 1915.

Ahead, further along the track, you will enter an area of scrub which covers what is left of the former redoubt. Amongst the scrub, the ground is still riven with the remains of deep craters and is in effect a mass grave.

Returning to your vehicle, retrace your route to St. Mary's ADS Cemetery and continue towards Hulluch. At the roundabout, turn right for Lens and Loos. Very quickly you will pass beyond the houses situated immediately on each side of the road and you will notice a stretch of scrubby trees bordering the road on your right. Here is a farm track that you can pull into on your right. Amongst the trees bordering the road you will discover the distinct remains of a trench line. This is in fact a small portion of the German front line trench that the 10th Gloucesters assaulted on the afternoon of October 13th 1915. The field immediately in front of the trees is therefore where the Gloucesters lost 150 men killed wounded and missing.

The area was continually fought over for much of the remaining war years and the ground on which you stand was very heavily cratered from the effects of underground mines being detonated. In fact a look at Google Earth reveals the faint outline of the German trenches alongside the road and traces of 'scarring' in the fields where the craters once existed.

Continuing on towards Lens, you are following the La Bassée to Lens road which plays such a large part in the narrative. It was roughly along the line of this road, from Hulluch and up onto Hill 70, that the battlefront settled after Loos. In the open farmland to your left ran the German second line, in front of which the 24th Division suffered so many casualties, causing the Germans to refer to it as **"The Corpse Field of Loos."**

As you start the gentle rise up onto the former Hill 70, you will notice a collection of industrial buildings on your right, concealing a large, modern chalk pit. This is now the former site of the Chalk Pit and Chalk Pit Wood.

At this point to your left is a modern day aerodrome. It was here, on the afternoon of September 26th that Sergeant 3/10133 Arthur Frederick Saunders of the 9th (Service Battalion) The Suffolk Regiment, 24th Division, won his Victoria Cross. Although minus a leg, he stoutly fired a Lewis light machine gun from the cover of a shell hole to protect the retreat of his battalion and to decisively thwart the German counter attack developing in his immediate vicinity. Later, Saunders was lucky enough to be found by British stretcher-bearers and was carried to safety.

You will very quickly encounter a roundabout where the buildings on your right mark the former location of Puits 14Bis. The wooded area on your left is therefore all that remains of Bois Hugo where the 8th Lincolns were overrun on the morning of September 26th.

Exit the roundabout at 9 o'clock towards the Commercial Park. The wood to your right is Chalet Wood, which still occupies its original 1915 position and conceals a German trench system at its eastern extremity.

During the roundabout's construction in July 2001, the remains of two British soldiers were discovered. No identity discs were found, but a shoulder title identified one of the men as a Queen's Own Cameron Highlander. This tied in nicely with the history of the 6th Battalion Cameron Highlanders of the 15th Scottish Division. The battalion, having been forced out of Chalet Wood on the morning of September 26th, made a series of bayonet charges led by Lieutenant Colonel Angus Falconer Douglas-Hamilton in an attempt to recapture the position. Douglas-Hamilton finally perished at the head of just fifty of his remaining men and is commemorated on Panels 119-124 at Dud Corner. Aged 52 at his death, he was awarded a posthumous Victoria Cross for his fearless leadership.

It seemed that for 86 years, these men had lain where they had fallen, and were perhaps buried by earth thrown up by shellfire. After much research, it was satisfactorily established that one of the soldiers was Lance Corporal S/12807 John Young Brown of the 6th Camerons. Before the war he had been a postman at Giffnock near Glasgow and with his bones was found a fountain pen engraved, 'Postman's Gazette Pen'. John Young Brown was buried with full military honours at Loos British Cemetery on October 20th 2004. A piper played 'Flowers of the Forest' at his graveside, in the presence of family members.

If you require refreshments, carry on into the Commercial Park where there is a large supermarket, restaurants, toilets and a fuel station.

Once you are refreshed, a visit to the small museum at the Mairie in the centre of Loos is well worthwhile. It is necessary to book beforehand and there is a small charge. The museum contains many interesting artefacts recovered from the Loos battlefield.

Association 'Sur les traces de la Grande Guerre'
Mairie de Loos-en-Gohelle
Place de la République
62750 LOOS-EN-GOHELLE
FRANCE
Tel: 0033 3 21 69 88 77
Email: a.villedieu@infonie.fr

From the centre of Loos follow the Commonwealth War Graves signs to Loos British Cemetery and St. Patrick's Cemetery. Both these cemeteries contain the graves of soldiers killed in 1915, 1916 and 1917, but Loos British, in particular, was used after the war for the reburial of soldier's remains brought in from the battlefield and from a number of smaller cemeteries in the immediate vicinity.

It is here that Second Lieutenant George Egerton Clairmonte and his men of the 1st Gloucester's machine gun section were buried following the discovery of their bodies in Bois Hugo in the 1920s.

A series of tunnels dug by Royal Engineers under Hill 70 in 1917, contain dozens of carvings and pencilled messages on the chalk walls, made by Canadian and British troops just before the Hill was finally captured in August 1917. Unfortunately, due to health and safety issues, these tunnels are no longer open to the public.

A cricket ball bomb, still lying on the battlefield after nearly 90 years.

Postscript

The 10th Gloucester's participation in the great Somme battles of 1916 opened a completely new chapter in the battalion's history. However, I feel a brief description of the battalion's continued sacrifice is necessary, as many of those who survived Loos perished on the Somme and in the final months of the war.

On July 10th 1916, having travelled south to Albert by rail, the 1st Division was marched to the front line, which at that date had established itself north of the pulverised village of Fricourt. The British Army had broken into the fearsome enemy defences each side of the village on July 1st and had captured Fricourt on July 2nd.

Occupying the British support lines immediately north of Fricourt, the men of the 1st Division were astounded to find the whole area totally devastated by shellfire of an intensity far beyond that experienced at Loos. Literally hundreds of corpses, both British and German, choked the blasted trenches and lay thickly in the open. The 10th worked flat out for four days to bury between four and five hundred bodies. During this work, five men were killed and twenty-four wounded, nearly all by shellfire.

As July progressed and the huge offensive ground on, the 1st Division became embroiled in the struggle around the villages of Contalmaison, Bazentin Le Grand, Bazentin Le Petit and the push towards Martinpuich.

By mid July, the British offensive had stuck on the undulating farmland north of Bazentin Le Petit, between Pozieres, High Wood and Delville Wood. The 10th Gloucesters lost 13 men killed whilst digging assault trenches just north of Bazentin Le Petit.

On the night of July 22nd - 23rd the 1st Brigade attacked the stoutly defended enemy Switch Line in front of the village of Martinpuich. The 10th Gloucesters lost 150 men, mostly reported as missing but in reality dead. The Switch Line and High Wood held out against attacks by a number of British divisions until tanks broke the deadlock on September 15th. During this time the 10th Gloucesters lost hundreds more men, killed, wounded and captured in fruitless attacks on both these positions and on the bravely defended enemy Intermediate Line.

On Christmas Eve 1916, the battalion's survivors held a solemn service amidst the splintered shambles of High Wood. Here, they erected a wooden cross crafted by Sergeant Meulbrouck and dedicated to their lost comrades. Many more memorials stood alongside the 10th Gloucester's cross, honouring thousands of men from numerous battalions that had fallen whilst trying to capture the notorious wood.

In 1927, following French representations to have only official memorials remaining on their land, the cross was retrieved by Lieutenant Colonel Pritchard who had it brought to Cheltenham and placed in Christ Church, where the 10th had worshipped in 1914 and 1915. Here it remains to this day, along with the battalion's Colours, which were laid up in 1932.

Following the cessation of the Somme battles, the 1st Division remained on the Somme front for much of 1917. Casualties were mercifully few. However, in July of that year the 1st Division was earmarked for a daring and ambitious venture that would, if successful, add a massive punch to the effectiveness of the huge offensive just launched by the British in the Ypres Salient. This battle would become known as the 3rd Battle of Ypres, or Passchendaele.

The cross brought from High Wood on the Somme.

General Haig's intention was for the British Army to break out of the Ypres Salient and to advance seven miles northeastward into Belgium, where the town of Staden would be captured. At this point the 1st Division would be landed on the Belgian coast around Middelkerke, behind the German lines. The Division would then capture the nearby port of Ostende, supported by the heavy guns of the Royal Navy.

The operation faced a number of difficulties. At the selected landing areas the sea was very shallow. The solution was to construct three massive shallow draft pontoons each 600 feet long and 30 feet wide. Each was capable of carrying a whole brigade of troops with their equipment and would be pushed by heavily gunned shallow draft monitors up against the sea wall under the cover of darkness. The sea wall itself presented a formidable obstacle being constructed of concrete and sloping to a height of 30 feet surmounted by a vertical rise of 4 feet with an overhanging coping. Clearly the assault troops would need some intensive training.

A specially prepared camp was constructed amongst the dunes at Le Clipon on the French coast, six miles west of Dunkirk, in fact where the current ferry port is today. Secrecy was of the utmost importance and entry and exit to the camp was strictly controlled. The official line was that the Division was being quarantined following the outbreak of an infectious disease. The training was tough and intensive with much emphasis on the men being able to overcome a fearsome obstacle

Lieutenant Colonel Pritchard is saluted at the inauguration of the 10th Gloucester's Memorial Cross at Christ Church in Cheltenham, 1927.

A group of 10th Gloucesters veterans at Cheltenham in 1927.

course, loaded down with equipment and ammunition. A scale model of the sea wall was also constructed on which the troops continually practised. The plan also allowed for the landing of tanks.

Unfortunately, this audacious operation was never launched as the Ypres offensive quickly ground to a halt, bogged down in a glutinous morass of mud created by shellfire and unseasonable rainfall. By mid November 1917 the battalions of the 1st Division found themselves occupying miserable battle positions in the moonscape around Ypres.

On February 19th 1918, following a reorganisation of the British Army, the 10th Gloucesters were officially disbanded at the Belgian village of Merckeghem, just north of St. Omer. However, the story of the men of the 10th Gloucesters was far from over.

The battalion's fighting strength was distributed between two other famous Gloucestershire battalions. On February 7th, 5 officers and 100 other ranks were transferred to the 1st Gloucesters and on February 11th, 7 officers and 150 other ranks went to the 8th Gloucesters. The remaining officers and men became the 13th Entrenching Battalion under the command of the redoubtable Lieutenant Colonel James G. Kirkwood, who had earlier been promoted to command the 10th Gloucesters.

The 13th Entrenching Battalion, now reduced to approximately 350 men and officers, was transferred to General Sir Hubert Gough's Fifth Army which was responsible for holding a large sector of 42 miles between Gouzeaucourt and Barisis, directly east of Amiens. The battalion was employed digging and wiring the numerous defensive positions that General Gough deemed necessary to slow and halt the expected German spring offensive.

On March 21st 1918, the Germans struck, launching a huge offensive, code name 'Michael', against the British Fifth Army and also the Third Army, situated immediately to the north. Although the British were expecting the attack, its ferocity was such that the Fifth Army in particular, was forced back towards Amiens.

By March 23rd, Gough's III Corps, consisting of the 14th Light Division, the 18th Division and the 58th London Division, had retreated nearly four miles to the line of the Crozat Canal, south of St. Quentin. The canal is now known as the St. Quentin Canal. All the infantry battalions, which made up these divisions, had been very severely mauled and were badly in need of reinforcements. There was none, other than dismounted cavalry, engineers and support units, including the 13th Entrenching Battalion. The fighting was fierce and desperate, but the Germans forced their way over the canal on March 24th and advanced for two miles. The 13th Entrenching Battalion lost 11 men killed and a number wounded and was lucky to escape, falling back to Compiegne to the southwest by March 28th.

Gough's III Corps was now in a pitiful state and had to be relieved by three fresh French divisions. The 13th Entrenching Battalion, together with the remnants of III Corps, was moved north towards Amiens. Such was the critical situation on the Fifth Army front that III Corps would only receive a few days respite before again being put into the line on the night of April 3rd near the village of Le Hamel in the Somme valley.

Occupying the firing line just east of Le Hamel, was the 14th Light Division with two seriously under strength battalions, the 9th Rifle Brigade and the 5th Oxfordshire and Buckinghamshire Light Infantry manning the firing line. To bolster their numbers, 12 officers and 130 other ranks

Lt. Col. James George Kirkwood became the final Commanding Officer of the 10th Gloucesters. He also commanded the 13th Entrenching Battalion and the 25th King's Royal Rifle Corps. He died in Kenya in about 1954 from a heart attack following a motoring accident.

LT.-COL. J. G. KIRKWOOD

Lieutenant-Colonel James George Kirkwood, C.M.G., D.S.O., a member of the Legislative Council of Kenya from 1927 to 1944, has died in hospital at Nyeri, in Kenya, from injuries received in a motoring accident. He was 83.

The son of William Kirkwood, of Greymouth, New Zealand, he was born in 1872 and was educated at Wanganui Public School. For a time he saw service with the Wanganui Rifles (New Zealand Forces), and during the South African War he served with Brabant's Horse, and Kitchener's Fighting Scouts. He also saw action in the Bambarta rebellion of 1907 and during the 1914-18 War he served with The King's Royal Rifle Corps, being promoted lieutenant-colonel in 1917. He was mentioned in dispatches, awarded a D.S.O. in 1916, and made a C.M.G. in 1919.

He was twice married and had one son.

were drafted from the 13th Entrenching Battalion to the 9th Rifle Brigade and a similar number went to the 5th OXBLI. Intelligence reports suggested that the Germans would attack the following day.

At dawn on the morning of April 4th, following a short but powerful bombardment, the Germans did indeed attack and overran the positions held by these two battalions. Accusations of cowardice were levelled at the 14th Light Division, but although there is no doubt that some men did retreat in the face of the enemy, elements of this battle weary division did put up a stiff resistance. Twenty-six former 10th Gloucesters perished in the fighting, with three dying of wounds. Many more were wounded and captured with four later dying as prisoners.

The village of Le Hamel was lost, however the critical situation was saved by fresh Australian and British troops that managed to stop the Germans from advancing to Amiens. Although the Germans made subsequent attacks on other parts of the Western Front, this critical moment marked the high tide of their advance on this sector.

The end for the 13th Entrenching Battalion came on April 15th 1918, when the battalion was disbanded. Lieutenant Colonel Kirkwood, the Adjutant, Captain Mackenzie, their servants, Privates Fennell and Ellis and six others were by that time all that remained.

The 9th Rifle Brigade and 5th OXBLI did not last much longer. The whole 14th Light Division was reduced to a cadre with many of the troops being drafted to other battalions in different divisions. Fittingly, a number of the very few remaining 10th Gloucesters that had fought at Loos, found their way to the 12th Gloucesters where some, such as Privates Robert Henn from Birmingham and Sydney Tubb from Marlow in Buckinghamshire, sadly fell in the final advance to victory. Many more of the men that had been drafted into the 1st Gloucesters and 8th Gloucesters in February also perished, or were wounded or captured before victory was finally achieved.

And so the long and heroic story of the men of the 10th Gloucesters and their sacrifice in the Great War ends here. In 1921, General Sir Hubert Gough paid this reverent and lasting tribute to the valiant men of the British Army who tenaciously resisted the German onslaught in 1918 to ensure that the Allies finally won the Great War:

> There is a broad wreath of British dead in that desolate land, which has now become once again a smiling countryside. The rows of crosses mark for ever the scenes of their valiant deeds: history at least will give them the great honour they earned. Britain can ill spare such men: they are of the breed which has made her honoured and powerful throughout the world.

Date	Name	Rank Number	Birthplace	Age	Death	Comemorated
9/12/1914	THOMPSON John	Pte 13415	Pembroke Docks		Died	Mere Cem Wilts
18/2/1915	NEWMAN Charles Richard	Pte 17415	Minchinhampton Glos	19	Died	Minchinhampton
16/5/1915	KING Frederick William	Pte 17467	Bredon Worcs	27	Died	Bredon St Giles Worcs
15/9/1915	GEORGE Eric Coe	2Lt		19	Dow	Chocques Mil Cem
24/9/1915	BETTERIDGE Ernest Linden H	Sgt 13334	Cheltenham	24	Kia	Dud Corner Mil Cem
25/9/1915	ARKELL John	Pte 13455	Drybrook Glos	20	Kia	Loos Memorial Dud Corner
	ARTUS Ernest Richard	Sgt 3178	All Saints Gloucester	35	Kia	Dud Corner Mil Cem
	BAGLIN Arthur	Pte 17528	Aston Birmingham	19	Kia	St Mary's ADS Mil Cem
	BAKER Ernest	Cpl 12483	Aston Birmingham	29	Kia	Loos Memorial Dud Corner
	BARNFIELD John	Pte 13002	Avening Glos	21	Kia	Loos Memorial Dud Corner
	BATTY James	Pte 15779	Moseley Birmingham	20	Kia	Dud Corner Mil Cem
	BEACHAM John	Pte 15613	Bourton on Water Glos	20	Kia	Loos Memorial Dud Corner
	BETTERIDGE Reginald James	Sgt 12532	Chelsea London	25	Kia	Loos Memorial Dud Corner
	BISHOP George	Pte 16031	Birmingham	20	Kia	Loos Memorial Dud Corner
	BOND Sidney	Pte 15612	Hambledon Bucks	22	Kia	Loos Memorial Dud Corner
	BOOKER William	Pte 13637	Lydiard Wilts	23	Kia	Loos Memorial Dud Corner
	BOX William Henry	Pte 17319	Hillesley Glos	22	Kia	Loos Memorial Dud Corner
	BRIDGEMAN Frederick E	Sgt 13335	Cheltenham	20	Kia	Cabaret Rouge Mil Cem
	BROOKES Charles Edward	Pte 15737	Netherton Worcs		Kia	Loos Brit Mil Cem
	BUSHELL Henry	Pte 17412	Hillesley Glos	34	Kia	Loos Memorial Dud Corner
	BUTCHER Albert Frederick	Pte 15620	Moulsoe Bucks	22	Kia	Loos Memorial Dud Corner
	BUTLER Hubert Fred Arnold	Pte 12495	Hucknall Torkard Notts	17	Kia	Loos Memorial Dud Corner
	CALLAHAN Alfred Oliver	Pte 13914	Birmingham	26	Kia	Loos Memorial Dud Corner
	CARTER Alfred Lloyd	Pte 16266	Childswickham Worcs		Kia	Cabaret Rouge Mil Cem
	CLARKE Arthur	Pte 15728	Aston Birmingham	24	Kia	Loos Memorial Dud Corner
	COOKNELL Edgar James	Pte 13467	St Mary's Leamington	22	Kia	Dud Corner Mil Cem
	COOMBY Thomas	Sgt 13283	Whitbourne Worcs	30	Kia	Loos Memorial Dud Corner
	COOPER John Lewis	L/Cpl 15832	Shirburn Oxon	19	Kia	Loos Memorial Dud Corner
	CULLIMORE George	Pte 11636	Iron Acton Glos		Kia	Dud Corner Mil Cem
	DALLEN William	Cpl 13204	Gloucester	25	Kia	St Mary's ADS Mil Cem
	DANIELLS Ernest	Pte 15675	Newport Pagnell Bucks	21	Kia	Dud Corner Mil Cem
	DARKES Thomas Henry	Pte 15741	Duddeston Birmingham	21	Kia	Loos Memorial Dud Corner
	DARVELL Edward	L/Cpl 15680	Chesham Bucks	21	Kia	Loos Memorial Dud Corner
	DAVIS Arthur	Sgt 15869	Winson Green Birm	33	Kia	Loos Memorial Dud Corner
	DAVIS Ernest	Pte 13345	Cheltenham		Kia	Loos Memorial Dud Corner
	DAY George Henry James	Pte 16022	Gloucester	25	Kia	Dud Corner Mil Cem
	DELANEY Cecil James	Pte 19253	Cheltenham	18	Kia	Loos Memorial Dud Corner
	DISTON William	Pte 13349	Walsall	20	Kia	Loos Memorial Dud Corner
	DRISCOLL Frank Maurice	L/Sgt 13347	St Paul's Cheltenham	20	Kia	Cabaret Rouge Mil Cem
	EDWARDS Frank	Cpl 13291	Birmingham		Kia	Loos Memorial Dud Corner
	ELLIOTT Robert	Pte 16293	Cheltenham		Kia	Loos Memorial Dud Corner
	EVANS George	Pte 13441	Cinderford Glos	33	Kia	Loos Memorial Dud Corner

EVANS Thomas	Pte 16039	Cheltenham	29	Kia	Loos Memorial Dud Corner
FIELD George Walton	2Lt	Birmingham	19	Kia	St Mary's ADS Spec Mem
FENNEMORE Anthony Joseph	Pte 15666	Leckhampstead Bucks	30	Kia	Loos Memorial Dud Corner
FLETCHER Charles William	Pte 13413	Avening Glos	30	Kia	Loos Memorial Dud Corner
FOWLER Frederick Walter	Pte 15583	Charlbury Oxon	22	Kia	Loos Memorial Dud Corner
FREEMAN Arthur Frederick	Pte 13635	Norton Glos	23	Kia	Loos Memorial Dud Corner
FROWEN Ernest Harry	L/Cpl 13158	Woolaston Glos	24	Kia	Loos Memorial Dud Corner
GABB Alfred Dennis	Pte 13840	Cinderford Glos	17	Kia	Loos Memorial Dud Corner
GAPPER Frank Reginald	Pte 17376	Cheltenham	18	Kia	Loos Memorial Dud Corner
GAPPER James	L/Cpl 13363	Cheltenham	18	Kia	Loos Memorial Dud Corner
GARNER Horace	Sgt 3198	Cheltenham	35	Kia	Loos Memorial Dud Corner
GIBBS Ivan Richard	Capt	Cheltenham	23	Kia	St Mary's ADS Spec Mem
GILDER Reginald William	Pte 16264	Childswickham Worcs	19	Kia	Loos Memorial Dud Corner
GLEED William Alfred	Pte 17368	Gloucester	39	Kia	Loos Memorial Dud Corner
GOODMAN James	Pte 23125	Taunton		Kia	Loos Memorial Dud Corner
GORE James Bonsey	Sgt 3044	St Philip's Bristol	23	Kia	Loos Memorial Dud Corner
GOSTLOW Albert George	L/Cpl 15771	Willesden Middx	23	Kia	Loos Memorial Dud Corner
GRIFFIN Ernest Alfred	Pte 17355	Cold Aston Birmingham	22	Kia	Dud Corner Mil Cem
GROVES Frederick Stephen	Pte 16261	Hawling Glos	28	Kia	Loos Memorial Dud Corner
HAIGH William Edward	Pte 12006	St Michael's Coventry		Kia	St Mary's ADS Mil Cem
HAILE Frank Thomas	Pte 13162	Llandaff Glamorgan	29	Kia	Loos Memorial Dud Corner
HALL Frederick Richard	Pte 17252	Kingscote Glos	18	Kia	Loos Memorial Dud Corner
HALL Thomas	Sgt 12769	Tewkesbury Glos		Kia	Dud Corner Mil Cem
HANKS George Henry	Pte 17385	Horsley Glos	35	Kia	Cabaret Rouge Mil Cem
HARRIS Frederick	L/Cpl 11307	Yardley Birmingham	26	Kia	Loos Memorial Dud Corner
HARRIS Leonard Benjamin	L/Cpl 13524	St Luke's Gloucester	24	Kia	Loos Memorial Dud Corner
HARRISON Arthur	L/Cpl 17281	Accrington Lancs	45	Kia	Dud Corner Mil Cem
HART William Sidney C	Pte 17525	Castle Morton Worcs	19	Kia	Loos Memorial Dud Corner
HAWKINS Francis Clare	Pte 17333	Cinderford Glos	22	Kia	St Mary's ADS Mil Cem
HAWKINS William John	Pte 15881	Nechells Birmingham		Kia	Loos Memorial Dud Corner
HAWLING David	Pte 12721	St Paul's Cheltenham		Kia	Dud Corner Mil Cem
HEAD Ernest William	Pte 13754	Chard Somerset	23	Kia	Loos Memorial Dud Corner
HEDGES William Charles	Pte 17514	Campden Glos	23	Kia	Loos Memorial Dud Corner
HICKS Walter John	Pte 20421	Crudwell Wilts	23	Kia	St Mary's ADS Mil Cem
HIGGINS Albert Edward	Pte 17495	Gloucester		Kia	Loos Memorial Dud Corner
HILL Arthur	Pte 12784	Gloucester		Kia	Loos Memorial Dud Corner
HILL Harry	Pte 15756	Old Hill Worcs	17	Kia	Loos Memorial Dud Corner
HITCHCOX Herbert	Pte 15652	Wroxton Oxon	30	Kia	Loos Memorial Dud Corner
HODGKINS Frank Wilford	Pte 16331			Kia	Loos Memorial Dud Corner
HODSON Frederick	Pte 15849	Ladywood Birmingham	35	Kia	Loos Memorial Dud Corner
HOGG Frank Albert	Pte 13543	Whiteshill Glos	23	Kia	Loos Memorial Dud Corner
HOLDEN Henry William	Pte 15875	Birmingham	22	Kia	Loos Memorial Dud Corner
HOLFORD Ernest	Pte 13147	Longhope Glos	23	Kia	Loos Memorial Dud Corner

HOMER Frederick	Pte 23130	Cradley Birmingham	25	Kia	Loos Memorial Dud Corner
HOPKINS Thomas	Pte 15851	Birmingham	24	Kia	Loos Memorial Dud Corner
HORTON William John	Pte 17400	Birmingham		Kia	Loos Memorial Dud Corner
JACKLYN Ted	Pte 17379	Wotton-u-Edge Glos		Kia	Loos Memorial Dud Corner
JEFFERIES Evan James	L/Cpl 11643	St George's Bristol	17	Kia	Loos Memorial Dud Corner
JONES Ernest Alfred	Ptc 15294	West Dean Glos	21	Kia	Loos Memorial Dud Corner
LEACH Albert Edward	Pte 17251	Northleach Glos	20	Kia	Loos Memorial Dud Corner
LEAMAN William	Pte 17531	Aston Birmingham	16	Kia	Loos Memorial Dud Corner
LEARY George Godfrey W	Lt			Kia	St Mary's ADS Spec Mem
LOCKEY Arthur Granville	Pte 13643	Cheltenham		Kia	Loos Memorial Dud Corner
LONG Frank Thomas	Pte 13675	Gotherington Glos	25	Kia	Loos Memorial Dud Corner
LONG Walter Joseph	Sgt 13167	Leonard Stanley Glos	24	Kia	Loos Memorial Dud Corner
MATHEWS Alfred	Pte 13330	St Peter's Cheltenham	22	Kia	Loos Memorial Dud Corner
MAYALL George	Pte 16269	Prestbury Glos	23	Kia	Loos Memorial Dud Corner
MAYO Arthur Blackford	Cpl 2892	Barton St Mary Glos		Kia	Loos Memorial Dud Corner
MERRICK Horace Clive	Pte 15836	Ladywood Birmingham	20	Kia	Loos Memorial Dud Corner
MOORE Thomas	Pte 15847	Runcorn Cheshire		Kia	Loos Memorial Dud Corner
MORGAN Albert	Pte 17341	Lydney Glos		Kia	Dud Corner Mil Cem
MOSS Edward Hampton	Capt		37	Kia	Loos Memorial Dud Corner
MUNDY William Charles A	Pte 17351	Ewelme Oxon		Kia	Dud Corner Mil Cem
MUNT James	Pte 15724	Waterbury Oxon	22	Kia	Loos Memorial Dud Corner
MURRELL Charles	Pte 16037	Littledean Glos	24	Dow	Dud Corner Mil Cem
NASH Thomas	L/Cpl 12543	St Alban's Birmingham		Kia	Loos Memorial Dud Corner
NORMAN Thomas	L/Cpl 13170	St Philip's Bristol		Kia	Loos Memorial Dud Corner
NUNNEY Ernest Victor S	Pte 16068	Tewkesbury Glos	21	Kia	Loos Memorial Dud Corner
PAGE Herbert	L/Cpl 13465	Watford Beds		Kia	Loos Memorial Dud Corner
PALMER Charles	Pte 17354	Naunton Glos	24	Kia	Loos Memorial Dud Corner
PARTLOW George	Pte 17353	Stow on Wold Glos	29	Kia	Loos Memorial Dud Corner
PEGLER Alonzo	Pte 13755	Horsley Glos	19	Kia	Loos Memorial Dud Corner
PERRY Frederick James	Pte 15820	Brierley Hill Staffs		Kia	Loos Memorial Dud Corner
PHELPS Thomas	Pte 12795	Gloucester		Kia	Loos Memorial Dud Corner
PRICE John	Pte 16034	St Jude's Leicester		Kia	Loos Memorial Dud Corner
REEVES Frederick	Pte 16011	Cam Glos	25	Kia	Loos Memorial Dud Corner
RICHARDS Albert James	Pte 15889	Birmingham		Kia	Dud Corner Mil Cem
RICHARDS Thomas	Pte 12340	Lydney Glos		Kia	Loos Memorial Dud Corner
RIDDING Thomas Arthur	Pte 15708	St George's Birm	28	Kia	Loos Memorial Dud Corner
RIVERS William	Pte 13311	St John's Cheltenham		Kia	Loos Memorial Dud Corner
ROBINSON George Ernest	Sgt 12455	St Paul's Cheltenham		Kia	Loos Memorial Dud Corner
ROBINSON Geffrey Wathen	Lt	Redland Bristol	20	Kia	St Mary's ADS Spec Mem
ROWLEY Levi	Pte 13259	Tipton Staffs	18	Kia	Loos Memorial Dud Corner
RUMBOLD Henry	Pte 13639	Longborough Glos	23	Kia	Cabaret Rouge Mil Cem
SALE Edward Hanson	Capt	Atherstone Warks	25	Kia	St Mary's ADS Spec Mem
SANDFORD Cecil Walter F	L/Cpl 13517	Draycott Worcs	20	Kia	Dud Corner Mil Cem

	SARGENT William Thomas	Pte 17318	Wotton-u-Edge Glos		Kia	Dud Corner Mil Cem
	SEALEY Sidney William	Pte 15893	Leamington Warks	34	Kia	Loos Memorial Dud Corner
	SELBY Maurice	Sgt 3123	Bristol		Kia	Loos Memorial Dud Corner
	SHIPWAY Joseph Ewart	Pte 13663	Minchinhampton Glos	19	Kia	Loos Memorial Dud Corner
	SIMMS John Arthur	Cpl 13676	Rosehill Cardigan		Kia	Loos Memorial Dud Corner
	SIMPSON Thomas	Pte 13309	Toddington Glos	20	Kia	Dud Corner Mil Cem
	SKINNER William Henry	Pte 12871	East Malling Kent	20	Kia	Loos Memorial Dud Corner
	SMART Charles Alfred	Pte 16168	Jabalpur India	28	Kia	Loos Memorial Dud Corner
	SMITH Frederick	Pte 13622	Oxford	34	Kia	Loos Memorial Dud Corner
	SMITH Frederick Samuel	Pte 17347	St George's Bristol		Kia	Cabaret Rouge Mil Cem
	SMITH Frederick William	Pte 13303	Beckford Glos	21	Kia	Loos Memorial Dud Corner
	SMITH Thomas	Pte 17510	Mickleton Glos		Kia	Loos Memorial Dud Corner
	SMITH Walter Joseph	Pte 16048	Birmingham	25	Kia	Loos Memorial Dud Corner
	SMITH William Frank	Pte 11994	Edinburgh	30	Kia	Loos Memorial Dud Corner
	SPENCER Arthur William	Pte 17523	Northleach Glos	24	Kia	Loos Memorial Dud Corner
	STANILAND Walter Edwin	Cpl 13253	Abingdon Oxon	31	Kia	Loos Memorial Dud Corner
	STRATFORD Henry Charles	Pte 15726	Minster Lovell Oxon	22	Kia	Loos Memorial Dud Corner
	SYMONS Clement Aubrey	Lt	Banbury Oxon	21	Kia	Loos Memorial Dud Corner
	TAYLOR Bertram Harry	Pte 12776	Draycott Glos	20	Kia	Loos Memorial Dud Corner
	TAYLOR James Henry	L/Sgt 12450	Cheltenham	22	Kia	Loos Memorial Dud Corner
	THOMAS William Henry	Sgt 12420	Blakeney Glos	33	Kia	Loos Memorial Dud Corner
	TIMPSON William Herbert	Pte 15697	Hughenden Bucks	21	Kia	Loos Memorial Dud Corner
	TOMSETT William George	Pte 13633	English Bicknor Glos	25	Kia	Loos Memorial Dud Corner
	TONGUE John William Collis	Capt	Birmingham	23	Kia	St Mary's Spec Mem
	WARD Albert Frederick	Pte 23129	Sturton Candle Dorset	21	Kia	St Mary's Mil Cem
	WATERS Frank	Pte 13527	Mickleton Glos		Kia	Dud Corner Mil Cem
	WHIFFEN Hartley Allen	Lt	Edinburgh Scotland	38	Kia	St Mary's Spec Mem
	WHING John Edmund	Pte 15586	Wroxton Oxon	30	Kia	Loos Memorial Dud Corner
	WICKS Charles	Pte 16184		38	Kia	Loos Memorial Dud Corner
	WILDING Benjamin	Pte 12541	Worcester	22	Kia	Loos Memorial Dud Corner
	WILLIAMS Albert John	L/Cpl 13386	Winstone Glos	27	Kia	Loos Memorial Dud Corner
	WILLIAMS William	Sgt 2988	Gloucester		Kia	Loos Memorial Dud Corner
	WILLOCK James	Pte 15786	Birmingham		Kia	Loos Memorial Dud Corner
	WITNEY Henry James	Pte 20433	Dalston Middx	26	Kia	Cabaret Rouge Mil Cem
	WOODIN George	Pte 17530	Birmingham	22	Kia	Loos Memorial Dud Corner
	WRIGHT Ernest William	L/Cpl 13509	Mickleton Glos	21	Kia	Loos Memorial Dud Corner
	WYNIATT Frank Charles	Pte 13301	Wood Stanway Glos	23	Kia	Loos Memorial Dud Corner
	YOUNG Ernest	Pte 17535	Oakridge Lynch Glos		Kia	Dud Corner Mil Cem
	YOUNG Isaac	Pte 16002	Blaengarw Glamorgan	20	Kia	Loos Memorial Dud Corner
26/9/1915	CHARLETT Thomas George	Pte 15601	Yarnton Oxon	20	Dow	Béthune Town Cem
	COLLINS Archibald William	Pte 16263	Broadway Worcs	19	Dow	Nouex Les Mines Com Cem
	GAINER Gilbert James	Pte 13287	Cheltenham	20	Dow	Nouex Les Mines Com Cem
	LEE Herbert Horace	Cpl 3147	East Dereham Norfolk		Dow	Nouex Les Mines Com Cem

27/9/1915	GREY Wallace	Cpl 13621	Minchinhampton Glos	21	Dow	Lillers Com Cem
	LOCKEY Ernest George	L/Cpl 12427	East Ampney Glos	19	Dow	Verquin Com Cem
	RAVEN Henry Edward	L/Cpl 13222	St Mark's Cheltenham	28	Dow	Nouex Les Mines Com Cem
28/9/1915	WILSON Horace Edward	Pte 15688	High Wycombe	18	Dow	Lillers Com Cem
29/9/1915	LOVE Arthur	Pte 17321	Berkely Glos	32	Dow	Le Treport Mil Cem
1/10/1915	PUSEY William	Pte 15718	Lane End Bucks	20	Dow	Wimereux Com Cem
	SEABRIGHT John Franklin	Sgt 7409	Winchcombe Glos		Dow	Etaples Mil Cem
	YOUNG Ernest Albert	Pte 15298	Castle Combe Wilts	37	Dow	Etaples Mil Cem
3/10/1915	LITTLEFIELD Walter Edward	Pte 15766	Aston Birmingham	17	Dow	Boulogne Eastern Mil Ccm
5/10/1915	HARDING Albert	Cpl 13491	Prestbury Glos	27	Kia	Loos Memorial Dud Corner
	LADBROOK Thomas	Pte 17503	Stow on the Wold	19	Dow	Cabaret Rouge Mil Cem
8/10/1915	KING Joseph Sydney	Pte 16169	Cheltenham	16	Dow	Prestbury Cheltenham
	SMITH William Frank	Pte 13304	Cheltenham	22	Dow	Etaples Mil Cem
	WHITE William	Pte 15876	Clent Worcs	29	Kia	Loos Memorial Dud Corner
9/10/1915	BARNFIELD William	Pte 13358	St Luke's Cheltenham	25	Kia	Dud Corner Mil Cem
	BOSTON Oliver	Pte 12471	Rinningham Warks	24	Dow	Béthune Town Cem
	HAIL David	Pte 17332	East Dean Glos	27	Dow	Chocques Mil Cem
	NEEMS Percy Vincent Nigel	2Lt	Bristol	19	Dow	Sopworth Wilts
	WYMAN Sidney James	L/Cpl 12437	Stonehouse Glos		Dow	Chocques Mil Cem
11/10/1915	MOSSOP Bernard Alfred	Cpl 15835	Eccleshall Staffs	27	Kia	Loos Memorial Dud Corner
13/10/1915	ARBLASTER George T	Pte 15864	Aston Birmingham		Kia	Loos Memorial Dud Corner
	BALLINGER Percival Louis	Cpl 17566	Leckhampton Glos	22	Kia	Loos Memorial Dud Corner
	BARBER Charles Samuel	L/Cpl 13411	Weston Somerset	24	Kia	Loos Memorial Dud Corner
	BARNES John	Pte 16062	Tibberton Glos	21	Kia	Loos Memorial Dud Corner
	BAYLISS Frank	Pte 15900	Stratford on Avon		Kia	Loos Memorial Dud Corner
	BELSON Frederick Jesse	L/Cpl 15627	Chalgrove Oxon	25	Kia	Loos Memorial Dud Corner
	BOWKETT Frederick Charles	Pte 16064	Longhope Glos	22	Kia	Loos Memorial Dud Corner
	CARNEGY Fredereick A	Lt	Ireland	20	Kia	Loos Memorial Dud Corner
	CARROLL Malachy	L/Cpl 16041	Ilkeston Derby	22	Kia	Loos Memorial Dud Corner
	CLARKE Fred	L/Cpl 13490	Teddesley Staffs	24	Kia	Loos Memorial Dud Corner
	COFIELD Alfred Edward	L/Cpl 11130	Sutton Coldfield	28	Kia	Loos Memorial Dud Corner
	DORRINGTON Alfred	L/Cpl 11843	Romford Essex	24	Kia	Loos Memorial Dud Corner
	DRAPER Ralph Piercy	Pte 13348	Redford Notts	19	Kia	Loos Memorial Dud Corner
	FISHER William Henry	Pte 21121	Cubberley Glos	21	Kia	Loos Memorial Dud Corner
	FLETCHER Christopher C	Pte 16043	Naunton Glos	27	Kia	Loos Memorial Dud Corner
	FLETCHER Samuel	Pte 17398	Avening Glos	25	Kia	Loos Memorial Dud Corner
	FRANCIS Stephen	Pte 15545	St George's Bristol	19	Kia	Loos Memorial Dud Corner
	FREETH Arthur Henry	Pte 15772	Winson Green Birm	20	Kia	Loos Memorial Dud Corner
	GOODALL John	Pte 16195	Southam Glos		Kia	Loos Memorial Dud Corner
	GRINNELL Joseph	Pte 15662	Pershore Worcs		Kia	Loos Memorial Dud Corner
	HARDING Joseph Frederick	Pte 16049	Birmingham		Kia	Loos Memorial Dud Corner
	HARDWICK John Thomas	L/Cpl 15743	Hartlebury Worcs	19	Kia	Loos Memorial Dud Corner
	HOLLOWAY Richard	Pte 23121	Kinver Worcs		Kia	Loos Memorial Dud Corner

	HUMPHREY Arthur	Pte 11128	Putney London	32	Kia	Loos Memorial Dud Corner
	INGLES William DCM	Cpl 13488	Willersley Worcs	27	Kia	Loos Memorial Dud Corner
	INGRAM Ernest	Pte 15790	Aston Birmingham		Kia	Loos Memorial Dud Corner
	IRELAND Frederick James	Pte 17410	Painswick Glos	25	Kia	Loos Memorial Dud Corner
	IRELAND John Francis	Pte 17411	Painswick Glos	32	Kia	Loos Memorial Dud Corner
	JONES William	Pte 23670	Cheltenham		Kia	Loos Memorial Dud Corner
	JONES William Alfred	Pte 13879	Kentish Town London		Kia	Loos Memorial Dud Corner
	LANE Francis	Pte 16238	Pershore Worcs	32	Kia	Loos Memorial Dud Corner
	LEA George	Pte 12434	Newmarket Cambs		Kia	Loos Memorial Dud Corner
	LEE William Edward	Cpl 13837	Battersea London		Kia	Loos Memorial Dud Corner
	LOCKEY Albert	Pte 23593	Lower Hampden Glos	20	Kia	Loos Memorial Dud Corner
	MAISEY Edmund John	Pte 11988	Leckhampton Glos	30	Kia	Loos Memorial Dud Corner
	MARTIN John Douglas	Cpl 12460	Cheltenham	23	Kia	Loos Memorial Dud Corner
	NOAD Arthur	Pte 16052	Gossington Glos	21	Kia	Dud Corner Mil Cem
	NOYES Leonard Percival	Pte 17565	Gloucester	23	Kia	Loos Memorial Dud Corner
	PAY James Henry	Pte 12138	Kingsdown Kent	19	Kia	Loos Memorial Dud Corner
	PAYNE David	Pte 19042	St Wymondley Herts	24	Kia	Loos Memorial Dud Corner
	PEART William Arthur	Pte 16448	Arle Glos	20	Kia	Loos Memorial Dud Corner
	PEGRUM John Charles	Cpl 11803	Stratford Essex	25	Kia	Loos Memorial Dud Corner
	PERROTT John	Pte 15577	Wincham Somerset	23	Kia	Loos Memorial Dud Corner
	PHILLIPS Albert James	Pte 23566	Forest of Dean Glos	26	Kia	Loos Memorial Dud Corner
	POTTER Henry	Pte 16057	Ashchurch Glos	35	Kia	Loos Memorial Dud Corner
	RIGSBY William Albert	Cpl 12422	Plymouth	19	Kia	Loos Memorial Dud Corner
	RUSSELL Harley Raymond	Lt	Clifton Bristol	24	Kia	Loos Memorial Dud Corner
	SAWYER Reginald	Pte 17494	Horsley Glos	19	Kia	Loos Memorial Dud Corner
	SHILHAM Frank Allen	Pte 16056	Chalford Glos	19	Kia	Rue Petillon Mil Cem
	SMITH Charles Edward	Pte 15581	Handsworth Birm		Kia	Loos Memorial Dud Corner
	SMITH John	L/Cpl 15751	Birmingham		Kia	Loos Memorial Dud Corner
	SOLWAY William	Pte 16063	Tibberton Glos		Kia	Loos Memorial Dud Corner
	STAHR Ralph	Pte 17329		32	Kia	Loos Memorial Dud Corner
	STEWART Ernest Henry	Pte 13496	Winchcombe Glos		Kia	Loos Memorial Dud Corner
	TOWNSEND William Vernand	Cpl 8422	Watlinch Glos	24	Kia	Loos Memorial Dud Corner
	WALDRON James	Pte 15892	Salford Manchester	28	Kia	Loos Memorial Dud Corner
	WALL Henry Thomas	Pte 15819	Staunton on Arrow		Kia	Loos Memorial Dud Corner
	WALLINGTON Frederick C	Pte 21111			Kia	Loos Memorial Dud Corner
	WEBB Walter Joseph	Pte 15580	Holton Oxon	23	Kia	Loos Memorial Dud Corner
	WHEELER William Edward	Pte 23048	Kirkdean Glos	21	Kia	Loos Memorial Dud Corner
	WHITE Alexander Milton	L/Cpl 15579	Longstone Cambs	23	Kia	Loos Memorial Dud Corner
	WILLIAMS William John	Pte 13445	East Dean Glos	22	Kia	Loos Memorial Dud Corner
14/10/1915	GEE Ernest	L/Cpl 13121	Birmingham	25	Dow	Chocques Mil Cem
22/10/1915	BARNES Ernest John	Sgt 15614	Milton-U-Wychwood	22	Dow	Lapugnoy Mil Cem
27/10/1915	TRUSSLER Thomas W	Sgt 12451	Mells Somerset	21	Dow	Etaples Mil Cem
18/11/1915	BEDWELL George John H	Pte 16045	Cheltenham	33	Kia	Loos Memorial Dud Corner

Date	Name	Rank/No.	Place	Age	Fate	Cemetery/Memorial
19/11/1915	WILCOX Henry Joseph	Pte 17776	Wickwar Glos	19	Kia	Loos Memorial Dud Corner
29/11/1915	WINTER Alfred Jesse	Pte 17576	Withington Glos	25	Dow	Chocques Mil Cem
4/12/1915	HANKS Richard Hubert	Pte 17419	Painswick Glos	25	Dow	Painswick Hill Cem Glos
19/12/1915	BAILEY Charles Henry	Pte 16165	Tewkesbury	19	Kia	Dud Corner Mil Cem
	NASH George Harold	L/Cpl 15318	Gloucester	22	Kia	Loos Memorial Dud Corner
2/1/1916	PIERCE James	Pte 21414	N'castle W-Limmerick		Kia	Loos Memorial Dud Corner
3/1/1916	YOUNG Thomas William	Pte 12517	Eastcombe Glos		Kia	Ninth Avenue Mil Cem
21/1/1916	CHIDDINGTON George	Pte 15603	Horspath Oxon	20	Kia	Loos Memorial Dud Corner
14/3/1916	STOCKWELL Felix H	Pte 13497	Maidstone Kent	17	Kia	St Patrick's Mil Cem Loos
16/3/1916	SIMMS Frederick Albert	Pte 23690	Bledington Glos	20	Dow	Nouex Les Mines Mil Cem
18/3/1916	HUNT George William	Pte 23687	Upper Slaughter Glos	24	Dow	Nouex Les Mines Mil Cem
21/3/1916	GARDNER Norman H	Pte 23534	Harefield Glos	23	Kia	St Patrick's Mil Cem Loos
22/3/1916	HARRIS Frederick	Pte 15292	West Dean Glos	19	Died	St Sever Cem Rouen
25/3/1916	PHILLIPS Arthur	Pte 2031	Cinderford Glos	19	Died	Le Treport Mil Cem
2/4/1916	AKERS Albert	Sgt 13088	Naunton Glos	21	Dow	Béthune Town Cem
4/4/1916	FRYER Charles William	Pte 18922	Pinton Glos	26	Kia	Maroc British Cem
	GRIFFITHS Frederick	Pte 408	Westbury Glos		Kia	Maroc British Cem
	KINGSTONE Charles Robert	Pte 16276	Cheltenham Glos	36	Kia	Maroc British Cem
18/4/1916	NEGUS Ralph Albert	2Lt	Cheltenham	30	Kia	Maroc British Cem
19/4/1916	CORKE Hubert William	2Lt	Lyneham Wilts	21	Dow	Maroc British Cem
	HOWARD Arthur Frederick	Pte 11875	Enfield Essex	18	Kia	St Patrick's Mil Cem Loos
	LEWIS Charles Frederick	Pte 21349	Hornsey Middx		Kia	St Patrick's Mil Cem Loos
	TANNER Ernest George	Pte 24374	Whiteshill Glos	29	Kia	St Patrick's Mil Cem Loos
20/4/1916	STEPHENS Edgar William	Sgt 13631	Winchcombe Glos	24	Kia	St Patrick's Mil Cem Loos
21/4/1916	TRUMAN William John	L/Cpl 15696	Welford Glos	22	Dow	Béthune Town Cem
22/4/1916	DARCH Stanley Percival	2Lt	Gloucester	23	Kia	Maroc British Cem
27/4/1916	*MATHEWS Walter	Pte 20415	Leeds	22	Dow	Lapugnoy Mil Cem
30/4/1916	FRUIN Walter William John	Cpl 12430	Woodchester Glos	20	Dow	Abbeville Communal Cem
2/5/1916	LOVELL Albert Howard	Pte 11648	Wickwar Glos	30	Died	Longuenesse Souvenir
5/5/1916	MARTIN Joseph Noel	Pte 13357	Cheltenham	22	Kia	Maroc British Cem
11/5/1916	TAYLOR William Henry	Pte 12190	Milkwall Glos		Kia	Maroc British Cem
14/5/1916	DIXON William	Pte 23686	Bourton on Water Glos	35	Dow	Béthune Town cem
23/5/1916	TOVEY Frank Arthur	Pte 24719	Stroud Glos	17	Kia	Loos British Cem
25/5/1916	DENNIS Walter	Pte 9495	Aston Birmingham	21	Dow	Béthune Town cem
26/5/1916	WORLOCK Albert	Pte 25267	Oldland Common Brist'l	29	Dow	Nouex Les Mines Mil Cem
28/5/1916	WATTS Trewren Daniel	Pte 16114	Dursley Glos	32	Died	Lillers Communal Cem
12/6/1916	PAGE Thomas	Pte 25596	Whitchurch Somerset	35	Kia	Maroc British Cem
15/6/1916	JONES Charles Lambert	Lt	Cheltenham	20	Kia	Maroc British Cem
	WILLIAMS Urbin	Pte 23584	Coln St Aldwyn's Glos	21	Dow	Nouex Les Mines Mil Cem
16/6/1916	CHAFFEY Herbert Edgar	L/Cpl 21396	Taunton	20	Dow	Béthune Town cem
	JORDAN Percy	L/Cpl 13193	Lydney Glos	19	Kia	Maroc British Cem
	WILLIAMS Frederick B	Pte 24223	Charlton Kings Glos	31	Kia	Maroc British Cem
17/6/1916	MILES William George	Pte 23639	Gloucester	17	Dow	Longuenesse Souvenir

27/6/1916	BAILEY James	Pte 23663	Stourton Worcs	21	Kia	Loos British Cem
30/6/1916	CARELESS Arthur	Pte 23341	Wapping London	45	Kia	Maroc British Cem
	CROFTS Edwin James	Pte 15250	Radstock Somerset	27	Kia	Loos British Cem
	RICHINGS George Herbert	Pte 17666	Tyfield Glos	26	Kia	Loos British Cem
	STITSON Alfred	Pte 23747	Plymouth	18	Kia	Loos British Cem
	WATTS James Albert	Pte 19126	Cheltenham	26	Kia	Loos British Cem
	WILTSHIRE William Francis	Pte 21281	Fishponds Bristol	19	Died	Longuenesse Souvenir
	*MATHEWS Walter	Served as	GOODALL William			

Acknowledgements

I have sadly to report that a number of those who so generously helped and encouraged me back in 1996 have now passed away. Several of these fine people became my personal friends and I would particularly like to pay tribute to the valued friendship of a wonderfully kind lady, Olive Dorrington, the daughter of Private John 'Jack' Kear.

My father too, has passed on during these intervening years, leaving me an enduring interest and legacy that I am most grateful for.

I would like to thank the families of the following soldiers for providing me with a plethora of photographs, documents, letters, maps, and all manner of fascinating information. Charles Anscombe, John Barnes, Fred Bowkett, Ernest Chadband, The Chandler Brothers, Evan Davies, George Evans, Reg Fennell, Edward Farrell, Leonard Freeman, Dennis Gabb, Frank Haile, Albert Higgins, Onslowe Holtham, Edmund Lord, John Halifax Roberts, The Tuffley Brothers, Leslie Smith, John Webb, Alfred Wildsmith, Albert Yemm.

I would also like to acknowledge the vital help provided by the following institutions. Avril Williams and her superb Tea Rooms at Auchonvillers on the Somme, The Commonwealth War Graves Commission, The Public Records Office – Kew, The Imperial War Museum, The Gloucester Citizen, The Gloucestershire Echo, The Forester, The Forest and Wye Valley Review, The Ross Gazette, Gloucester City Library, Cheltenham Library, The Royal Regiments of Gloucestershire Museum, The South Wales Borderers and Monmouthshire Regimental Museum, The Welch Regiment Museum, Gloucestershire County Archives.

I am also grateful for the generous assistance and guidance received from the following persons. Alfredo and Emma Baglivi, Geoff Barnes, John Bright, Eva Brogniart, Matt Christian, Sam Christian, Steve Cooper Sam Eedle, Lloyd Gill, Madeline Guillemant, Paul Hughes, Mike Jenkins, Rose Jones, Sybil Katzmarek, Donald "Lofty" Large, Peter Last, Dean Marks, Carol Maxwell, June Minchin, Pete Moore, Nan Morse, Eric Nicholls, Francis Roger, Gary Sandford, Andrew Tatham, Dave Tuffley, Peter Wilson, Hilary Woolley.

Over nearly two decades I have enjoyed many exciting excursions to the battlefields of northern France and to Loos in particular. Without the great companionship of a few very good friends, my experiences there would not have been half so much fun, thought provoking, poignant, or informative. And so to Peter and Sharon Weston, Wayne and Michelle Young, Steve Cooper and Dave Tuffley, I owe my very deepest thanks and I look forward to many more years spent in their company; not least every September 25th when we gather at the New Lone Tree at the hour the Gloucesters 'went over the top'.

I must also thank Wayne and Michelle for producing the superb and extraordinarily detailed maps that enhance this edition.

To Jean Fouquenelle, his late wife Marguerite and all their family raised at Le Rutoire Farm, I cannot thank them enough for their continued superb hospitality each September 25th and for their kind help and co-operation in the planting and nurturing of the new Lone Tree.

A special thanks to Penny Ely, Trustee for the Estate of the Gloucestershire poet Ivor Gurney, for allowing me to include the poem "To Certain Comrades, E.S. and J.H."

Finally in the course of my research I was privileged to meet Arch Freeman and Bill Simmonds, fine old gentlemen, who in the vigour of their youth were actually there on the Western Front, risking their lives on the unspeakably brutal battlefields of the Great War.

Selected Bibliography

Batchelor, Peter. Matson, Christopher. VCs of The First World War, The Western Front 1915, Sutton Publishing Limited, 1997.

Cherry, Niall. Most Unfavourable Ground, Helion and Company Ltd, 2005.

Clark, A. First and Second Days, William Morrow and Co, 1961.

Coppard, George. With a Machine Gun to Cambrai, Cassel Military Paperbacks, 1969.

Corrigan, Gordon. Loos 1915 – The Unwanted Battle, Spellmount, 2006.

Dolden, A. S. Cannon Fodder, Blandford Press, 1980.

Fox, C. Cull, I. Chapman, J. McIntyre, M. Webb, L.
Responding to the Call – The Kitchener Battalions of the Royal Berkshire Regiment at the Battle of Loos 1915, The Centre for Continuing Education, The University of Reading, 1997.

Fox, C. Cull, I. Chapman, J. McIntyre, M. Webb, L.
Arras To Cambrai – The Kitchener Battalions of the Royal Berkshire Regiment 1917, The Centre for Continuing Education, The University of Reading, 1998.

Gibbs, P. Realities of War, Hutchinson and Co, 1938.

Gough, Hubert. General Sir. The Fifth Army, Hodder And Stoughton Ltd, 1921.

Graves, R. Goodbye To All That, Jonathon Cape, 1929.

Hartcup, G. The War of Invention, Brassey's Defence Publishers Ltd, 1988.

Hammerton, J. I Was There – Human Story of the Great War 1914 -1918,
The Amalgamated Press Ltd.

James, E.A. Brig. British Regiments 1914 - 1918,
Naval and Military Press and the Liverpool Medal Co.

MacDonald, L. 1915, The Death Of Innocence, Headline Book Publishing, 1993.

MacGill, Patrick. The Great Push, Herbert Jenkins Limited, 1916.

Moore, W. Gas Attack, Leo Cooper, 1987.

Purnell, History Of The First World War, Volume 3, Number 5, BPC Publishing, 1970.

Richter, Donald. Chemical Soldiers, Leo Cooper, 1994.

Soldiers Died, J.B. Hayward and Son, 1920.

The Back Badge – Gloucestershire Regimental Association, 1934.

Warner, Philip. The Battle of Loos, William Kimber and Co. Ltd, 1976.

Ward, Dudley C. Major. The Welsh Regiment of Foot Guards 1915 – 1918, John Murray, 1936.

Unpublished Sources

The Autobiography of Ernest Chadband.

The Diary of Reginald Fennell.

The Autobiography of Leonard Freeman.

To Certain Comrades E.S. and J.H.

Living we loved you, yet withheld our praises
Before your faces;

And though our spirits had you high in honour,
After the English manner,

We said no word. Yet, as such comrades would,
You understood.

Such friendship is not touched by Death's disaster,
But stands the faster;

Nor all the shocks and trials of time cannot
Shake it one jot.

Beside the fire at night some far December,
We shall remember,

And tell men, unbegotten as yet, the story
Of your sad glory –

Of your plain strength, your truth of heart, your Splendid
Coolness, all ended !

All ended . . . and the aching hearts of lovers
Joy over-covers,

Glad in their sorrow; hoping that if they must
Come to the dust,

An ending such as yours may be their portion,
And great good fortune –

That if we may not live to serve in peace
England, watching increase –

Then death with you, honoured and swift, and high;
And so - Not Die.

Ivor Gurney
Western Front 1916

Index

Kenny, Henry, Private, VC, 100
Kenya, 199
King George V, 167, 168
King, Joseph, Private, 24, 115, 116
Kingstone, Charles, Private, 169
Kipling, John, Lieutenant, 148, 149
Kipling, Rudyard, 149
Kirkwood, James, G., Lieutenant Colonel, 35, 43, 118, 145, 199, 200
Kitchener, 13, 15, 38, 63, 164, 174, 198
Kitchener's New Army, 9, 22, 33, 52
Kitchener Blue, 26, 38
Kitchener's Fighting Scouts, 35

L.
La Bassée, 74, 77, 95, 123, 148
La Bassée Canal, 104, 119
La Bassée to Lens Road, 74, 77, 95, 104, 106, 107, 121, 124, 126, 128, 129, 130, 150, 154, 157, 185, 193
La Haie, 66, 74, 77, 80, 87, 102, 104
Landalls, Len, 176
Lansdown Crescent, Cheltenham, 29, 30, 37, 41, 139
Langley, A.A., Lieutenant, 35
Large, David "Lofty", 5, 209
Larner, George, Private, 14, 17, 89
Laventie, 161, 185
Lawrence, L.C., Captain, 35
Lea, George, Private, 14, 16, 27
Leadbeater, Mr., 19
Leaman, William, Private, 24
Leary, George Godfrey W., Lieutenant, 35, 37, 141, 142
Leckhampton Hill, Glos, 35
Le Clipon, 197
Lee Enfield Rifle, 33, 41
Lee Metford Rifle, 33
Le Hamel, Somme, 173, 199, 200
La Havre, 49, 50, 114
Le Morquet Wood, 69, 71
Lens, 51, 74, 77, 95, 123, 148, 179, 192
Lens Road Redoubt, 108, 179
Les Brebis, 68, 131, 134, 145, 174
Le Rutoir Alley, 109, 113
Le Rutoir Farm, 49, 66, 67, 71, 74, 78, 102, 113, 124, 125, 147, 167, 180, 182, 209
Le Rutoir Hamlet, 180
Le Rutoir Keep, 113
Lewis Gun, 129, 164, 193
Lievin, 179
Lightmoor Colliery, Glos, 151

Lillers, 68, 114, 121, 162, 167, 168
Littledean, Glos, 141
Littlefield, Walter, Private, 114, 117
Little London, Glos, 159, 161
Little Willie Trench, 191
Lockey, Albert, Private, 161
Lone Pine, 54
Lone Tree, 7, 54, 55, 64, 65, 71, 74, 90, 95, 97, 98, 100, 101, 102, 103, 104, 106, 107, 119, 124, 125, 139, 177, 180, 182, 185, 186, 188, 209
Lone Tree Ridge, 55, 104, 109, 123, 125, 129, 133, 139, 162
Longbridge Deveril, 41
Longdon, Glos, 137
Longhope, Glos, 159, 161
Loos, 7, 9, 12, 20, 24, 25, 27, 36, 37, 41, 48, 54, 57, 58, 59, 61, 63, 66, 68, 69, 70, 71, 74, 77, 88, 89, 90, 93, 94, 95, 96, 104, 105, 111, 112, 114, 117, 118, 119, 121, 122, 124, 125, 126, 128, 129, 131, 132, 135, 139, 144, 147, 161, 162, 163, 164, 165, 167, 168, 169, 170, 171, 172, 173, 175, 177, 179, 180, 182, 185, 186, 188, 189, 192, 193, 194, 195, 200, 210, 211
Loos British Cemetery, 193, 194
Lord, Edmund, Lance Corporal, 47, 111, 209
Lovell, Alfred, Private, 172
Lovell, George, Private, 172, 173
Lower Harford, Glos, 161
Lydney, Glos, 73, 95, 96, 136, 168

M.
MacGill, Patrick, 113, 165, 178
Mackenzie, Captain, 200
Marfell, Mr., Cosy Corner, Cheltenham, 38
Marks, Dean, 209
Marlow, Bucks, 200
Maroc, 171, 172
Maroc Military Cemetery, 171
Martinpuich, Somme, 195
Maxim Machine Gun, 13, 50, 93
Maxwell, Carol, 209
Mazingarbe, 168, 179, 180
Memorial Cross, 10th Gloucesters, 197
Merckeghem, Belgium, 198
Meulbrouck, Alphonse, Sergeant, 133, 195
Michael, Operation, 199
Mickleton, Glos, 19
Middlekirke, Belgium, 197
Midland Road Rail Station, Cheltenham, 116
Mikra, British Cemetery, Greece, 136

The GLOSTERS are
"holding their own"